The
Pocket
Aristotle

Edited and with an Introduction
and Prefatory Notes by
Justin D. Kaplan

Translated under the Editorship of
W. D. Ross

Selections from
*Psychology, Physics, Politics,
Nicomachean Ethics, Metaphysics*
and *Poetics*

D1450301

WASHINGTON SQUARE PRESS
PUBLISHED BY POCKET BOOKS NEW YORK

The translations used in this edition are from *The Student's Oxford Aristotle*, translated under the editorship of W D. Ross, copyright 1942 by the Oxford University Press, and are reprinted by special arrangement with the Delegates of the Oxford University Press

A Washington Square Press Publication of
POCKET BOOKS, a division of Simon & Schuster, Inc.
1230 Avenue of the Americas, New York, N.Y. 10020

ISBN: 0-671-46377-2

First Pocket Books printing October 1958

20   19   18   17   16

WASHINGTON SQUARE PRESS and WSP colophon are
registered trademarks of Simon & Schuster, Inc.

Printed in the U.S.A.

CONTENTS

∾∾∾∾∾∾∾∾∾∾∾∾∾∾∾∾∾∾∾∾∾∾∾∾∾∾∾∾∾∾∾∾∾

The
Pocket
Aristotle

INTRODUCTION

~~~~~~

In Athens, nearly 2,500 years ago, one man set out to be the master of all reality. Aristotle surveyed what the men of his time had thought and questioned; he invented new instruments and modes of inquiry; and he devoted his life to codifying and rationalizing what was then the sum of human knowledge.

He worked within the severest limitations. He was an astronomer without a telescope, a biologist without a laboratory, a physiologist and psychologist without apparatus. He was a natural historian who had to rely for his data partly on hearsay and tradition, partly on the miscellaneous specimens and prodigies that reached him from the itinerant agents of Alexander the Great. In an age when written records were few, he devoted himself to placing phenomena in historical and causal perspective.

Aristotle was also among the first to study comparative government and to analyze the life history of institutions. In his attempt to relate the individual to the state, and education to law, he became an ethical theorist of prime importance. He was a literary and dramatic critic of rare insight and extraordinary influence. And underlying all these achievements was this: he was a logician of subtlety and strength, and a searcher after the knowledge that transcends and exists independent of all other knowledge. He called this knowledge "first philosophy" or "wisdom," and it has since become known as metaphysics and often as theology.

Many of the questions Aristotle asked—about the nature of man and society, science and knowledge and art—are very much alive today. But it cannot be denied that some of the answers he gave are no longer valid. His aristocratic bias and his relative insularity now seem to vitiate some of his conclusions about ethical, social, and political goals, while his particular scientific conclusions have since been denied by fact and experience. The keystone of Aristotle's logic, the syllogism—which seemed to promise a steplike progression from the certain to the ascertainable—now has little real function, even though for centuries it was regarded as one of the more potent instruments of human inquiry. Similarly, Aristotle's doctrine of causes, which he considered his chief and distinctive contribution to philosophy, has lost its usefulness, even though its schematic and semantic beauty is still appealing.

Like Francis Bacon, who led the reaction against him, Aristotle could have proclaimed that he took all knowledge for his province. He left behind a true *summa*, a majestic structure which has aesthetic wholeness, the element of drama, and—in an age of specialized and fragmented knowledge—a certain emotional appeal. It is a body of knowledge and theory which for centuries dominated and shaped Western thought, which entered into the main intellectual tradition of Christianity, and which lies at the heart of some of the great expressions of Western genius. For Dante, Aristotle was "the Master of those that know"; for St. Thomas Aquinas, he was simply, and to the exclusion of all others, "The Philosopher."

Although his name is associated with Athens, Aristotle was a foreigner, a native of Stagira in Thrace, where he was born in 384 B.C. His father, Nicomachus, who died while Aristotle was young, was physician at the Macedonian court, and the son's fortunes were always to be closely tied to those of the Macedonian rulers.

In 368/7 B.C., when he was about seventeen, Aristotle came to Athens to study with Plato at the Academy. He stayed there for twenty years. Unfortunately, little is known about the personal relationship between the two greatest thinkers of their time, the one bringing to a close a long, productive career, the other in his formative years. Aristotle is supposed to have had a sharp and bitter tongue, and this, together with his later criticisms of Plato, suggested to classical writers that he had broken with Plato and was ready to leave the Academy before the latter's death in 348/7.

That same year Philip of Macedon attacked Stagira. Nearly forty, his master dead and his ancestral home destroyed, Aristotle left Athens and the Academy. He was away for thirteen years. He probably taught for three years at Assos in Asia Minor, where he lived under the protection of the ruler Hermias, a former member of the Academy. There also he married Hermias' niece, Pythias, who bore him a daughter; by another woman, a native of Stagira, he was later to have a son, Nicomachus, for whom he named the *Nicomachean Ethics*. For another three years he lived at Mytilene, on the island of Lesbos, and then, at the invitation of King Philip, Aristotle came to the Macedonian court as tutor to the thirteen-year-old heir to the throne, the future Alexander the Great. From this association, which lasted about eight years, Aristotle gained not only firsthand experience of politics but also the friendship and protection of the man who was to be the most powerful ruler of his time.

After Alexander ascended to the throne in 336, Aristotle returned to Athens to enter upon the most productive phase of his career. He already had a considerable reputation as the brilliant protégé of Plato and the intimate of Alexander, and when he founded his own school in Athens it took precedence over the Academy. Situated in, and named after, a grove sacred to Apollo Lyceius and the Muses, Aristotle's Lyceum (like Plato's "Academy," the word "Lyceum" was to become a generic term for schools that would come after) consisted of a Temple of the Muses, an altar, several lecture rooms, and a library and map room. These were surrounded by a large garden in which the masters and students walked while discoursing (hence members of the school are known as Peripatetics, from the Greek word *peripatein,* meaning "to walk about"). In the mornings, according to tradition, Aristotle lectured to the students; in the afternoons, the public was admitted to lectures on relatively easy subjects, such as rhetoric. Apparently more highly organized and comprehensive in its curriculum than the Academy, the Lyceum was close to being a university in the modern sense. Aristotle used it not only as a forum for the development and exposition of his philosophy but as a training ground for students who would carry on his program and methods of research.

Now a radical change in the political climate upset all his plans. To the rising nationalist party in Athens, Aristotle had always been suspect for his Macedonian connections, and his position became dangerous when Alexander the Great died in 323. A charge of impiety was brought against him, and remembering the fate of Socrates, Aristotle left Athens lest, as he is supposed to have said, the Athenians "sin twice against philosophy." He fled to Chalcis, where he died the following year at the age of about 62, supposedly of a stomach ailment aggravated by overwork.

It was chiefly through his students at the Lyceum rather than through his written work that Aristotle's thought remained alive and influential in the centuries immediately after his death. The more or less popular works—dialogues and treatises—which were circulated during his lifetime were lost, as were many of the collections he had made of material on history and natural science; these two categories of lost work we know of through lists and allusions in classical authors.

According to one traditional account, the works that survive today consist of manuscripts which were carefully guarded by Aristotle's friend and successor as head of the Lyceum, Theophrastus. Fearing that the anti-Macedonian party in Athens might try to destroy the manuscripts, Theophrastus is supposed to have sent them off to Asia Minor where they remained hidden for 150 years.

In the first century B.C., a Greek edition was compiled by Andronicus of Rhodes, and this edition represents substantially the form and order in which we have Aristotle's writings today. But even with an accepted edition, the Western world —in which the knowledge of Greek became increasingly rare— continued to have little direct contact with Aristotle's writings, for it was not until the thirteenth century that they became generally available in Latin translations, and these Latin translations were often not from the Greek originals but from versions in Arabic.

Quite aside from the complexity of thought, Aristotle's writings present textual problems. Often fragmentary, repetitious, digressive, they are obviously not finished work, and since most of them probably date from the Lyceum period it has been conjectured that they represent Aristotle's notes for lectures or perhaps notes taken down by his listeners. It is fairly generally agreed now that the writings probably represent Aristotle's memoranda of lectures already given. Hence the alternation of eloquent and rough passages, the occasional self-contradiction, as Aristotle, trying to set down and systematize his teaching, continued to explore, reconsider, and revise.

After centuries of commentary and criticism, adulation, and even repudiation, it is difficult to read Aristotle freshly, or on his own terms. His medieval and scholastic commentators, for example, were almost exclusively concerned with the abstract and theoretical side of his program; and later, with the first stirrings of the modern scientific spirit, it was inevitable that there should be a bitter reaction against him. He was regarded as the enemy of the specific and concrete, a tyrant over thought, the embodiment of pointless speculation. "He did not consult experience as he should have done," Francis Bacon wrote in 1620; "but, having first determined the question according to his will, he then resorted to experience and led her about like a captive in a procession."

Yet if we go back to Aristotle himself, bypassing the commentators, we find that few philosophers have been as dedicated to the particular and the concrete, to empirical observation (although not, it is true, to applications). He made a detailed, lifelong study of animal and plant forms; his analysis of 158 Greek constitutions was the first compilation of its kind; he studied local records, including those of dramatic performances and even athletic competitions. In his hands, empirical investigation and the study of the individual form and function became goals in themselves, and this was a revolutionary innovation for his time.

Other schools of interpretation and criticism have tried to reconcile him with Plato, to emphasize the break with Plato, to reconcile him with Christianity—in short, to do everything with him but read him within the framework of his central purpose: to organize the knowledge and thought of his time into a significant unity, to relate all material phenomena, all motion and change, to a concept of order and unswerving purpose.

To do this he established broad working categories. Under the heading of the theoretic sciences he grouped metaphysics, mathematics, and physics. The goal of these sciences is knowledge for its own sake, for they deal with things we can only observe, that exist independent of human will. The special province of metaphysics, the science of first principles, was to examine the otherwise unquestioned bases of all knowledge.

Under the heading of the practical sciences—the purpose of which is not merely to know but to act in the light of knowledge—Aristotle grouped politics and ethics; these can be modified by human behavior. A third category, although Aristotle did not make explicit provision for it, can be called the productive sciences: poetry and rhetoric, for example. Here the purpose is not merely to know but to produce in the light of knowledge.

Of course this basic terminology has to be reconciled with

modern usage. The word "science" is used in its broadest
sense of systematized knowledge, and we have to
remember that we are likely to transpose Aristotle's classifications and
think of physics as a practical science and ethics as a purely
theoretic one. But once we have accepted Aristotle's broad
divisions of knowledge, we can see the relationship in his
work between the particular and the general, the observed
phenomenon and the immutable principle. Then his universality and basic wholeness become apparent, the psychological
marvel of this sweep and ambition within the mind of a single
man.

The influence of both Plato and Aristotle has been so pervasive, their differences so heightened by commentators, that
they have come to stand not only for divergent systems of
thought but for polarities of temperament. We can be skeptical of the dictum that every man is born either a Platonist or
an Aristotelian, but there is a very real tension between the
two philosophies; and as the antitheses are popularly formulated, Aristotle—and the Aristotelian approach—seems to come
off second best.

To many, Plato represents the lyrical, soaring imagination,
while Aristotle represents investigation, prosaic and earthbound. Plato seems inspired and inspiring, while Aristotle
seems tied to an inflexible system and an unrelenting logic.
One is a reformer, a prophet, and an artist, the other a compiler, an observer, and an organizer. Plato seems to represent
the highest nobility of thought and aspiration; Aristotle seems
content to accept and work within the day-to-day limitations
of human behavior. Where Plato is mythic, plastic, sensuous,
Aristotle is scientific, conceptual, analytic.

These conventional contrasts hardly do justice to Aristotle.
For the modern reader he may be more difficult to approach
than Plato because his text is not essentially literary and
dramatic and because of the abstruseness of his first principles. Yet he offers his own unique and lasting rewards: directness of thought and expression; astounding nimbleness of
analysis and reasoning; a dedication to tracing things from

their beginnings; a system which embraced, and attempted to unify, both science and philosophy. He impresses us not only by his pioneering ambition and scope, by his quest for unity, but also by the role he played in shaping Western thought. How far he succeeded in creating a philosophical system which has not only aesthetic and intellectual excitement but also pertinence to contemporary thought we can judge only by remembering his aims while we read his work.

—JUSTIN D. KAPLAN

PHYSICS

Translated by R. P. Hardie and R. K. Gaye

Together with mathematics and metaphysics, physics falls into Aristotle's category of the theoretic sciences, the goal of which is knowledge rather than action. Physics deals specifically with things which are both material and capable of motion and change. Such things come under the heading of Nature, which Aristotle defines in Book II.

In the PHYSICS, Aristotle presents the basic definitions and principles which, in other works (on meteorology and astronomy, biology and psychology), he applies to specific categories of natural bodies, both organic and inorganic. Although he acknowledges the role of chance and the spontaneous, his basic purpose is to rationalize motion and change, to relate them to a concept of an ordered universe.

Aristotle's prime instrument in reconciling particular phenomena and transcendent order is his doctrine of causes, which he considered his distinctive contribution to philosophy. All motion or change, he reasons, can be explained by one or more of the following four "causes": the *material* cause ("that out of which a thing comes to be and which persists, e. g., the bronze of the statue, the silver of the bowl"); the *formal* cause (the pattern or formula of the thing in question); the *efficient* cause (the primary source of the change or coming to rest—the immediate stimulus or agent); and the *final* cause (the ultimate goal, "that for the sake of which a thing is done"). It should be remembered that only two of these, the efficient and the final, correspond to the normal way in which we now use the word "cause."

PHYSICS

BOOK I

1. [*The scope and method of this book.*] When the objects
of an inquiry, in any department, have principles, conditions,
or elements, it is through acquaintance with these that knowledge, that is to say scientific knowledge, is attained. For we
do not think that we know a thing until we are acquainted
with its primary conditions or first principles, and have carried our analysis as far as its simplest elements. Plainly therefore in the science of Nature, as in other branches of study,
our first task will be to try to determine what relates to its
principles.

The natural way of doing this is to start from the things
which are more knowable and obvious to us and proceed towards those which are clearer and more knowable by nature; for the same things are not "knowable relatively to us"
and "knowable" without qualification. So in the present inquiry we must follow this method and advance from what
is more obscure by nature, but clearer to us, towards what
is more clear and more knowable by nature.

Now what is to us plain and obvious at first is rather confused masses, the elements and principles of which become
known to us later by analysis. Thus we must advance from
generalities to particulars; for it is a whole that is best known
to sense perception, and a generality is a kind of whole, com-
prehending many things within it, like parts. Much the same

4

thing happens in the relation of the name to the formula. A name, e. g., "round," means vaguely a sort of whole: its definition analyses this into its particular senses. Similarly a child begins by calling all men "father," and all women "mother," but later on distinguishes each of them.

2. [*The problem: The number and character of the first principles of nature.*] The principles in question must be either (*a*) one or (*b*) more than one.

If (*a*) one, it must be either (i) motionless, as Parmenides and Melissus assert, or (ii) in motion, as the physicists hold, some declaring air to be the first principle, others water.

If (*b*) more than one, then either (i) a finite or (ii) an infinite plurality. If (i) finite (but more than one), then either two or three or four or some other number. If (ii) infinite, then either as Democritus believed one in kind, but differing in shape or form; or different in kind and even contrary.

A similar inquiry is made by those who inquire into the number of *existents*: for they inquire whether the ultimate constituents of existing things are one or many, and if many, whether a finite or an infinite plurality. So they too are inquiring whether the principle or element is one or many.

Now to investigate whether Being is one and motionless is not a contribution to the science of Nature. For just as the geometer has nothing more to say to one who denies the principles of his science—this being a question for a different science or for one common to all—so a man investigating *principles* cannot argue with one who denies their existence. For if Being is just one, and one in the way mentioned, there is a principle no longer, since a principle must be the principle of some thing or things.

To inquire therefore whether Being is one in this sense would be like arguing against any other position maintained for the sake of argument (such as the Heraclitean thesis, or such a thesis as that Being is one man) or like refuting a merely contentious argument—a description which applies to the arguments both of Melissus and of Parmenides: their premisses are false and their conclusions do not follow. Or rather the argument of Melissus is gross and palpable and offers no difficulty at all: accept one ridiculous proposition and the rest follows—a simple enough proceeding.

We physicists, on the other hand, must take for granted that the things that exist by nature are, either all or some of them, in motion—which is indeed made plain by induction. Moreover, no man of science is bound to solve every kind of difficulty that may be raised, but only as many as are drawn falsely from the principles of the science; it is not our business to refute those that do not arise in this way; just as it is the duty of the geometer to refute the squaring of the circle by means of segments, but it is not his duty to refute Antiphon's proof. At the same time the holders of the theory of which we are speaking do incidentally raise physical questions, though Nature is not their subject; so it will perhaps be as well to spend a few words on them, especially as the inquiry is not without scientific interest.

The most pertinent question with which to begin will be this: In what sense is it asserted that all things *are* one? For "is" is used in many senses. Do they mean that all things "are" *substance* or *quantities* or *qualities?* And, further, are all things *one* substance—one man, one horse, or one soul—or quality and that one and the same—white or hot or something of the kind? These are all very different doctrines and all impossible to maintain.

For if *both* substance and quantity and quality are, then, whether these exist independently of each other or not, Being will be many.

If on the other hand it is asserted that all things are quality or quantity, then, whether substance exists or not, an absurdity results, if indeed the impossible can properly be called absurd. For none of the others can exist independently; substance alone is independent; for everything is predicated of substance as subject. Now Melissus says that Being is infinite. It is then a quantity. For the infinite is in the category of quantity, whereas substance or quality or affection cannot be infinite except through a concomitant attribute, that is, if at the same time they are also quantities. For to define the infinite you must use quantity in your formula, but not substance or quality. If then Being is both substance and quantity, it is two, not one; if only substance, it is not infinite and has no magnitude; for to have that it will have to be a quantity.

Again, "one" itself, no less than "being," is used in many senses, so we must consider in what sense the word is used when it is said that the All is one.

Now we say that (a) the continuous is one or that (b) the indivisible is one, or (c) things are said to be "one," when their essence is one and the same, as "liquor" and "drink."

If (a) their One is one in the sense of continuous, it is many, for the continuous is divisible *ad infinitum*.

There is, indeed, a difficulty about part and whole, perhaps not relevant to the present argument, yet deserving consideration on its own account—namely, whether the part and the whole are one or more than one, and how they can be one or many, and, if they are more than one, in what sense they are more than one. (Similarly with the parts of wholes which are not continuous.) Further, if each of the two parts is indivisibly one with the whole, the difficulty arises that they will be indivisibly one with each other also.

But to proceed: If (b) their One is one as indivisible, nothing will have quantity or quality, and so the one will not be infinite, as Melissus says—nor, indeed, limited, as Parmenides says, for though the limit is indivisible, the limited is not.

But if (c) all things are one in the sense of having the same definition, like "raiment" and "dress," then it turns out that they are maintaining the Heraclitean doctrine, for it will be the same thing "to be good" and "to be bad," and "to be good" and "to be not good," and so the same thing will be "good" and "not good," and man and horse; in fact, their view will be, not that all things are one, but that they are nothing; and that "to be of such-and-such a quality" is the same as "to be of such-and-such a size."

Even the more recent of the ancient thinkers were in a pother lest the same thing should turn out in their hands both one and many. So some, like Lycophron, were led to omit "is," others to change the mode of expression and say "the man has been whitened" instead of "is white," and "walks" instead of "is walking," for fear that if they added the word "is" they should be making the one to *be* many—as if "one" and "being" were always used in one and the same sense. What "is" may be many either in definition (for example, "to be white" is one thing, "to be musical" another, yet the same thing may be both, so the one is many) or by division, as the whole and its parts. On this point, indeed, they were already getting into difficulties and admitted that the one was many—as if there was any difficulty about the same thing being both one and many, provided that these are not opposites; for "one" may mean either "potentially one" or "actually one."

3. [*Refutation of the arguments of Parmenides and Melissus.*] If, then, we approach the thesis in this way it seems impossible for all things to be one. Further, the arguments they use to prove their position are not difficult to expose. For both of them reason contentiously—I mean both Melissus and Parmenides. Their premisses are false and their conclusions do not follow. Or rather the argument of Melissus is gross and palpable and offers no difficulty at all: admit one ridiculous proposition and the rest follows—a simple enough proceeding.

The fallacy of Melissus is obvious. For he supposes that the assumption "what has come into being always has a beginning" justifies the assumption "what has not come into being has no beginning." Then this also is absurd, that in every case there should be a beginning of the *thing*—not of the time and not only in the case of coming to be in the full sense but also in the case of coming to have a quality—as if change never took place suddenly. Again, does it follow that Being, if one, is motionless? Why should it not move, the whole of it within itself, as parts of it do which are unities, e. g., this water? Again, why is qualitative change impossible? But, further, Being cannot be one in form, though it may be in what it is made of. (Even some of the physicists hold it to be one in the latter way, though not in the former.) Man obviously differs from horse in form, and contraries from each other.

The same kind of argument holds good against Parmenides also, besides any that may apply specially to his view, the answer to him being that "*this* is not true" and "*that* does not follow." His assumption that one is used in a single sense only is false, because it is used in several. His conclusion does not follow, because if we take only white things, and if "white" has a single meaning, none the less what is white will be many and not one. For what is white will not be one either in the sense that it is continuous or in the sense that it must be defined in only one way. "Whiteness" will be different from "what has whiteness." Nor does this mean that there is anything that can exist separately, over and above what is white. For "whiteness" and "that which is white" differ in definition, not in the sense that they are things which can exist apart from each other. But Parmenides had not come in sight of this distinction.

It is necessary for him, then, to assume not only that "being" has the same meaning, of whatever it is predicated, but further that it means (1) what *just is* and (2) what is *just one*.

It must be so, for (1) an attribute is predicated of some subject, so that the subject to which "being" is attributed will not be, as it is something different from "being." Something, therefore, which is not will be. Hence "substance" will not be a predicate of anything else. For the subject cannot be a *being*, unless "being" means several things, in such a way that each *is* something. But *ex hypothesi*, "being" means only one thing.

If, then, "substance" is not attributed to anything, but other things are attributed to it, how does "substance" mean what is rather than what is not? For suppose that "substance" is also "white." Since the definition of the latter is different (for being cannot even be attributed to white, as nothing is which is not "substance"), it follows that "white" is not-being—and that not in the sense of a particular not-being, but in the sense that it is not all. Hence "substance" is not; for it is true to say that it is white, which we found to mean not-being. If to avoid this we say that even "white" means substance, it follows that "being" has more than one meaning.

In particular, then, Being will not have magnitude, if it is substance. For each of the two parts must *be* in a different sense.

(2) Substance is plainly divisible into other substances, if we consider the mere nature of a definition. For instance, if "man" is a substance, "animal" and "biped" must also be substances. For if not substances, they must be attributes—and if attributes, attributes either of (a) man or of (b) some other subject. But neither is possible.

(a) An attribute is either that which may or may not belong to the subject or that in whose definition the subject of which it is an attribute is involved. Thus "sitting" is an example of a separable attribute, while "snubness" contains the definition of "nose," to which we attribute snubness. Further, the definition of the whole is not contained in the definitions of the contents or elements of the definitory formula; that of "man" for instance in "biped," or that of "white man" in "white." If then this is so, and if "biped" is supposed to be an attribute of "man," it must be either separable, so that "man" might possibly not be "biped," or the definition of "man" must come into the definition of "biped"—which is impossible, as the converse is the case.

(b) If, on the other hand, we suppose that "biped" and "animal" are attributes not of man but of something else, and are not each of them a substance, then "man" too will be an attribute of something else. But we must assume that substance is *not* the attribute of anything, and that the subject of which both "biped" and "animal" and each separately are predicated is the subject also of the complex "biped animal."

Are we then to say that the All is composed of indivisible substances? Some thinkers did, in point of fact, give way to both arguments. To the argument that all things are one if being means one thing, they conceded that not-being is;

to that from bisection, they yielded by positing atomic magnitudes. But obviously it is not true that if being means one
thing, and cannot at the same time mean the contradictory
of this, there will be nothing which is not, for even if what
is not cannot *be* without qualification, there is no reason why
it should not be a particular not-being. To say that all things
will be one, if there is nothing besides Being itself, is absurd.
For who understands "being itself" to be anything but a particular substance? But if this is so, there is nothing to prevent
there being many beings, as has been said.

It is, then, clearly impossible for Being to be one in this
sense.

4. [*Statement and examination of the opinions of the natural
philosophers.*] The physicists on the other hand have two
modes of explanation.

The first set make the underlying body one—either one of
the three or something else which is denser than fire and
rarer than air—then generate everything else from this, and
obtain multiplicity by condensation and rarefaction. Now
these are contraries, which may be generalized into "excess
and defect." (Compare Plato's "Great and Small"—except that
he makes these his matter, the one his form, while the others
treat the one which underlies as matter and the contraries as
differentiae, i. e., forms.)

The second set assert that the contrarieties are contained in
the one and emerge from it by segregation, for example,
Anaximander and also all those who assert that "what is" is
one and many, like Empedocles and Anaxagoras; for they
too produce other things from their mixture by segregation.
These differ, however, from each other in that the former
imagines a cycle of such changes, the latter a single series.
Anaxagoras again made both his "homœomerous" substances
and his contraries infinite in multitude, whereas Empedocles
posits only the so-called elements.

The theory of Anaxagoras that the principles are infinite in
multitude was probably due to his acceptance of the common opinion of the physicists that nothing comes into being

from not-being. For this is the reason why they use the phrase "all things were together" and the coming into being of such and such a kind of thing is reduced to change of quality, while some spoke of combination and separation. Moreover, the fact that the contraries proceed from each other led them to the conclusion. The one, they reasoned, must have already existed in the other; for since everything that comes into being must arise either from what is or from what is not, and it is impossible for it to arise from what is not (on this point all the physicists agree), they thought that the truth of the alternative necessarily followed, namely that things come into being out of existent things, i. e., out of things already present, but imperceptible to our senses because of the smallness of their bulk. So they assert that everything has been mixed in everything, because they saw everything arising out of everything. But things, as they say, appear different from one another and receive different names according to the nature of the particles which are numerically predominant among the innumerable constituents of the mixture. For nothing, they say, is purely and entirely white or black or sweet, bone or flesh, but the nature of a thing is held to be that of which it contains the most.

Now (1) the infinite *qua* infinite is unknowable, so that what is infinite in multitude or size is unknowable in quantity, and what is infinite in variety of kind is unknowable in quality. But the principles in question are infinite both in multitude and in kind. Therefore it is impossible to know things which are composed of them; for it is when we know the nature and quantity of its components that we suppose we know a complex.

Further (2) if the parts of a whole may be of any size in the direction either of greatness or of smallness (by "parts" I mean components into which a whole can be divided and which are actually present in it), it is necessary that the whole thing itself may be of any size. Clearly, therefore, since it is impossible for an animal or plant to be indefinitely big or small, neither can its parts be such, or the whole will be the same. But flesh, bone, and the like are the parts of animals, and the fruits are the parts of plants. Hence it is obvious that neither flesh, bone, nor any such thing can be of indefinite size in the direction either of the greater or of the less.

Again (3) according to the theory all such things are already present in one another and do not come into being but are constituents which are separated out, and a thing receives its designation from its chief constituent. Further, anything may come out of anything—water by segregation from flesh and flesh from water. Hence, since every finite body is exhausted by the repeated abstraction of a finite body, it seems obviously to follow that everything *cannot* subsist in everything else. For let flesh be extracted from water and again more flesh be produced from the remainder by repeating the process of separation; then, even though the quantity separated out will continually decrease, still it will not fall below a certain magnitude. If, therefore, the process comes to an end, everything will not be in everything else (for there will be no flesh in the remaining water); if on the other hand it does not, and further extraction is always possible, there will be an infinite multitude of finite equal particles in a finite quantity—which is impossible. Another proof may be added: Since every body must diminish in size when something is taken from it, and flesh is quantitatively definite in respect both of greatness and smallness, it is clear that from the minimum quantity of flesh no body can be separated out; for the flesh left would be less than the minimum of flesh.

Lastly (4) in each of his infinite bodies there would be already present infinite flesh and blood and brain—having a distinct existence, however, from one another, and no less real than the infinite bodies, and each infinite; which is contrary to reason.

The statement that complete separation never will take place is correct enough, though Anaxagoras is not fully aware of what it means. For affections are indeed inseparable. If then colours and states had entered into the mixture, and if separation took place, there would be a "white" or a "healthy" which was nothing *but* white or healthy, i. e., was not the predicate of a subject. So his "Mind" is an absurd person aiming at the impossible, if he is supposed to wish to separate them, and it is impossible to do so, both in respect of quantity and of quality—of quantity, because there is no minimum magnitude, and of quality, because affections are inseparable.

Nor is Anaxagoras right about the coming to be of homogeneous bodies. It is true there is a sense in which clay is divided into pieces of clay, but there is another in which it is not. Water and air are, and are generated, "from" each other, but not in the way in which bricks come "from" a house and again a house "from" bricks; and it is better to assume a smaller and finite number of principles, as Empedocles does.

5. [*The principles are contraries.*] All thinkers then agree in making the contraries principles, both those who describe the All as one and unmoved (for even Parmenides treats hot and cold as principles under the names of fire and earth) and those too who use the rare and the dense. The same is true of Democritus also, with his plenum and void, both of which exist, he says, the one as being, the other as not-being. Again he speaks of differences in position, shape, and order, and these are genera of which the species are contraries, namely, of position, above and below, before and behind; of shape, angular and angle-less, straight and round.

It is plain then that they all in one way or another identify the contraries with the principles. And with good reason. For first principles must not be derived from one another nor from anything else, while everything has to be derived from them. But these conditions are fulfilled by the primary contraries, which are not derived from anything else because they are primary, nor from each other because they are contraries.

But we must see how this can be arrived at as a reasoned result, as well as in the way just indicated.

Our first presupposition must be that in nature nothing acts on, or is acted on by, any other thing at random, nor may anything come from anything else, unless we mean that it does so in virtue of a concomitant attribute. For how could "white" come from "musical," unless "musical" happened to be an attribute of the not-white or of the black? No, "white" comes from "not-white"—and not from *any* "not-white," but from black or some intermediate colour. Similarly, "musical" comes to be from "not-musical," but not from *any* thing other than musical, but from "unmusical" or any intermediate state there may be.

Nor again do things pass into the first chance thing; "white" does not pass into "musical" (except, it may be, in virtue of a concomitant attribute), but into "not-white"—and not into any chance thing which is not white, but into black or an intermediate colour; "musical" passes into "not-musical"—and not into any chance thing other than musical, but into "unmusical" or any intermediate state there may be.

The same holds of other things also; even things which are not simple but complex follow the same principle, but the opposite state has not received a name, so we fail to notice the fact. What is in tune must come from what is not in tune, and *vice versa;* the tuned passes into untunedness—and not into *any* untunedness, but into the corresponding opposite. It does not matter whether we take attunement, order, or composition for our illustration; the principle is obviously the same in all, and in fact applies equally to the production of a house, a statue, or any other complex. A house comes from certain things in a certain state of separation instead of conjunction, a statue (or any other thing that has been shaped) from shapelessness—each of these objects being partly order and partly composition.

If then this is true, everything that comes to be or passes away comes from, or passes into, its contrary or an intermediate state. But the intermediates are derived from the contraries—colours, for instance, from black and white. Everything, therefore, that comes to be by a natural process is either a contrary or a product of contraries.

Up to this point we have practically had most of the other writers on the subject with us, as I have said already; for all of them identify their elements, and what they call their principles, with the contraries, giving no reason indeed for the theory, but constrained as it were by the truth itself. They differ, however, from one another in that some assume contraries which are more primary, others contraries which are less so; some those more knowable in the order of explanation, others those more familiar to sense. For some make hot and cold, or again moist and dry, the conditions of becoming; while others make odd and even, or again Love and Strife; and these differ from each other in the way mentioned.

Hence their principles are in one sense the same, in another different; different certainly, as indeed most people think, but the same inasmuch as they are analogous; for all are taken from the same table of columns, some of the pairs being wider, others narrower in extent. In this way then their theories are both the same and different, some better, some worse; some, as I have said, take as their contraries what is more knowable in the order of explanation, others what is more familiar to sense. (The universal is more knowable in the order of explanation, the particular in the order of sense; for explanation has to do with the universal, sense with the particular.) "The great and the small," for example, belong to the former class, "the dense and the rare" to the latter.

It is clear then that our principles must be contraries.

6. [*The principles are two, or three, in number.*] The next question is whether the principles are two or three or more in number.

One they cannot be, for there cannot be one contrary. Nor can they be innumerable, because, if so, Being will not be knowable; and in any one genus there is only one contrariety, and substance is one genus; also a finite number is sufficient, and a finite number, such as the principles of Empedocles, is better than an infinite multitude; for Empedocles professes to obtain from his principles all that Anaxagoras obtains from his innumerable principles. Lastly, some contraries are more primary than others, and some arise from others—for example sweet and bitter, white and black—whereas the principles must always remain principles.

This will suffice to show that the principles are neither one nor innumerable.

Granted, then, that they are a limited number, it is plausible to suppose them more than two. For it is difficult to see how either density should be of such a nature as to act in any way on rarity or rarity on density. The same is true of any other pair of contraries; for Love does not gather Strife together and make things out of it, nor does Strife make anything out of Love, but both act on a third thing different from both. Some indeed assume more than one such thing from which they construct the world of nature.

Other objections to the view that it is not necessary to assume a third principle as a substratum may be added. (1) We do not find that the contraries constitute the *substance* of any thing. But what is a first principle ought not to be the *predicate* of any subject. If it were, there would be a principle of the supposed principle; for the subject is a principle, and prior presumably to what is predicated of it. Again (2) we hold that a substance is not contrary to another substance. How then can substance be derived from what are not substances? Or how can non-substance be prior to substance?

If then we accept both the former argument and this one, we must, to preserve both, assume a third somewhat as the substratum of the contraries, such as is spoken of by those who describe the All as one nature—water or fire or what is intermediate between them. What is intermediate seems preferable; for fire, earth, air, and water are already involved with pairs of contraries. There is, therefore, much to be said for those who make the underlying substance different from these four; of the rest, the next best choice is air, as presenting sensible differences in a less degree than the others; and after air, water. All, however, agree in this, that they differentiate their One by means of the contraries, such as density and rarity and more and less, which may of course be generalized, as has already been said, into excess and defect. Indeed this doctrine too (that the One and excess and defect are the principles of things) would appear to be of old standing, though in different forms; for the early thinkers made the two the active and the one the passive principle, whereas some of the more recent maintain the reverse.

To suppose then that the elements are three in number would seem, from these and similar considerations, a plausible view, as I said before. On the other hand, the view that they are more than three in number would seem to be untenable.

For the one substratum is sufficient to be acted on; but if we have four contraries, there will be two contrarieties, and we shall have to suppose an intermediate nature for each pair separately. If, on the other hand, the contrarieties, being two, can generate from each other, the second contrariety will be superfluous. Moreover, it is impossible that there should be more than one *primary* contrariety. For substance is a single genus of being, so that the principles can differ only as prior and posterior, *not* in genus; in a single genus there is always a single contrariety, all the other contrarieties in it being held to be reducible to one.

It is clear then that the number of elements is neither one nor more than two or three; but whether two or three is, as I said, a question of considerable difficulty.

7. [*The number and nature of the principles.*] We will now give our own account, approaching the question first with reference to becoming in its widest sense; for we shall be following the natural order of inquiry if we speak first of common characteristics, and then investigate the characteristics of special cases.

We say that one thing comes to be from another thing, and one sort of thing from another sort of thing, both in the case of simple and of complex things. I mean the following. We can say (1) the "man becomes musical," (2) what is "not-musical becomes musical," or (3) the "not-musical man becomes a musical man." Now what becomes in (1) and (2) —"man" and "not musical"—I call *simple*, and what each becomes—"musical"—simple also. But when (3) we say the "not-musical man becomes a musical man," both what becomes and what it becomes are *complex*.

As regards one of these simple "things that become" we say not only "this becomes so-and-so," but also "from being this, comes to be so-and-so," as "from being not-musical comes to be musical"; as regards the other we do not say this in all cases, as we do not say (1) "from being a man he came to be musical" but only "the man became musical."

When a "simple" thing is said to become something, in one case (1) it survives through the process, in the other (2) it does not. For the man remains a man and is such even when he becomes musical, whereas what is not musical or is unmusical does not continue to exist, either simply or combined with the subject.

These distinctions drawn, one can gather from surveying the various cases of becoming in the way we are describing that, as we say, there must always be an underlying something, namely that which becomes, and that this, though always one numerically, in form at least is not one. (By that I mean that it can be described in different ways.) For "to be man" is not the same as "to be unmusical." One part survives, the other does not; what is not an opposite survives (for "man" survives), but "not-musical" or "unmusical" does not survive, nor does the compound of the two, namely "unmusical man."

We speak of "becoming that from this" instead of "this becoming that" more in the case of what does not survive the change—"becoming musical from unmusical," not "from man" —but there are exceptions, as we sometimes use the latter form of expression even of what survives; we speak of "a statue coming to be from bronze," not of the "bronze becoming a statue." The change, however, from an opposite which does not survive is described indifferently in both ways, "becoming that from this" or "this becoming that." We say both that "the unmusical becomes musical," and that "from unmusical he becomes musical." And so both forms are used of the complex, "becoming a musical man from an unmusical man," and "an unmusical man becoming a musical man."

But there are different senses of "coming to be." In some

cases we do not use the expression "come to be," but "come to be so-and-so." Only substances are said to "come to be" in the unqualified sense.

Now in all cases other than substance it is plain that there must be some subject, namely, that which becomes. For we know that when a thing comes to be of such a quantity or quality or in such a relation, time, or place, a subject is always presupposed, since substance alone is not predicated of another subject, but everything else of substance.

But that substances too, and anything else than can be said "to be" without qualification, come to be from some substratum, will appear on examination. For we find in every case something that underlies from which proceeds that which comes to be; for instance, animals and plants from seed.

Generally things which come to be, come to be in different ways: (1) by change of shape, as a statue; (2) by addition, as things which grow; (3) by taking away, as the Hermes from the stone; (4) by putting together, as a house; (5) by alteration, as things which "turn" in respect of their material substance.

It is plain that these are all cases of coming to be from a substratum.

Thus, clearly, from what has been said, whatever comes to be is always complex. There is, on the one hand, (a) something which comes into existence, and again (b) something which becomes that—the latter (b) in two senses, either the subject or the opposite. By the "opposite" I mean the "unmusical," by the "subject" "man," and similarly I call the absence of shape or form or order the "opposite," and the bronze or stone or gold the "subject."

Plainly then, if there are conditions and principles which constitute natural objects and from which they primarily are or have come to be—have come to be, I mean, what each is said to be in its essential nature, not what each is in respect of a concomitant attribute—plainly, I say, everything comes to be from both subject and form. For "musical man" is composed (in a way) of "man" and "musical": you can analyse it into the definitions of its elements. It is clear then that what comes to be will come to be from these elements.

Now the subject is one numerically, though it is two in form. (For it is the man, the gold—the "matter" generally— that is counted, for it is more of the nature of a "this," and what comes to be does not come from it in virtue of a concomitant attribute; the privation, on the other hand, and the contrary *are* incidental in the process.) And the positive form is one—the order, the acquired art of music, or any similar predicate.

There is a sense, therefore, in which we must declare the principles to be two, and a sense in which they are three; a sense in which the contraries are the principles—say for example the musical and the unmusical, the hot and the cold, the tuned and the untuned—and a sense in which they are not, since it is impossible for the contraries to be acted on by each other. But this difficulty also is solved by the fact that the substratum is different from the contraries, for it is itself not a contrary. The principles therefore are, in a way, not more in number than the contraries, but as it were two, nor yet precisely two, since there is a difference of essential nature, but three. For "to be man" is different from "to be unmusical," and "to be unformed" from "to be bronze."

We have now stated the number of the principles of natural objects which are subject to generation, and how the number is reached; and it is clear that there must be a substratum for the contraries, and that the contraries must be two. (Yet in another way of putting it this is not necessary, as one of the contraries will serve to effect the change by its successive absence and presence.)

The underlying nature is an object of scientific knowledge, by an analogy. For as the bronze is to the statue, the wood to the bed, or the matter and the formless before receiving form to any thing which has form, so is the underlying nature to substance, i. e., the "this" or existent.

This then is one principle (though not one or existent in the same sense as the "this"), and the definition was one as we agreed; then further there is its contrary, the privation. In what sense these are two, and in what sense more, has been stated above. Briefly, we explained first that only the contraries were principles, and later that a substratum was indispensable, and that the principles were three; our last statement has elucidated the difference between the contraries, the mutual relation of the principles, and the nature of the substratum. Whether the form or the substratum is the essential nature of a physical object is not yet clear. But that the principles are three, and in what sense, and the way in which each is a principle, is clear.

So much then for the question of the number and the nature of the principles.

8. [*The true opinion removes the difficulty felt by the early philosophers.*] We will now proceed to show that the difficulty of the early thinkers, as well as our own, is solved in this way alone.

The first of those who studied science were misled in their search for truth and the nature of things by their inexperience, which as it were thrust them into another path. So they say that none of the things that are either comes to be or passes out of existence, because what comes to be must do so either from what is or from what is not, both of which are impossible. For what is cannot come to be (because it *is* already), and from what is not nothing could have come to be (because something must be present as a substratum). So too they exaggerated the consequence of this, and went so far as to deny even the *existence* of a plurality of things, maintaining that only Being itself is. Such then was their opinion, and such the reason for its adoption.

Our explanation on the other hand is that the phrases "something comes to be from what is or from what is not," "what is not or what is does something or has something done to it or becomes some particular thing," are to be taken (in the first way of putting our explanation) in the same sense as "a doctor does something or has something done to him," "is or becomes something from being a doctor." These expressions may be taken in two senses, and so too, clearly, may "from being," and "being acts or is acted on." A doctor builds a house, not *qua* doctor, but *qua* housebuilder, and turns gray, not *qua* doctor, but *qua* dark-haired. On the other hand he doctors or fails to doctor *qua* doctor. But we are using words most appropriately when we say that a doctor does something or undergoes something, or becomes something from being a doctor, if he does, undergoes, or becomes *qua* doctor. Clearly then also "to come to be so-and-so from not-being" means "*qua* not-being."

It was through failure to make this distinction that those thinkers gave the matter up, and through this error that they went so much farther astray as to suppose that nothing else comes to be or exists apart from Being itself, thus doing away with all becoming.

We ourselves are in agreement with them in holding that nothing can be said without qualification to come from what is not. But nevertheless we maintain that a thing may "come to be from what is not"—that is, in a qualified sense. For a thing comes to be from the privation, which in its own nature is not-being—this not surviving as a constituent of the result. Yet this causes surprise, and it is thought impossible that something should come to be in the way described from what is not.

In the same way we maintain that nothing comes to be from being, and that being does not come to be except in a qualified sense. In that way, however, it does, just as animal might come to be from animal, and an animal of a certain kind from an animal of a certain kind. Thus, suppose a dog to come to be from a horse. The dog would then, it is true, come to be from animal (as well as from an animal of a certain kind) but not as *animal*, for that is already there. But if anything is to become an animal, *not* in a qualified sense, it will not be from animal; and if being, not from being—nor from not-being either, for it has been explained that by "from not-being" we mean from not-being *qua* not-being.

Note further that we do not subvert the principle that everything either is or is not.

This then is one way of solving the difficulty. Another consists in pointing out that the same things can be explained in terms of potentiality and actuality. But this has been done with greater precision elsewhere.

So as we said, the difficulties which constrain people to deny the existence of some of the things we mentioned are now solved. For it was this reason which also caused some of the earlier thinkers to turn so far aside from the road which leads to coming to be and passing away and change generally. If they had come in sight of this nature, all their ignorance would have been dispelled.

9. [*Further reflections on the first principles of nature.*] Others, indeed, have apprehended the nature in question, but not adequately.

In the first place they allow that a thing may come to be without qualification from not-being, accepting on this point the statement of Parmenides. Secondly, they think that if the substratum is one numerically, it must have also only a single potentiality—which is a very different thing.

Now we distinguish matter and privation, and hold that one of these, namely the matter, is not-being only in virtue of an attribute which it has, while the privation in its own nature is not-being; and that the matter is nearly, in a sense *is*, substance, while the privation in no sense is. They, on the other hand, identify their Great and Small alike with not-being, and that whether they are taken together as one or separately. Their triad is therefore of quite a different kind from ours. For they got so far as to see that there must be some underlying nature, but they make it one—for even if one philosopher makes a dyad of it, which he calls Great and Small, the effect is the same, for he overlooked the other nature. For the one which persists is a joint cause, with the form, of what comes to be—a mother, as it were. But the negative part of the contrariety may often seem, if you concentrate your attention on it as an evil agent, not to exist at all.

For admitting with them that there is something divine,

good, and desirable, we hold that there are two principles, the one contrary to it, the other such as of its own nature to desire and yearn for it. But the consequence of their view is that the contrary desires its own extinction. Yet the form cannot desire itself, for it is not defective; nor can the contrary desire it, for contraries are mutually destructive. The truth is that what desires the form is matter, as the female desires the male and the ugly the beautiful—only the ugly or the female not *per se* but *per accidens*.

The matter comes to be and ceases to be in one sense, while in another it does not. As that which contains the privation, it ceases to be in its own nature, for what ceases to be—the privation—is contained within it. But as potentiality it does not cease to be in its own nature, but is necessarily outside the sphere of becoming and ceasing to be. For if it came to be, something must have existed as a primary substratum from which it should come and which should persist in it; but this is its own special nature, so that it will be before coming to be. (For my definition of matter is just this—the primary substratum of each thing, from which it comes to be without qualification, and which persists in the result.) And if it ceases to be it will pass into that at the last, so it will have ceased to be before ceasing to be.

The accurate determination of the first principle in respect of form, whether it is one or many and what it is or what they are, is the province of the primary type of science; so these questions may stand over till then. But of the natural, i. e., perishable, forms we shall speak in the expositions which follow.

The above, then, may be taken as sufficient to establish that there are principles and what they are and how many there are. Now let us make a fresh start and proceed.

1. [*Nature and the natural.*] Of things that exist, some exist by nature, some from other causes.

"By nature" the animals and their parts exist, and the plants and the simple bodies (earth, fire, air, water)—for we say that these and the like exist "by nature."

All the things mentioned present a feature in which they differ from things which are *not* constituted by nature. Each of them has *within itself* a principle of motion and of stationariness (in respect of place, or of growth and decrease, or by way of alteration). On the other hand, a bed and a coat and anything else of that sort, *qua* receiving these designations—i. e., in so far as they are products of art—have no innate impulse to change. But in so far as they happen to be composed of stone or of earth or of a mixture of the two, they *do* have such an impulse, and just to that extent—which seems to indicate that *nature is a source or cause of being moved and of being at rest in that to which it belongs primarily,* in virtue of itself and not in virtue of a concomitant attribute.

I say "not in virtue of a concomitant attribute," because (for instance) a man who is a doctor might cure himself. Nevertheless it is not in so far as he is a patient that he possesses the art of medicine; it merely has happened that the same man is doctor and patient—and that is why these attributes are not always found together. So it is with all other artificial products. None of them has in itself the source of its own production. But while in some cases (for instance, houses and the other products of manual labour) that principle is in something else external to the thing, in others—

those which may cause a change in themselves in virtue of a concomitant attribute—it lies in the things themselves (but not in virtue of what they are).

"Nature" then is what has been stated. Things "have a nature" which have a principle of this kind. Each of them is a substance; for it is subject, and nature always implies a subject in which it inheres.

The term "according to nature" is applied to all these things and also to the attributes which belong to them in virtue of what they are, for instance the property of fire to be carried upwards—which is not a "nature" nor "has a nature" but is "by nature" or "according to nature."

What nature is, then, and the meaning of the terms "by nature" and "according to nature," has been stated. *That* nature exists, it would be absurd to try to prove; for it is obvious that there are many things of this kind, and to prove what is obvious by what is not is the mark of a man who is unable to distinguish what is self-evident from what is not. (This state of mind is clearly possible. A man blind from birth might reason about colours. Presumably therefore such persons must be talking about words without any thought to correspond.)

Some identify the nature or substance of a natural object with that immediate constituent of it which taken by itself is without arrangement, e. g., the wood is the "nature" of the bed, and the bronze the "nature" of the statue.

As an indication of this Antiphon points out that if you planted a bed and the rotting wood acquired the power of sending up a shoot, it would not be a bed that would come up, but *wood*—which shows that the arrangement in accordance with the rules of the art is merely an incidental attribute, whereas the real nature is the other, which, further, persists continuously through the process of making.

But if the material of each of these objects has itself the same relation to something else, say bronze (or gold) to water, bones (or wood) to earth and so on, *that* (they say) would be their nature and essence. Consequently some assert earth, others fire or air or water or some or all of these, to be the nature of the things that are. For whatever any one of them supposed to have this character—whether one thing or more than one thing—this or these he declared to be the whole of substance, all else being its affections, states, or dispositions. Every such thing they held to be eternal (for it could not pass into anything else), but other things to come into being and cease to be times without number.

This then is one account of "nature," namely that it is the immediate material substratum of things which have in themselves a principle of motion or change.

Another account is that "nature" is the shape or form which is specified in the definition of the thing.

For the word "nature" is applied to what is according to nature and the natural in the same way as "art" is applied to what is artistic or a work of art. We should not say in the latter case that there is anything artistic about a thing, if it is a bed only potentially, not yet having the form of a bed; nor should we call it a work of art. The same is true of natural compounds. What is potentially flesh or bone has not yet its own "nature," and does not exist "by nature," until it receives the form specified in the definition, which we name in defining what flesh or bone is. Thus in the second sense of "nature" it would be the shape or form (not separable except in statement) of things which have in themselves a source of motion. (The combination of the two, e. g., man, is not "nature" but "by nature" or "natural.")

The form indeed is "nature" rather than the matter; for a thing is more properly said to be what it is when it has attained to fulfillment than when it exists potentially. Again man is born from man, but not bed from bed. That is why people say that the figure is not the nature of a bed, but the wood is—if the bed sprouted not a bed but wood would come up. But even if the figure *is* art, then on the same principle the shape of man is his nature. For man is born from man.

We also speak of a thing's nature as being exhibited in the process of growth by which its nature is attained. The "nature" in this sense is not like "doctoring," which leads not to the art of doctoring but to health. Doctoring must start from the art, not lead to it. But it is not in this way that nature (in the one sense) is related to nature (in the other.) What grows *qua* growing grows from something into something. Into what then does it grow? Not into that from which it arose but into that to which it tends. The shape then is nature.

"Shape" and "nature," it should be added, are used in two senses. For the privation too is in a way form. But whether in unqualified coming to be there is privation, i. e., a contrary to what comes to be, we must consider later.

2. [*Distinction of the natural philosopher from the mathematician and the metaphysician.*] We have distinguished, then, the different ways in which the term "nature" is used.

The next point to consider is how the mathematician differs from the physicist. Obviously physical bodies contain surfaces and volumes, lines and points, and these are the subject matter of mathematics.

Further, is astronomy different from physics or a department of it? It seems absurd that the physicist should be supposed to know the nature of sun or moon, but not to know any of their essential attributes, particularly as the writers on physics obviously do discuss their shape also and whether the earth and the world are spherical or not.

Now the mathematician, though he too treats of these things, nevertheless does not treat of them as the limits of a physical body; nor does he consider the attributes indicated as the attributes of such bodies. That is why he separates them; for in thought they are separable from motion, and it makes no difference, nor does any falsity result, if they are separated. The holders of the theory of Forms do the same, though they are not aware of it; for they separate the objects of physics, which are less separable than those of mathematics. This becomes plain if one tries to state in each of the two cases the definitions of the things and of their attributes. "Odd" and "even," "straight" and "curved," and likewise "number," "line," and "figure," do not involve motion; not so "flesh" and "bone" and "man"—*these* are defined like "snub nose," not like "curved."

Similar evidence is supplied by the more physical of the branches of mathematics, such as optics, harmonics, and astronomy. These are in a way the converse of geometry. While geometry investigates physical lines but not *qua* physical, optics investigates mathematical lines, but *qua* physical, not *qua* mathematical.

Since "nature" has two senses, the form and the matter, we must investigate its objects as we would the essence of snubness. That is, such things are neither independent of matter nor can be defined in terms of matter only. Here too indeed one might raise a difficulty. Since there are two natures, with which is the physicist concerned? Or should he investigate the combination of the two? But if the combination of the two, then also each severally. Does it belong then to the same or to different sciences to know each severally?

If we look at the ancients, physics would seem to be concerned with the *matter*. (It was only very slightly that Empedocles and Democritus touched on the forms and the essence.)

But if on the other hand art imitates nature, and it is the part of the same discipline to know the form and the matter up to a point (e. g., the doctor has a knowledge of health and also of bile and phlegm, in which health is realized, and the builder both of the form of the house and of the matter, namely that it is bricks and beams, and so forth); if this is so, it would be the part of physics also to know nature in both its senses.

Again, "that for the sake of which," or the end, belongs to the same department of knowledge as the means. But the nature is the end or "that for the sake of which." For if a thing undergoes a continuous change and there is a stage which is last, this stage is the end or "that for the sake of which." (That is why the poet was carried away into making an absurd statement when he said "he has the end for the sake of which he was born." For not every stage that is last claims to be an end, but only that which is best.)

For the arts make their material (some simply "make" it, others make it serviceable), and we use everything as if it was there for our sake. (We also are in a sense an end. "That for the sake of which" has two senses: the distinction is made in our work *On Philosophy*.) The arts, therefore, which govern the matter and have knowledge are two, namely the art which uses the product and the art which directs the production of it. That is why the using art also is in a sense directive; but it differs in that it knows the form, whereas the art which is directive as being concerned with production knows the matter. For the helmsman knows and prescribes what sort of form a helm should have, the other from what wood it should be made and by means of what operations. In the products of art, however, we make the material with a view to the function, whereas in the products of nature the matter is there all along.

Again, matter is a relative term: to each form there corresponds a special matter. How far then must the physicist know the form or essence? Up to a point, perhaps, as the doctor must know sinew or the smith bronze (i. e., until he understands the purpose of each); and the physicist is concerned only with things whose forms are separable indeed, but do not exist apart from matter. Man is begotten by man and by the sun as well. The mode of existence and essence of the separable it is the business of the primary type of philosophy to define.

3. [*The essential conditions of change.*] Now that we have established these distinctions, we must proceed to consider causes, their character and number. Knowledge is the object of our inquiry, and men do not think they know a thing till they have grasped the "why" of it (which is to grasp its primary cause). So clearly we too must do this as regards both coming to be and passing away and every kind of physical change, in order that, knowing their principles, we may try to refer to these principles each of our problems.

In one sense, then, (1) that out of which a thing comes to be and which persists, is called "cause," e. g., the bronze of the statue, the silver of the bowl, and the genera of which the bronze and the silver are species.

In another sense (2) the form or the archetype, i. e., the statement of the essence, and its genera, are called "causes" (e. g., of the octave the relation of 2 : 1, and generally number), and the parts in the definition.

Again (3) the primary source of the change or coming to rest; e. g., the man who gave advice is a cause, the father is cause of the child, and generally what makes of what is made and what causes change of what is changed.

Again (4) in the sense of end or "that for the sake of which" a thing is done, e. g., health is the cause of walking about. ("Why is he walking about?" we say. "To be healthy," and, having said that, we think we have assigned the cause.) The same is true also of all the intermediate steps which are brought about through the action of something else as means towards the end, e. g., reduction of flesh, purging, drugs, or surgical instruments are means towards health. All these things are "for the sake of" the end, though they differ from one another in that some are activities, others instruments.

This then perhaps exhausts the number of ways in which the term "cause" is used.

As the word has several senses, it follows that there are several causes of the same thing (not merely in virtue of a concomitant attribute), e. g., both the art of the sculptor and the bronze are causes of the statue. These are causes of the statue *qua* statue, not in virtue of anything else that it may be—only not in the same way, the one being the material cause, the other the cause whence the motion comes. Some things cause each other reciprocally, e. g., hard work causes fitness and *vice versa,* but again not in the same way, but the one as end, the other as the origin of change. Further the same thing is the cause of contrary results. For that which by its presence brings about one result is sometimes blamed for bringing about the contrary by its absence. Thus we ascribe the wreck of a ship to the absence of the pilot whose presence was the cause of its safety.

All the causes now mentioned fall into four familiar divisions. The letters are the causes of syllables, the material of artificial products, fire, etc., of bodies, the parts of the whole, and the premisses of the conclusion, in the sense of "that from which." Of these pairs the one set are causes in the sense of substratum, e. g., the parts, the other set in the sense of essence—the whole and the combination and the form. But the seed and the doctor and the adviser, and generally the maker, are all sources whence the change or stationariness originates, while the others are causes in the sense of the end or the good of the rest; for "that for the sake of which" means what is best and the end of the things that lead up to it. (Whether we say the "good itself" or the "apparent good" makes no difference.)

Such then is the number and nature of the kinds of cause. Now the modes of causation are many, though when brought under heads they too can be reduced in number. For "cause" is used in many senses and even within the same kind one may be prior to another (e. g., the doctor and the expert are causes of health, the relation 2 : 1 and number of the octave), and always what is inclusive to what is particular. Another mode of causation is the incidental and its genera, e. g., in one way "Polyclitus," in another "sculptor" is the cause of a statue, because "being Polyclitus" and "sculptor" are incidentally conjoined. Also the classes in which the incidental attribute is included; thus "a man" could be said to be the cause of a statue or, generally, "a living creature." An incidental attribute too may be more or less remote, e. g., suppose that "a pale man" or "a musical man" were said to be the cause of the statue.

All causes, both proper and incidental, may be spoken of either as potential or as actual; e. g., the cause of a house being built is either "housebuilder" or "housebuilder building."

Similar distinctions can be made in the things of which the causes are causes, e. g., of "this statue" or of "statue" or of "image" generally, of "this bronze" or of "bronze" or of "material" generally. So too with the incidental attributes. Again we may use a complex expression for either and say,

e. g., neither "Polyclitus" nor "sculptor" but "Polyclitus, sculptor."

All these various uses, however, come to six in number, under each of which again the usage is twofold. Cause means either what is particular or a genus, or an incidental attribute or a genus of that, and these either as a complex or each by itself; and all six either as actual or as potential. The difference is this much, that causes which are actually at work and particular exist and cease to exist simultaneously with their effect, e. g., this healing person with this being-healed person and that housebuilding man with that being-built house; but this is not always true of potential causes—the house and the housebuilder do not pass away simultaneously.

In investigating the cause of each thing it is always necessary to seek what is most precise (as also in other things); thus man builds because he is a builder, and a builder builds in virtue of his art of building. This last cause then is prior; and so generally.

Further, generic effects should be assigned to generic causes, particular effects to particular causes, e. g., statue to sculptor, this statue to this sculptor; and powers are relative to possible effects, actually operating causes to things which are actually being effected.

This must suffice for our account of the number of causes and the modes of causation.

4. [*The opinions of others about chance and spontaneity.*] But chance also and spontaneity are reckoned among causes; many things are said both to be and to come to be as a result of chance and spontaneity. We must inquire therefore in what manner chance and spontaneity are present among the causes enumerated, and whether they are the same or different, and generally what chance and spontaneity are.

Some people even question whether they are real or not. They say that nothing happens by chance, but that everything which we ascribe to chance or spontaneity has some definite cause, e. g., coming "by chance" into the market and finding there a man whom one wanted but did not expect to meet is due to one's wish to go and buy in the market. Similarly in other cases of chance it is always possible, they maintain, to find something which is the cause; but not chance, for if chance were real, it would seem strange indeed, and the question might be raised, why on earth none of the wise men of old in speaking of the causes of generation and decay took account of chance; whence it would seem that they too did not believe that anything is by chance. But there is a further circumstance that is surprising. Many things both come to be and are by chance and spontaneity, and although all know that each of them can be ascribed to some cause (as the old argument said which denied chance), nevertheless they speak of some of these things as happening by chance and others not. For this reason also they ought to have at least referred to the matter in some way or other.

Certainly the early physicists found no place for chance among the causes which they recognized—love, strife, mind, fire, or the like. This is strange, whether they supposed that there is no such thing as chance or whether they thought there is but omitted to mention it—and that too when they sometimes used it, as Empedocles does when he says that the air is not always separated into the highest region, but "as it may chance." At any rate he says in his cosmogony that "it happened to run that way at that time, but it often ran otherwise." He tells us also that most of the parts of animals came to be by chance.

There are some too who ascribe this heavenly sphere and all the worlds to spontaneity. They say that the vortex arose spontaneously, i. e., the motion that separated and arranged in its present order all that exists. This statement might well cause surprise. For they are asserting that chance is not responsible for the existence or generation of animals and plants, nature or mind or something of the kind being the cause of them (for it is not any chance thing that comes from a given seed but an olive from one kind and a man from another); and yet at the same time they assert that the heavenly sphere and the divinest of visible things arose spontaneously, having no such cause as is assigned to animals and plants. Yet if this is so, it is a fact which deserves to be dwelt upon, and something might well have been said about it. For besides the other absurdities of the statement, it is the more absurd that people should make it when they see nothing coming to be spontaneously in the heavens, but much happening by chance among the things which as they say are not due to chance; whereas we should have expected exactly the opposite.

Others there are who, indeed, believe that chance is a cause, but that it is inscrutable to human intelligence, as being a divine thing and full of mystery.

Thus we must inquire what chance and spontaneity are, whether they are the same or different, and how they fit into our division of causes.

5. [*Do chance and spontaneity exist? What is chance and what are its characteristics?*] First then we observe that some things always come to pass in the same way, and others for the most part. It is clearly of neither of these that chance is said to be the cause, nor can the "effect of chance" be identified with any of the things that come to pass by necessity and always, or for the most part. But as there is a third class of events besides these two—events which all say are "by chance"—it is plain that there is such a thing as chance and spontaneity; for we know that things of this kind are due to chance and that things due to chance are of this kind.

But, secondly, some events are for the sake of something, others not. Again, some of the former class are in accordance with deliberate intention, others not, but both are in the class of things which are for the sake of something. Hence it is clear that even among the things which are outside the necessary and the normal, there are some in connexion with which the phrase "for the sake of something" is applicable. (Events that are for the sake of something include whatever may be done as a result of thought or of nature.) Things of this kind, then, when they come to pass incidentally are said to be "by chance." For just as a thing is something either in virtue of itself or incidentally, so may it be a cause. For instance, the housebuilding faculty is in virtue of itself the cause of a house, whereas the pale or the musical is the incidental cause. That which is *per se* cause of the effect is determinate, but the incidental cause is indeterminable, for the possible attributes of an individual are innumerable. To resume then; when a thing of this kind comes to pass among events which are for the sake of something, it is said to be spontaneous or by chance. (The distinction between the two must be made later—for the present it is sufficient if it is plain that both are in the sphere of things done for the sake of something.)

Example: A man is engaged in collecting subscriptions for a feast. He would have gone to such and such a place for the purpose of getting the money, if he had known. He actually went there for another purpose, and it was only incidentally that he got his money by going there; and this was not due to the fact that he went there as a rule or necessarily, nor is the end effected (getting the money) a cause present in himself —it belongs to the class of things that are intentional and the result of intelligent deliberation. It is when these conditions are satisfied that the man is said to have gone "by chance." If he had gone of deliberate purpose and for the sake of this —if he always or normally went there when he was collecting payments—he would not be said to have gone "by chance."

It is clear then that chance is an incidental cause in the sphere of those actions for the sake of something which involve purpose. Intelligent reflection, then, and chance are in the same sphere, for purpose implies intelligent reflection.

It is necessary, no doubt, that the causes of what comes to pass by chance be indefinite; and that is why chance is supposed to belong to the class of the indefinite and to be inscrutable to man, and why it might be thought that, in a way, nothing occurs by chance. For all these statements are correct, because they are well grounded. Things *do*, in a way, occur by chance, for they occur incidentally and chance is an *incidental cause*. But strictly it is not the *cause*—without qualification—of anything; for instance, a housebuilder is the cause of a house; incidentally, a flute-player may be so.

And the causes of the man's coming and getting the money (when he did not come for the sake of that) are innumerable. He may have wished to see somebody or been following somebody or avoiding somebody, or may have gone to see a spectacle. Thus to say that chance is a thing contrary to rule is correct. For "rule" applies to what is always true or true for the most part, whereas chance belongs to a third type of event. Hence, to conclude, since causes of this kind are indefinite, chance too is indefinite. (Yet in some cases one might raise the question whether *any* incidental fact might be the cause of the chance occurrence, e. g., of health the fresh air or the sun's heat may be the cause, but having had one's hair cut *cannot*; for some incidental causes are more relevant to the effect than others.)

Chance or fortune is called "good" when the result is good, "evil" when it is evil. The terms "good fortune" and "ill fortune" are used when either result is of considerable magnitude. Thus one who comes within an ace of some great evil or great good is said to be fortunate or unfortunate. The mind affirms the presence of the attribute, ignoring the hair's breadth of difference. Further, it is with reason that good fortune is regarded as unstable; for chance is unstable, as none of the things which result from it can be invariable or normal.

Both are then, as I have said, incidental causes—both chance and spontaneity—in the sphere of things which are capable of coming to pass not necessarily, nor normally, and with reference to such of these as might come to pass for the sake of something.

6. [*Distinction between chance and spontaneity, and between both and the essential conditions of change.*] They differ in that "spontaneity" is the wider term. Every result of chance is from what is spontaneous, but not everything that is from what is spontaneous is from chance.

Chance and what results from chance are appropriate to agents that are capable of good fortune and of moral action generally. Therefore necessarily chance is in the sphere of

moral actions. This is indicated by the fact that good fortune
is thought to be the same, or nearly the same, as happiness,
and happiness to be a kind of moral action, since it is well-
doing. Hence what is not capable of moral action cannot do
anything by chance. Thus an inanimate thing or a lower animal or a child cannot do anything by chance, because it is
incapable of deliberate intention; nor can "good fortune" or
"ill fortune" be ascribed to them, except metaphorically, as
Protarchus, for example, said that the stones of which altars
are made are fortunate because they are held in honour,
while their fellows are trodden under foot. Even these things,
however, can in a way be affected by chance, when one who
is dealing with them does something to them by chance, but
not otherwise.

The spontaneous on the other hand is found both in the
lower animals and in many inanimate objects. We say, for
example, that the horse came "spontaneously," because,
though his coming saved him, he did not come for the sake
of safety. Again, the tripod fell "of itself," because, though
when it fell it stood on its feet so as to serve for a seat, it
did not fall for the sake of that.

Hence it is clear that events which (1) belong to the general class of things that may come to pass for the sake of
something, (2) do not come to pass for the sake of what
actually results, and (3) have an external cause, may be
described by the phrase "from spontaneity." These "spontaneous" events are said to be "from chance" if they have
the further characteristics of being the objects of deliberate
intention and due to agents capable of that mode of action.
This is indicated by the phrase "in vain," which is used when
A, which is for the sake of B, does not result in B. For instance, taking a walk is for the sake of evacuation of the
bowels; if this does not follow after walking, we say that
we have walked "in vain" and that the walking was "vain."
This implies that what is naturally the means to an end
is "in vain," when it does not effect the end towards which
it was the natural means—for it would be absurd for a man
to say that he had bathed in vain because the sun was not

eclipsed, since the one was not done with a view to the
other. Thus the spontaneous is even according to its deriva-
tion the case in which the thing itself happens in vain. The
stone that struck the man did not fall for the purpose of
striking him; therefore it fell spontaneously, because it might
have fallen by the action of an agent and for the purpose of
striking. The difference between spontaneity and what results by chance is greatest in things that come to be by nature; for when anything comes to be contrary to nature, we
do not say that it came to be by chance, but by spontaneity.
Yet strictly this too is different from the spontaneous proper;
for the cause of the latter is external, that of the former internal.

We have now explained what chance is and what spontaneity is, and in what they differ from each other. Both belong to the mode of causation "source of change," for either
some natural or some intelligent agent is always the cause;
but in this sort of causation the number of possible causes
is infinite.

Spontaneity and chance are causes of effects which, though
they might result from intelligence or nature, have in fact
been caused by something *incidentally*. Now since nothing
which is incidental is prior to what is *per se*, it is clear that
no incidental cause can be prior to a cause *per se*. Spontaneity
and chance, therefore, are posterior to intelligence and nature. Hence, however true it may be that the heavens are
due to spontaneity, it will still be true that intelligence
and nature will be prior causes of this All and of many things
in it besides.

7. [*The physicist demonstrates by means of the four conditions of change.*] It is clear then that there are causes, and
that the number of them is what we have stated. The number is the same as that of the things comprehended under
the question "why." The "why" is referred ultimately either
(1) in things which do not involve motion, e. g., in mathematics, to the "what" (to the definition of "straight line" or
"commensurable," etc.), or (2) to what initiated a motion,

e. g., "why did they go to war?—because there had been a raid"; or (3) we are inquiring "for the sake of what?"— "that they may rule"; or (4) in the case of things that come into being, we are looking for the matter. The causes, therefore, are these and so many in number.

Now, the causes being four, it is the business of the physicist to know about them all, and if he refers his problems back to all of them, he will assign the "why" in the way proper to his science—the matter, the form, the mover, "that for the sake of which." The last three often coincide; for the "what" and "that for the sake of which" are one, while the primary source of motion is the same in species as these (for man generates man), and so too, in general, are all things which cause movement by being themselves moved; and such as are not of this kind are no longer inside the province of physics, for they cause motion not by possessing motion or a source of motion in themselves, but being themselves incapable of motion. Hence there are three branches of study, one of things which are incapable of motion, the second of things in motion, but indestructible, the third of destructible things.

The question "why," then, is answered by reference to the matter, to the form, and to the primary moving cause. For in respect of coming to be it is mostly in this last way that causes are investigated—"what comes to be after what? what was the primary agent or patient?" and so at each step of the series.

Now the principles which cause motion in a physical way are two, of which one is not physical, as it has no principle of motion in itself. Of this kind is whatever causes movement, not being itself moved, such as (1) that which is completely unchangeable, the primary reality, and (2) the essence of that which is coming to be, i. e., the form; for this is the end or "that for the sake of which." Hence since nature is for the sake of something, we must know this cause also. We must explain the "why" in all the senses of the term, namely, (1) that from this that will necessarily result ("from this" either without qualification or in most cases);

(2) that "this must be so if that is to be so" (as the conclusion presupposes the premises); (3) that this was the essence of the thing; and (4) because it is better thus (not without qualification, but with reference to the essential nature in each case).

8. [*Does nature act for an end?*] We must explain then (1) that Nature belongs to the class of causes which act for the sake of something; (2) about the necessary and its place in physical problems, for all writers ascribe things to this cause, arguing that since the hot and the cold, etc., are of such and such a kind, therefore certain things *necessarily* are and come to be—and if they mention any other cause (one his "friendship and strife," another his "mind"), it is only to touch on it, and then goodbye to it.

A difficulty presents itself: why should not nature work, not for the sake of something, nor because it is better so, but just as the sky rains, not in order to make the corn grow, but of necessity? What is drawn up must cool, and what has been cooled must become water and descend, the result of this being that the corn grows. Similarly if a man's crop is spoiled on the threshing floor, the rain did not fall for the sake of this—in order that the crop might be spoiled—but that result just followed. Why then should it not be the same with the parts in nature, e. g., that our teeth should come up *of necessity*—the front teeth sharp, fitted for tearing, the molars broad and useful for grinding down the food—since they did not arise for this end, but it was merely a coincident result; and so with all other parts in which we suppose that there is purpose? Wherever then all the parts came about just what they would have been if they had come to be for an end, such things survived, being organized spontaneously in a fitting way; whereas those which grew otherwise perished and continue to perish, as Empedocles says his "man-faced ox-progeny" did.

Such are the arguments (and others of the kind) which may cause difficulty on this point. Yet it is impossible that this should be the true view. For teeth and all other natural things either invariably or normally come about in a given way; but of not one of the results of chance or spontaneity is this true. We do not ascribe to chance or mere coincidence the frequency of rain in winter, but frequent rain in summer we do; nor heat in the dog days, but only if we have it in winter. If then, it is agreed that things are either the result of coincidence or for an end, and these cannot be the result of coincidence or spontaneity, it follows that they must be for an end; and that such things are all due to nature even the champions of the theory which is before us would agree. Therefore action for an end is present in things which come to be and are by nature.

Further, where a series has a completion, all the preceding steps are for the sake of that. Now surely as in intelligent action, so in nature; and as in nature, so it is in each action, if nothing interferes. Now intelligent action is for the sake of an end; therefore the nature of things also is so. Thus if a house, e. g., had been a thing made by nature, it would have been made in the same way as it is now by art; and if things made by nature were made also by art, they would come to be in the same way as by nature. Each step then in the series is for the sake of the next; and generally art partly completes what nature cannot bring to a finish, and partly imitates her. If, therefore, artificial products are for the sake of an end, so clearly also are natural products. The relation of the later to the earlier terms of the series is the same in both.

This is most obvious in the animals other than man: they make things neither by art nor after inquiry or deliberation. Wherefore people discuss whether it is by intelligence or by some other faculty that these creatures work—spiders, ants, and the like. By gradual advance in this direction we come to see clearly that in plants too that is produced which is conducive to the end—leaves, e. g., grow to provide shade for the fruit. If then it is both by nature and for an end that the swallow makes its nest and the spider its web, and plants grow leaves for the sake of the fruit and send their roots down (not up) for the sake of nourishment, it is plain that this kind of cause is operative in things which come to be and are by nature. And since "nature" means two things, the matter and the form, of which the latter is the end, and since all the rest is for the sake of the end, the form must be the cause in the sense of "that for the sake of which."

Now mistakes come to pass even in the operations of art: the grammarian makes a mistake in writing and the doctor pours out the wrong dose. Hence clearly mistakes are possible in the operations of nature also. If then in art there are cases in which what is rightly produced serves a purpose, and if where mistakes occur there was a purpose in what was attempted, only it was not attained, so must it be also in natural products, and monstrosities will be failures in the purposive effort. Thus in the original combinations the "ox-progeny" if they failed to reach a determinate end must have arisen through the corruption of some principle corresponding to what is now the seed.

Further, seed must have come into being first, and not straightway the animals; the words "whole-natured first . . ." must have meant seed.

Again, in plants too we find the relation of means to end, though the degree of organization is less. Were there then in plants also "olive-headed vine-progeny," like the "man-headed ox-progeny," or not? An absurd suggestion; yet there must have been, if there were such things among animals.

Moreover, among the seeds anything must have come to be at random. But the person who asserts this entirely does away with "nature" and what exists "by nature." For those things are natural which, by a continuous movement originated from an internal principle, arrive at some completion; the same completion is not reached from every principle; nor any chance completion, but always the tendency in each is towards the same end, if there is no impediment.

The end and the means towards it may come about by chance. We say, for instance, that a stranger has come by chance, paid the ransom, and gone away, when he does so as if he had come for that purpose, though it was not for that that he came. This is incidental, for chance is an incidental cause, as I remarked before. But when an event takes place always or for the most part, it is not incidental or by chance. In natural products the sequence is invariable, if there is no impediment.

It is absurd to suppose that purpose is not present because we do not observe the agent deliberating. Art does not deliberate. If the shipbuilding art were in the wood, it would produce the same results *by nature*. If, therefore, purpose is present in art, it is present also in nature. The best illustration is a doctor doctoring himself; nature is like that.

It is plain then that nature is a cause, a cause that operates for a purpose.

9. [*The sense in which necessity is present in natural things.*] As regards what is "of necessity," we must ask whether the necessity is "hypothetical," or "simple" as well. The current view places what is of necessity in the process of production, just as if one were to suppose that the wall of a house necessarily comes to be because what is heavy is naturally carried downwards and what is light to the top, wherefore the stones and foundations take the lowest place, with earth above because it is lighter, and wood at the top of all as being the lightest. Whereas, though the wall does not come to be *without* these it is not *due* to these, except as its material cause; it comes to be for the sake of sheltering and guarding certain things. Similarly in all other things which involve production for an end; the product cannot come to be without things which have a necessary nature, but it is not due to these (except as its material); it comes to be for an end. For instance, why is a saw such as it is? To effect so-and-so and for the sake of so-and-so. This end, however, cannot be realized unless the saw is made of iron. It is, therefore, necessary for it to be of iron, *if* we are to have a saw and perform the operation of sawing. What is necessary then, is necessary *on a hypothesis*; it is not a result necessarily determined by antecedents. Necessity is in the matter, while "that for the sake of which" is in the definition.

Necessity in mathematics is in a way similar to necessity in things which come to be through the operation of nature. Since a straight line is what it is, it is necessary that the angles of a triangle should equal two right angles. But not conversely; though if the angles are *not* equal to two right angles, then the straight line is not what it is either. But in things which come to be for an end, the reverse is true. If the end is to exist or does exist, that also which precedes it will exist or does exist; otherwise just as there, if the conclusion is not true, the premiss will not be true, so here the end or "that for the sake of which" will not exist. For this too is itself a starting point, but of the reasoning, not of the action; while in mathematics the starting point is the starting point of the reasoning only, as there is no action. If then there is to be a house, such-and-such things must be made or be there already or exist, or generally the matter relative to the end, bricks and stones if it is a house. But the end is not due to these except as the matter, nor will it come to exist because of them. Yet if they do not exist at all, neither will the house, or the saw—the former in the absence of stones, the latter in the absence of iron—just as in the other case the premisses will not be true, if the angles of the triangle are not equal to two right angles.

The necessary in nature, then, is plainly what we call by the name of matter, and the changes in it. Both causes must be stated by the physicist, but especially the end; for that is the cause of the matter, not *vice versa;* and the end is "that for the sake of which," and the beginning starts from the definition or essence; as in artificial products, since a house is of such-and-such a kind, certain things must *necessarily* come to be or be there already, or since health is this, these things must necessarily come to be or be there already. Similarly if man is this, then these; if these, then those. Perhaps the necessary is present also in the definition. For if one defines the operation of sawing as being a certain kind of dividing, then this cannot come about unless the saw has teeth of a certain kind; and these cannot be unless it is of iron. For in the definition too there are some parts that are, as it were, its matter.

PSYCHOLOGY

~~~~~~

Translated by J. A. Smith

Aristotelian physics deals with natural bodies in general. His psychology deals with natural bodies which possess a soul, "the principle of animal life." Hence, in Aristotle's scheme of knowledge, psychology is the meeting point of physics and the biological sciences.

In order to pursue his inquiry into the nature of soul, Aristotle has to consider it as if it were a separate thing, but he is extremely careful to avoid a dualistic concept of spirit and matter. The soul is inseparable from the body, he attempts to demonstrate; and the affections of soul—such as pity and fear, joy, loving, and hating—are (in a characteristically Aristotelian definition) "enmattered formulable essences."

In analyzing the faculties or powers of soul which the various classes of natural life possess, Aristotle suggests a universal scheme in which all creatures are both linked to and distinguished from each other. In the lowest order of creation are such things as plants; they are capable of nutrition and growth. Next come the animals, which are capable of "sensitive" life; they perceive, they react, they desire, and they are able to move in order to fulfill their desires. On the highest natural level is man, who is capable of intellection; not driven simply by appetite, he is capable of seeking knowledge and virtue as goals in themselves. For each living thing there is a firm and fixed place in creation. By rationalizing this hierarchy, Aristotle helped establish that conception of the universe as a great chain of being which was to dominate much of Western thinking until the late eighteenth century.

PSYCHOLOGY

BOOK I

1. [*The dignity, usefulness, and difficulty of psychology.*]
Holding as we do that, while knowledge of any kind is a
thing to be honoured and prized, one kind of it may, either
by reason of its greater exactness or of a higher dignity and
greater wonderfulness in its objects, be more honourable and
precious than another, on both accounts we should naturally
be led to place in the front rank the study of the soul. The
knowledge of the soul admittedly contributes greatly to the
advance of truth in general, and, above all, to our understanding of Nature, for the soul is in some sense the principle
of animal life. Our aim is to grasp and understand, first its
essential nature, and secondly its properties; of these some
are thought to be affections proper to the soul itself, while
others are considered to attach to the animal owing to the
presence within it of soul.

To attain any assured knowledge about the soul is one of
the most difficult things in the world. As the form of question which here presents itself, viz., the question "What is
it?" recurs in other fields, it might be supposed that there
was some single method of inquiry applicable to all objects
whose essential nature we are endeavouring to ascertain (as
there *is* for derived properties the single method of demonstration); in that case what we should have to seek for
would be this unique method. But if there is no such single
and general method for solving the question of essence, our

task becomes still more difficult; in the case of each different subject we shall have to determine the appropriate process of investigation. If to this there be a clear answer, e. g., that the process is demonstration or division, or some other known method, difficulties and hesitations still beset us—with what facts shall we begin the inquiry? For the facts which form the starting points in different subjects must be different, as, e. g., in the case of numbers and surfaces.

First, no doubt, it is necessary to determine in which of the *summa genera* soul lies, what it *is*; is it "a this-somewhat," a substance, or is it a quale or a quantum, or some other of the remaining kinds of predicates which we have distinguished? Further, does soul belong to the class of potential existents, or is it not rather an actuality? Our answer to this question is of the greatest importance.

We must consider also whether soul is divisible or is without parts, and whether it is everywhere homogeneous or not; and if not homogeneous, whether its various forms are different specifically or generically. Up to the present time those who have discussed and investigated soul seem to have confined themselves to the human soul. We must be careful not to ignore the question whether soul can be defined in a single unambiguous formula, as is the case with animal, or whether we must not give a separate formula for each sort of it, as we do for horse, dog, man, God (in the latter case the "universal" animal—and so too every other "common predicate" —being treated either as nothing at all or as a later product). Further, if what exists is not a plurality of souls, but a plurality of parts of one soul, which ought we to investigate first, the whole soul or its parts? (It is also a difficult problem to decide which of these parts are in nature distinct from one another.) Again, which ought we to investigate first, these parts or their functions, mind or thinking, the faculty or the act of sensation, and so on? If the investigation of the functions precedes that of the parts, the further question suggests itself: ought we not before either to consider the correlative objects, e. g., of sense or thought? It seems not only useful for the discovery of the causes of the derived properties of substances to be acquainted with the essential nature of those substances (as in mathematics it is useful for the understanding of the property of the equality of the interior angles of a triangle to two right angles to know the essential nature of the straight and the curved or of the line and the plane) but also conversely, for the knowledge of the essential nature of a substance is largely promoted by an acquaintance with its properties; for, when we are able to give an account conformable to experience of all or most of the properties of a substance, we shall be in the most favourable position to say something worth saying about the essential nature of that subject; in all demonstration a definition of the essence is required as a starting point, so that definitions which do not enable us to discover the derived properties, or which fail to facilitate even a conjecture about them, must obviously, one and all, be dialectical and futile.

A further problem presented by the affections of soul is this: are they all affections of the complex of body and soul, or is there any one among them peculiar to the soul by itself? To determine this is indispensable but difficult. If we consider the majority of them, there seems to be no case in which the soul can act or be acted upon without involving the body, e. g., anger, courage, appetite, and sensation generally. Thinking seems the most probable exception; but if this too proves to be a form of imagination or to be impossible without imagination, it too requires a body as a condition of its existence. If there is any way of acting or being acted upon proper to soul, soul will be capable of separate existence; if there is none, its separate existence is impossible. In the latter case, it will be like what is straight, which has many properties arising from the straightness in it, e. g., that of touching a bronze sphere at a point, though straightness divorced from the other constituents of the straight thing cannot touch it in this way; it cannot be so divorced at all, since it is always found in a body. It therefore seems that all the affections of soul involve a body—passion, gentleness, fear, pity, courage, joy, loving, and hating; in all these there is a concurrent affection of the body. In support of this we may point to the fact that, while sometimes on the occasion of violent and striking occurrences there is no excitement or fear felt, on others faint and feeble stimulations produce these emotions, viz., when the body is already in a state of tension resembling its condition when we are angry. Here is a still clearer case: in the absence of any external cause of terror we find ourselves experiencing the feelings of a man in terror. From all this it is obvious that the affections of soul are enmattered formulable essences.

Consequently their definitions ought to correspond, e. g., anger should be defined as a certain mode of movement of such and such a body (or part or faculty of a body) by this or that cause and for this or that end. That is precisely why the study of the soul must fall within the science of Nature, at least so far as in its affections it manifests this double character. Hence a physicist would define an affection of soul differently from a dialectician; the latter would define, e. g., anger as the appetite for returning pain for pain, or something like that, while the former would define it as a boiling of the blood or warm substance surrounding the heart. The latter assigns the material conditions, the former the form or formulable essence; for what he states is the formulable essence of the fact, though for its actual existence there must be embodiment of it in a material such as is described by the other. Thus the essence of a house is assigned in such a formula as "a shelter against destruction by wind, rain, and heat"; the physicist would describe it as "stones, bricks, and timbers"; but there is a third possible description which would say that it was that form in that material with that purpose or end. Which, then, among these is entitled to be regarded as the genuine physicist? The one who confines himself to the material, or the one who restricts himself to the formulable essence alone? Is it not rather the one who combines both in a single formula? If this is so, how are we to characterize the other two? Must we not say that there is no type of thinker who concerns himself with those qualities or attributes of the material which are in fact inseparable from the material, and without attempting even in thought to separate them? The physicist is he who concerns himself with all the properties active and passive of bodies or materials thus or thus defined; attributes not considered as being of this character he leaves to others, in certain cases it may be to a specialist, e. g., a carpenter or a physician, in others (*a*) where they are inseparable in fact, but are separable from any particular kind of body by an effort of abstraction, to the mathematician, (*b*) where they are separate both in fact and in thought from body altogether, to the First Philosopher or metaphysician. But we must return from this digression, and repeat that the affections of soul are inseparable from the material substratum of animal life, to which we have seen that such affections, e. g., passion and fear, attach, and have not the same mode of being as a line or a plane.

* * *

4. [*The soul not a harmony, not moved with non-local movement, not a self-moving number.*] There is yet another theory about soul, which has commended itself to many as no less probable than any of those we have hitherto mentioned, and has rendered public account of itself in the court of popular discussion. Its supporters say that the soul is a kind of harmony, for (*a*) harmony is a blend or composition of contraries, and (*b*) the body is compounded out of contraries. Harmony, however, is a certain proportion or composition of the constituents blended, and soul can be neither the one nor the other of these. Further, the power of originating movement cannot belong to a harmony, while almost all concur in regarding this as a principal attribute of soul. It is more appropriate to call health (or generally one of the good states of the body) a harmony than to predicate it of the soul. The absurdity becomes most apparent when we try to attribute the active and passive affections of the soul to a harmony; the necessary readjustment of their conceptions is difficult. Further, in using the word "harmony" we have one or other of two cases in our mind; the most proper sense is in relation to spatial magnitudes which have motion and

position, where harmony means the disposition and cohesion of their parts in such a manner as to prevent the introduction into the whole of anything homogeneous with it, and the secondary sense, derived from the former, is that in which it means the ratio between the constituents so blended; in neither of these senses is it plausible to predicate it of soul. That soul is a harmony in the sense of the mode of composition of the parts of the body is a view easily refutable; for there are many composite parts and those variously compounded; of what bodily part is mind or the sensitive or the appetitive faculty the mode of composition? And what *is* the mode of composition which constitutes each of them? It is equally absurd to identify the soul with the ratio of the mixture; for the mixture which makes flesh has a different ratio between the elements from that which makes bone. The consequence of this view will therefore be that distributed throughout the whole body there will be many souls, since every one of the bodily parts is a different mixture of the elements, and the ratio of mixture is in each case a harmony, i. e., a soul.

From Empedocles at any rate we might demand an answer to the following question—for he says that each of the parts of the body is what it is in virtue of a ratio between the elements; is the soul identical with this ratio, or is it not rather something over and above this which is formed in the parts? Is love the cause of any and every mixture, or only of those that are in the right ratio? Is love this ratio itself, or is love something over and above this? Such are the problems raised by this account. But, on the other hand, if the soul is different from the mixture, why does it disappear at one and the same moment with that relation between the elements which constitutes flesh or the other parts of the animal body? Further, if the soul is not identical with the ratio of mixture, and it is consequently not the case that each of the parts has a soul, what is that which perishes when the soul quits the body?

That the soul cannot either be a harmony, or be moved in a circle, is clear from what we have said. Yet that it can be moved incidentally is, as we said above, possible, and even that in a sense it can move itself, i. e., in the sense that *the vehicle* in which it is can be moved, and moved by it; in no other sense can the soul be moved in space. More legitimate doubts might remain as to its movement in view of the following facts. We speak of the soul as being pained or pleased, being bold or fearful, being angry, perceiving, thinking. All these are regarded as modes of movement, and hence it might be inferred that the soul is moved. This, however, does not necessarily follow. We may admit to the full that being pained or pleased, or thinking, are movements (each of them a "being moved"), and that the movement is originated by the soul. For example we may regard anger or fear as such and such movements of the heart, and thinking as such and such another movement of that organ, or of some other; these modifications may arise either from changes of place in certain parts or from qualitative alterations (the special nature of the parts and the special modes of their changes being for our present purpose irrelevant). Yet to say that it is *the soul* which is angry is as inexact as it would be to say that it is the soul that weaves webs or builds houses. It is doubtless better to avoid saying that the soul pities or learns or thinks, and rather to say that it is the man who does this with his soul. What we mean is not that the movement is in the soul, but that sometimes it terminates in the soul and sometimes starts from it, sensation, e. g., coming from without inwards, and reminiscence starting from the soul and terminating with the movements, actual or residual, in the sense organs.

The case of mind is different; it seems to be an independent substance implanted within the soul and to be incapable of being destroyed. If it could be destroyed at all, it would be under the blunting influence of old age. What really happens in respect of mind in old age is, however, exactly parallel to what happens in the case of the sense organs; if the old man could recover the proper kind of eye, he would see just as well as the young man. The incapacity of old age is due to an affection not of the soul but of its vehicle, as occurs in drunkenness or disease. Thus it is that in old age the activity of mind or intellectual apprehension declines only through the decay of some other inward part; mind itself is impassible. Thinking, loving, and hating are affections not of mind, but of that which has mind, so far as it has it. That is why, when this vehicle decays, memory and love cease; they were activities not of mind, but of the composite which has perished; mind is, no doubt, something more divine and impassible. That the soul cannot be moved is therefore clear from what we have said, and if it cannot be moved at all, manifestly it cannot be moved by itself.

Of all the opinions we have enumerated, by far the most unreasonable is that which declares the soul to be a self-moving number; it involves in the first place all the impossibilities which follow from regarding the soul as moved, and in the second special absurdities which follow from calling it a number. How are we to imagine a unit being moved? By what agency? What sort of movement can be attributed to what is without parts or internal differences? If the unit is both originative of movement and itself capable of being moved, it must contain difference.

Further, since they say a moving line generates a surface and a moving point a line, the movements of the psychic units must be lines (for a point is a unit having position, and the number of the soul is, of course, somewhere and has position).

Again, if from a number a number or a unit is subtracted, the remainder is another number; but plants and many animals when divided continue to live, and each segment is thought to retain the same kind of soul.

It must be all the same whether we speak of units or corpuscles; for if the spherical atoms of Democritus became points, nothing being retained but their being a quantum, there must remain in each a moving and a moved part, just as there is in what is continuous; what happens has nothing to do with the size of the atoms, it depends solely upon their being a quantum. That is why there must be something to originate movement in the units. If in the animal what originates movement is the soul, so also must it be in the case of the number, so that not the mover and the moved together, but the mover only, will be the soul. But how is it possible for one of the units to fulfil this function of originating movement? There must be *some* difference between such a unit and all the other units, and what difference can there be between one placed unit and another except a difference of position? If then, on the other hand, these psychic units within the body are different from the points *of* the body, there will be two sets of units both occupying the same place; for each unit will occupy a point. And yet, if there can be two, why cannot there be an infinite number? For if things can occupy an indivisible place, they must themselves be indivisible. If, on the other hand, the points of the body are identical with the units whose number is the soul, or if the number of the points in the body is the soul, why have not all bodies souls? For all bodies contain points or an infinity of points.

Further, how is it possible for these points to be isolated or separated from their bodies, seeing that lines cannot be resolved into points?

5. [*The soul not composed of elements, not present in all things. The unity of the soul.*] The result is, as we have said, that this view, while on the one side identical with that of those who maintain that soul is a subtle kind of body, is on the other entangled in the absurdity peculiar to Democritus' way of describing the manner in which movement is originated by soul. For if the soul is present throughout the whole percipient body, there must, if the soul be a kind of body, be two bodies in the same place; and for those who call it a number, there must be many points at one point, or every body must have a soul, unless the soul be a different sort of number—other, that is, than the sum of the points existing in a body. Another consequence that follows is that the animal must be moved by its number precisely in the way that Democritus explained its being moved by his spherical psychic atoms. What difference does it make whether we

speak of small spheres or of large units, or, quite simply, of units in movement? One way or another, the movements of the animal must be due to their movements. Hence those who combine movement and number in the same subject lay themselves open to these and many other similar absurdities. It is impossible not only that these characters should give the definition of soul—it is impossible that they should even be attributes of it. The point is clear if the attempt be made to start from this as the account of soul and explain from it the affections and actions of the soul, e. g., reasoning, sensation, pleasure, pain, etc. For, to repeat what we have said earlier, movement and number do not facilitate even conjecture about the derivative properties of soul.

Such are the three ways in which soul has traditionally been defined; one group of thinkers declared it to be that which is most originative of movement because it moves itself, another group to be the subtlest and most nearly incorporeal of all kinds of body. We have now sufficiently set forth the difficulties and inconsistencies to which these theories are exposed. It remains now to examine the doctrine that soul is composed of the elements.

The reason assigned for this doctrine is that thus the soul may perceive or come to know everything that is, but the theory necessarily involves itself in many impossibilities. Its upholders assume that like is known only by like, and imagine that by declaring the soul to be composed of the elements they succeed in identifying the soul with the things it is capable of apprehending. But the elements are not the only things it knows; there are many others, or, more exactly, an infinite number of others, formed out of the elements. Let us admit that the soul knows or perceives the elements out of which each of these composites is made up; but by what means will it know or perceive the composite whole, e. g., what God, man, flesh, bone (or any other compound) is? For each *is*, not merely the elements of which it is composed, but those elements combined in a determinate mode or ratio, as Empedocles himself says of bone:

The kindly Earth in its broad-bosomed moulds
Won of clear Water two parts out of eight
And four of Fire; and so white bones were formed.

Nothing, therefore, will be gained by the presence of the elements in the soul, unless there be also present there the various formulae of proportion and the various compositions in accordance with them. Each element will indeed know its fellow outside, but there will be no knowledge of bone or man, unless they too are present in the constitution of the soul. The impossibility of this needs no pointing out; for who would suggest that stone or man could enter into the constitution of the soul? The same applies to "the good" and "the not-good," and so on.

Further, the word "is" has many meanings: it may be used of a "this" or substance, or of a quantum, or of a quale, or of any other of the kinds of predicates we have distinguished. Does the soul consist of all of these or not? It does not appear that all have common elements. Is the soul formed out of those elements alone which enter into substances? If so, how will it be able to know each of the other kinds of thing? Will it be said that each kind of thing has elements or principles of its own, and that the soul is formed out of the whole of these? In that case, the soul must be a quantum *and* a quale *and* a substance. But all that can be made out of the elements of a quantum is a quantum, not a substance. These (and others like them) are the consequences of the view that the soul is composed of all the elements.

It is absurd, also, to say both (*a*) that like is not capable of being affected by like, and (*b*) that like is perceived or known by like, for perceiving, and also both thinking and knowing, are, on their own assumption, ways of being affected or moved.

There are many puzzles and difficulties raised by saying, as Empedocles does, that each set of things is known by means of its corporeal elements and by reference to something in soul which is like them, and additional testimony is furnished by this new consideration; for all the parts of the animal body which consist wholly of earth such as bones, sinews, and hair seem to be wholly insensitive and consequently not perceptive even of objects earthy like themselves, as they ought to have been.

Further, each of the principles will have far more ignorance than knowledge, for though each of them will know one thing, there will be many of which it will be ignorant. Empedocles at any rate must conclude that his God is the least intelligent of all beings, for of him alone is it true that there is one thing, Strife, which he does not know, while there is nothing which mortal beings do not know, for there is nothing which does not enter into their composition.

In general, we may ask, Why has not everything a soul, since everything either is an element, or is formed out of one or several or all of the elements? Each must certainly know one or several or all.

The problem might also be raised, What is that which unifies the elements into a soul? The elements correspond, it would appear, to the matter; what unites them, whatever it is, is the supremely important factor. But it is impossible that there should be something superior to, and dominant over, the soul (and *a fortiori* over the mind); it is reasonable to hold that mind is by nature most primordial and dominant, while their statement is that it is the elements which are first of all that is.

All, both those who assert that the soul, because of its knowledge or perception of what is, is compounded out of the elements, and those who assert that it is of all things the most originative of movement, fail to take into consideration all kinds of soul. In fact (1) not all beings that perceive can originate movement; there appear to be certain animals which are stationary, and yet local movement is the only one, so it seems, which the soul originates in animals. And (2) the same objection holds against all those who construct mind and the perceptive faculty out of the elements; for it appears that plants live, and yet are not endowed with locomotion or perception, while a large number of animals are without discourse of reason. Even if these points were waived and mind admitted to be a part of the soul (and so too the perceptive faculty), still, even so, there would be kinds and parts of soul of which they had failed to give any account.

The same objection lies against the view expressed in the "Orphic" poems; there it is said that the soul comes in from the whole when breathing takes place, being borne in upon the winds. Now this cannot take place in the case of plants, nor indeed in the case of certain classes of animal, for not all classes of animal breathe. This fact has escaped the notice of the holders of this view.

If we must construct the soul out of the elements, there is no necessity to suppose that *all* the elements enter into its construction; one element in each pair of contraries will suffice to enable it to know both that element itself and its contrary. By means of the straight line we know both itself and the curved—the carpenter's rule enables us to test both—but what is curved does not enable us to distinguish either itself or the straight.

Certain thinkers say that soul is intermingled in the whole universe, and it is perhaps for that reason that Thales came to the opinion that all things are full of gods. This presents some difficulties. Why does the soul when it resides in air or fire not form an animal, while it does so when it resides in mixtures of the elements, and that although it is held to be of higher quality when contained in the former? (One might add the question, why the soul in air is maintained to be higher and more immortal than that in animals.) Both possible ways of replying to the former question lead to absurdity or paradox; for it is beyond paradox to say that fire or air is an animal, and it is absurd to refuse the name of animal to what has soul in it. The opinion that the elements have soul in them seems to have arisen from the doctrine that a whole must be homogeneous with its parts. If it is true that animals become animate by drawing into themselves a portion of what surrounds them, the partisans of this view are bound to say that the soul of the Whole too is homogeneous with all its parts. If the air sucked in is homogeneous, but soul heterogeneous, clearly while some part of soul will exist in the inbreathed air, some other part will not. The soul must either be homogeneous, or such that there are some parts of the Whole in which it is not to be found.

From what has been said it is now clear that knowing as an attribute of soul cannot be explained by soul's being composed of the elements, and that it is neither sound nor true to speak of soul as moved. But since (a) knowing, perceiving, opining, and further (b) desiring, wishing, and generally all other modes of appetition, belong to soul, and (c) the local movements of animals, and (d) growth, maturity, and decay are produced by the soul, we must ask whether each of these is an attribute of the soul as a whole, i. e., whether it is with the whole soul we think, perceive, move ourselves, act or are acted upon, or whether each of them requires a different part of the soul? So too with regard to life. Does it depend on one of the parts of soul? Or is it dependent on more than one? Or on all? Or has it some quite other cause?

Some hold that the soul is divisible, and that one part thinks, another desires. If, then, its nature admits of its being divided, what can it be that holds the parts together? Surely not the body; on the contrary it seems rather to be the soul that holds the body together; at any rate when the soul departs the body disintegrates and decays. If, then, there is something else which makes the soul one, this unifying agency would have the best right to the name of soul, and we shall have to repeat for it the question: Is *it* one or multipartite? If it is one, why not at once admit that "the soul" is one? If it has parts, once more the question must be put: What holds *its* parts together, and so *ad infinitum?*

The question might also be raised about the parts of the soul: What is the separate rôle of each in relation to the body? For, if the whole soul holds together the whole body, we should expect each part of the soul to hold together a part of the body. But this seems an impossibility; it is difficult even to imagine what sort of bodily part mind will hold together, or how it will do this.

It is a fact of observation that plants and certain insects go on living when divided into segments; this means that each of the segments has a soul in it identical in species, though not numerically identical in the different segments, for both of the segments for a time possess the power of sensation and local movement. That this does not last is not surprising, for they no longer possess the organs necessary for self-maintenance. But, all the same, in each of the bodily parts there are present all the parts of soul, and the souls so present are homogeneous with one another and with the whole; this means that the several parts of the soul are indisseverable from one another, although the whole soul is divisible. It seems also that the principle found in plants is also a kind of soul; for this is the only principle which is common to both animals and plants; and this exists in isolation from the principle of sensation, though there is nothing which has the latter without the former.

BOOK II

1. [*First definition of soul.*] Let the foregoing suffice as our account of the views concerning the soul which have been handed on by our predecessors; let us now dismiss them and make as it were a completely fresh start, endeavouring to give a precise answer to the question, What is soul? i. e., to formulate the most general possible definition of it.

We are in the habit of recognizing, as one determinate kind of what is, substance, and that in several senses, (*a*) in the sense of matter or that which in itself is not "a this," and (*b*) in the sense of form or essence, which is that precisely in virtue of which a thing is called "a this," and thirdly (*c*) in the sense of that which is compounded of both (*a*) and (*b*). Now matter is potentiality, form actuality; of the latter there are two grades related to one another as, e. g., knowledge to the exercise of knowledge.

Among substances are by general consent reckoned bodies and especially natural bodies; for they are the principles of all other bodies. Of natural bodies some have life in them, others not; by life we mean self-nutrition and growth (with its correlative decay). It follows that every natural body which has life in it is a substance in the sense of a composite.

But since it is also a *body* of such and such a kind, viz., having life, the *body* cannot be soul; the body is the subject or matter, not what is attributed to it. Hence the soul must be a substance in the sense of the form of a natural body having life potentially within it. But substance is actuality, and thus soul is the actuality of a body as above characterized. Now the word actuality has two senses corresponding respectively to the possession of knowledge and the actual exercise of knowledge. It is obvious that the soul is actuality in the first sense, viz., that of knowledge as possessed, for both sleeping and waking presuppose the existence of soul, and of these waking corresponds to actual knowing, sleeping to knowledge possessed but not employed, and, in the history of the individual, knowledge comes before its employment or exercise.

That is why the soul is the first grade of actuality of a natural body having life potentially in it. The body so described is a body which is organized. The parts of plants in spite of their extreme simplicity are "organs"; e. g., the leaf serves to shelter the pericarp, the pericarp to shelter the fruit, while the roots of plants are analogous to the mouth of animals, both serving for the absorption of food. If, then, we have to give a general formula applicable to all kinds of soul, we must describe it as the first grade of actuality of a natural organized body. That is why we can wholly dismiss as unnecessary the question whether the soul and the body are one; it is as meaningless as to ask whether the wax and the shape given to it by the stamp are one, or generally the matter of a thing and that of which it is the matter. Unity has many senses (as many as "is" has), but the most proper and fundamental sense of both is the relation of an actuality to that of which it is the actuality.

We have now given an answer to the question, What is soul?—an answer which applies to it in its full extent. It is substance in the sense which corresponds to the definitive formula of a thing's essence. That means that it is "the essential whatness" of a body of the character just assigned. Suppose that what is literally an "organ," like an axe, were a *natural* body, its "essential whatness" would have been its essence, and so its soul; if this disappeared from it, it would have ceased to be an axe, except in name. As it is, it is just an axe; it wants the character which is required to make its whatness or formulable essence a soul; for that, it would have had to be a *natural* body of a particular kind, viz., one having *in itself* the power of setting itself in movement and arresting itself. Next, apply this doctrine in the case of the "parts" of the living body. Suppose that the eye were an animal—sight would have been its soul, for sight is the substance or essence of the eye which corresponds to the formula, the eye being merely the matter of seeing; when seeing is removed the eye is no longer an eye, except in name—it is no more a real eye than the eye of a statue or of a painted figure. We must now extend our consideration from the "parts" to the whole living body; for what the departmental sense is to the bodily part which is its organ, that the whole faculty of sense is to the whole sensitive body as such.

We must not understand by that which is "potentially capable of living" what has lost the soul it had, but only what still retains it; but seeds and fruits are bodies which possess the qualification. Consequently, while waking is actuality in a sense corresponding to the cutting and the seeing, the soul is actuality in the sense corresponding to the power of sight and the power in the tool; the body corresponds to what exists in potentiality; as the pupil *plus* the power of sight constitutes the eye, so the soul *plus* the body constitutes the animal.

From this it indubitably follows that the soul is inseparable from its body, or at any rate that certain parts of it are (if it has parts)—for the actuality of some of them is nothing but the actualities of their bodily parts. Yet some may be separable because they are not the actualities of any body at all. Further, we have no light on the problem whether the soul may not be the actuality of its body in the sense in which the sailor is the actuality of the ship.

This must suffice as our sketch or outline determination of the nature of soul.

2. [*Second definition of soul.*] Since what is clear or logically more evident emerges from what in itself is confused but more observable by us, we must reconsider our results from this point of view. For it is not enough for a definitive formula to express as most now do the mere fact; it must include and exhibit the ground also. At present definitions are given in a form analogous to the conclusion of a syllogism; e. g., What is squaring? The construction of an equilateral rectangle equal to a given oblong rectangle. Such a definition is in form equivalent to a conclusion. One that tells us that squaring is the discovery of a line which is a mean proportional between the two unequal sides of the given rectangle discloses the ground of what is defined.

We resume our inquiry from a fresh starting point by calling attention to the fact that what has soul in it differs from what has not in that the former displays life. Now this word has more than one sense, and provided any one alone of these is found in a thing we say that thing is living. Living, that is, may mean thinking or perception or local movement and rest, or movement in the sense of nutrition, decay and growth. Hence we think of plants also as living, for they are observed to possess in themselves an originative power through which they increase or decrease in all spatial directions; they grow up *and* down, and everything that grows increases its bulk alike in both directions or indeed in all, and continues to live so long as it can absorb nutriment.

This power of self-nutrition can be isolated from the other powers mentioned, but not they from it—in mortal beings at least. The fact is obvious in plants; for it is the only psychic power they possess.

This is the originative power the possession of which leads us to speak of things as *living* at all, but it is the possession of sensation that leads us for the first time to speak of living things as animals; for even those beings which possess no power of local movement but do possess the power of sensation we call animals and not merely living things.

The primary form of sense is touch, which belongs to all animals. Just as the power of self-nutrition can be isolated from touch and sensation generally, so touch can be isolated from all other forms of sense. (By the power of self-nutrition we mean that departmental power of the soul which is common to plants and animals; all animals whatsoever are observed to have the sense of touch.) What the explanation of these two facts is, we must discuss later. At present we must confine ourselves to saying that soul is the source of these phenomena and is characterized by them, viz., by the powers of self-nutrition, sensation, thinking, and motivity.

Is each of these a soul or a part of a soul? And if a part, a part in what sense? A part merely distinguishable by definition or a part distinct in local situation as well? In the case of certain of these powers, the answers to these questions are easy, in the case of others we are puzzled what to say. Just as in the case of plants which when divided are observed to continue to live though removed to a distance from one another (thus showing that in *their* case the soul of each individual plant before division was actually one, potentially many), so we notice a similar result in other varieties of soul, i. e., in insects which have been cut in two; each of the segments possesses both sensation and local movement; and if sensation, necessarily also imagination and appetition; for, where there is sensation, there is also pleasure and pain, and, where these, necessarily also desire.

We have no evidence as yet about mind or the power to think; it seems to be a widely different kind of soul, differing as what is eternal from what is perishable; it alone is capable of existence in isolation from all other psychic powers. All the other parts of soul, it is evident from what we have said, are, in spite of certain statements to the contrary, incapable of separate existence though, of course, distinguishable by definition. If opining is distinct from perceiving, to be capable of opining and to be capable of perceiving must be distinct, and so with all the other forms of living above enumerated. Further, some animals possess all these parts of soul, some certain of them only, others one only (this is what enables us to classify animals); the cause must be considered later. A similar arrangement is found also within the field of the senses; some classes of animals have all the senses, some only certain of them, others only one, the most indispensable, touch.

Since the expression "that whereby we live and perceive" has two meanings, just like the expression "that whereby we know"—that may mean either (a) knowledge or (b) the soul, for we can speak of knowing by or with either, and similarly that whereby we are in health may be either (a) health or (b) the body or some part of the body; and since of the two terms thus contrasted knowledge or health is the name of a form, essence, or ratio, or if we so express it an actuality of a recipient matter—knowledge of what is capable of knowing, health of what is capable of being made healthy (for the operation of that which is capable of originating change terminates and has its seat in what is changed or altered); further, since it is the soul by or with which primarily we live, perceive, and think, it follows that the soul must be a ratio or formulable essence, not a matter or subject. For, as we said, the word substance has three meanings—form, matter, and the complex of both—and of these three what is called matter is potentiality, what is called form actuality. Since then the complex here is the living thing, the body cannot be the actuality of the soul; it is the soul which is the actuality of a certain kind of body. Hence the rightness of the view that the soul cannot be without a body, while it cannot *be* a body; it is not a body but something relative to a body. That is why it is *in* a body, and a body of a definite kind. It was a mistake, therefore, to do as former thinkers did, merely to fit it into a body without adding a definite specification of the kind or character of that body. Reflection confirms the observed fact; the actuality of any given thing can only be realized in what is already potentially that thing, i. e., in a matter of its own appropriate to it. From all this it follows that soul is an actuality or formulable essence of something that possesses a potentiality of being besouled.

3. [*The faculties of the soul.*] Of the psychic powers above enumerated, some kinds of living things, as we have said, possess all, some less than all, others one only. Those we have mentioned are the nutritive, the appetitive, the sensory, the locomotive, and the power of thinking. Plants have none but the first, the nutritive, while another order of living things has this *plus* the sensory. If any order of living things has the sensory, it must also have the appetitive; for appetite is the genus of which desire, passion, and wish are the species; now all animals have one sense at least, viz., touch, and whatever has a sense has the capacity for pleasure and pain and therefore has pleasant and painful objects present to it, and wherever these are present, there is desire, for desire is just appetition of what is pleasant. Further, all animals have the sense for food (for touch is the sense for food), the food of all living things consists of what is dry, moist, hot, cold, and these are the qualities apprehended by touch; all other sensible qualities are apprehended by touch only indirectly. Sounds, colours, and odours contribute nothing to nutriment; flavours fall within the field of tangible qualities. Hunger and thirst are forms of desire, hunger a desire for what is dry and hot, thirst a desire for what is cold and moist; flavour is a sort of seasoning added to both. We must later clear up these points, but at present it may be enough to say that all animals that possess the sense of touch have also appetition. The case of imagination is obscure; we must examine it later. Certain kinds of animals possess in addition the power of locomotion, and still another order of animate beings, i. e., man and possibly another order like man or superior to him, the power of thinking, i. e., mind. It is now evident that a

single definition can be given of soul only in the same sense as one can be given of figure. For, as in that case there is no figure distinguishable and apart from triangle, etc., so here there is no soul apart from the forms of soul just enumerated. It is true that a highly general definition can be given for figure which will fit all figures without expressing the peculiar nature of any figure. So here in the case of soul and its specific forms. Hence it is absurd in this and similar cases to demand an absolutely general definition, which will fail to express the peculiar nature of anything that *is,* or again, omitting this, to look for separate definitions corresponding to each *infima species.* The cases of figure and soul are exactly parallel; for the particulars subsumed under the common name in both cases—figures and living beings—constitute a series, each successive term of which potentially contains its predecessor, e. g., the square the triangle, the sensory power the self-nutritive. Hence we must ask in the case of each order of living things, What is its soul, i. e., What is the soul of plant, animal, man? Why the terms are related in this serial way must form the subject of later examination. But the facts are that the power of perception is never found apart from the power of self-nutrition, while—in plants—the latter is found isolated from the former. Again, no sense is found apart from that of touch, while touch *is* found by itself; many animals have neither sight, hearing, nor smell. Again, among living things that possess sense some have the power of locomotion, some not. Lastly, certain living beings— a small minority—possess calculation and thought, for (among mortal beings) those which possess calculation have all the other powers above mentioned, while the converse does not hold—indeed some live by imagination alone, while others have not even imagination. The mind that knows with immediate intuition presents a different problem.

It is evident that the way to give the most adequate definition of soul is to seek in the case of *each* of its forms for the most appropriate definition.

4. [*The nutritive faculty.*] It is necessary for the student of these forms of soul first to find a definition of each, expressive of what it is, and then to investigate its derivative properties, etc. But if we are to express what each is, viz., what the thinking power is, or the perceptive, or the nutritive, we must go farther back and first give an account of thinking or perceiving, for in the order of investigation the question of what an agent does precedes the question, what enables it to do what it does. If this is correct, we must on the same ground go yet another step farther back and have some clear view of the objects of each; thus we must *start* with these objects, e. g., with food, with what is perceptible, or with what is intelligible.

It follows that first of all we must treat of nutrition and reproduction, for the nutritive soul is found along with all the others and is the most primitive and widely distributed power of soul, being indeed that one in virtue of which all are said to have life. The acts in which it manifests itself are reproduction and the use of food—reproduction, I say, because for any living thing that has reached its normal development and which is unmutilated, and whose mode of generation is not spontaneous, the most natural act is the production of another like itself, an animal producing an animal, a plant a plant, in order that, as far as its nature allows, it may partake in the eternal and divine. That is the goal towards which all things strive, that for the sake of which they do whatsoever their nature renders possible. The phrase "for the sake of which" is ambiguous; it may mean either (*a*) the end to achieve which, or (*b*) the being in whose interest, the act is done. Since then no living thing is able to partake in what is eternal and divine by uninterrupted continuance (for nothing perishable can for ever remain one and the same), it tries to achieve that end in the only way possible to it, and success is possible in varying degrees; so it remains not indeed as the selfsame individual but continues its existence in something *like* itself—not numerically but specifically one.

The soul is the cause or source of the living body. The terms cause and source have many senses. But the soul is the cause of its body alike in all three senses which we explicitly recognize. It is (*a*) the source or origin of movement, it is (*b*) the end, it is (*c*) the essence of the whole living body.

That it is the last, is clear; for in everything the essence is identical with the ground of its being, and here, in the case of living things, their being is to live, and of their being and their living the soul in them is the cause or source. Further, the actuality of whatever is potential is identical with its formulable essence.

It is manifest that the soul is also the final cause of its body. For Nature, like mind, always does whatever it does for the sake of something, which something is its end. To that something corresponds in the case of animals the soul and in this it follows the order of nature; all natural bodies are organs of the soul. This is true of those that enter into the constitution of plants as well as of those which enter into that of animals. This shows that that for the sake of which they are is soul. We must here recall the two senses of "that for the sake of which," viz., (*a*) the end to achieve which, and (*b*) the being in whose interest, anything is or is done.

We must maintain, further, that the soul is also the cause of the living body as the original source of local movement. The power of locomotion is not found, however, in all living things. But change of quality and change of quantity are also due to the soul. Sensation is held to be a qualitative alteration, and nothing except what has soul in it is capable of sensation. The same holds of the quantitative changes which constitute growth and decay; nothing grows or decays naturally except what feeds itself, and nothing feeds itself except what has a share of soul in it.

Empedocles is wrong in adding that growth in plants is to be explained, the downward rooting by the natural tendency of earth to travel downwards, and the upward branching by the similar natural tendency of fire to travel upwards. For he misinterprets up and down; up and down are not for all things what they are for the whole Cosmos; if we are to distinguish and identify organs according to their *functions,* the roots of plants are analogous to the head in animals. Further, we must ask what is the force that holds together the earth and the fire which tend to travel in contrary directions; if there is no counteracting force, they will be torn asunder; if there is, this must be the soul and the cause of nutrition and growth. By some the element of fire is held to be *the* cause of nutrition and growth, for it alone of the primary bodies or elements is observed to feed and increase *itself*. Hence the suggestion that in both plants and animals it is it which is the operative force. A concurrent cause in a sense it certainly is, but not the principal cause; that is rather the soul; for while the growth of fire goes on without limit so long as there is a supply of fuel, in the case of all complex wholes formed in the course of nature there is a limit or ratio which determines their size and increase, and limit and ratio are marks of soul but not of fire, and belong to the side of formulable essence rather than that of matter.

Nutrition and reproduction are due to one and the same psychic power. It is necessary first to give precision to our account of food, for it is by this function of absorbing food that this psychic power is distinguished from all the others. The current view is that what serves as food to a living thing is what is contrary to it—not that in every pair of contraries each is food to the other; to be food a contrary must not only be transformable into the other and vice versa, it must also in so doing increase the bulk of the other. Many a contrary is transformed into its other and vice versa, where neither is even a quantum and so cannot increase in bulk, e. g., an invalid into a healthy subject. It is clear that not even those contraries which satisfy both the conditions mentioned above are food to one another in precisely the same sense; water may be said to feed fire, but not fire water. Where the members of the pair are elementary bodies only one of the contraries, it would appear, can be said to feed the other. But there is a difficulty here. One set of thinkers assert that like is fed, as well as increased in amount, by like. Another set, as we have said, maintain the very reverse, viz., that what feeds and what is fed are contrary to one another; like, they argue, is incapable of being affected by like; but food is changed in the process of digestion, and change is always *to* what is opposite or to what is intermediate. Further, food is acted upon by what is nourished by it, not the other way round, as timber is worked by a carpenter and not conversely; there is a change in the carpenter but it is merely a change from not-working to working. In answering this problem it makes all the difference whether we mean by "the food" the "finished" or the "raw" product. If we use the word food of both, viz., of the completely undigested and the completely digested matter, we can justify both the rival accounts of it; taking food in the sense of undigested matter, it is the contrary of what is fed by it, taking it as digested it is like what is fed by it. Consequently it is clear that in a certain sense we may say that both parties are right, both wrong.

Since nothing except what is alive can be fed, what is fed is the besouled body and just because it has soul in it. Hence food is essentially related to what has soul in it. Food has a power which is other than the power to increase the bulk of what is fed by it; so far forth as what has soul in it is a quantum, food may increase its quantity, but it is only so far as what has soul in it is a "this-somewhat" or substance that food acts *as* food; in that case it maintains the being of what is fed, and that continues to be what it is so long as the process of nutrition continues. Further, it is the agent in generation, i. e., not the generation of the individual fed but the reproduction of another like it; the substance of the individual fed is already in existence; the existence of no substance is a self-generation but only a self-maintenance.

Hence the psychic power which we are now studying may be described as that which tends to maintain whatever has this power in it of continuing such as it was, and food helps it to do its work. That is why, if deprived of food, it must cease to be.

The process of nutrition involves three factors, (*a*) what is fed, (*b*) that wherewith it is fed, (*c*) what does the feeding; of these (*c*) is the first soul, (*a*) the body which has that soul in it, (*b*) the food. But since it is right to call things after the ends they realize, and the end of this soul is to generate another being like that in which it is, the first soul ought to be named the reproductive soul. The expression (b) "wherewith it is fed" is ambiguous just as is the expression "wherewith the ship is steered"; that may mean either (i) the hand or (ii) the rudder, i. e., either (i) what is moved and sets in movement, or (ii) what is merely moved. We can apply this analogy here if we recall that all food must be capable of being digested, and that what produces digestion is warmth; that is why everything that has soul in it possesses warmth.

We have now given an outline account of the nature of food; further details must be given in the appropriate place.

5. [*Sense perception.*] Having made these distinctions let us now speak of sensation in the widest sense. Sensation depends, as we have said, on a process of movement or affection from without, for it is held to be some sort of change of quality. Now some thinkers assert that like is affected only by like; in what sense this is possible and in what sense impossible, we have explained in our general discussion of acting and being acted upon.

Here arises a problem: why do we not perceive the senses themselves as well as the external objects of sense, or why without the stimulation of external objects do they not produce sensation, seeing that they contain in themselves fire, earth, and all the other elements, which are the direct or indirect objects of sense? It is clear that what is sensitive is so only potentially, not actually. The power of sense is parallel to what is combustible, for that never ignites itself spontaneously, but requires an agent which has the power of starting ignition; otherwise it could have set itself on fire, and would not have needed actual fire to set it ablaze.

In reply we must recall that we use the word "perceive" in two ways, for we say (a) that what has the power to hear or see, "sees" or "hears," even though it is at the moment asleep, and also (b) that what is actually seeing or hearing, "sees" or "hears." Hence "sense" too must have two meanings, sense potential, and sense actual. Similarly "to be a sentient" means either (*a*) to have a certain power or (*b*) to manifest a certain activity. To begin with, for a time, let us speak as if there were no difference between (i) being moved or affected, and (ii) being active, for movement is a kind of activity—an imperfect kind, as has elsewhere been explained. Everything that is acted upon or moved is acted upon by an agent which is actually at work. Hence it is that in one sense, as has already been stated, what acts and what is acted upon are like, in another unlike, i. e., prior to and during the change the two factors are unlike, after it like.

But we must now distinguish not only *between* what is potential and what is actual but also different senses in which things can be said to be potential or actual; up to now we have been speaking as if each of these phrases had only one sense. We can speak of something as "a knower" either (*a*) as when we say that man is a knower, meaning that man falls within the class of beings that know or have knowledge, or (*b*) as when we are speaking of a man who possesses a knowledge of grammar; each of these is so called as having in him a certain potentiality, but there is a difference between their respective potentialities, the one (*a*) being a potential knower, because his kind or matter is such and such, the other (*b*), because he can in the absence of any external counteracting cause realize his knowledge in actual knowing at will. This implies a third meaning of "a knower" (*c*), one who is already realizing his knowledge—he is a knower in actuality and in the most proper sense is knowing, e. g., this A. Both the former are potential knowers, who realize their respective potentialities, the one (*a*) by change of quality, i. e., repeated transitions from one state to its opposite under instruction, the other (*b*) by the transition from the inactive possession of sense or grammar to their active exercise. The two kinds of transition are distinct.

Also the expression "to be acted upon" has more than one meaning; it may mean either (*a*) the extinction of one of two contraries by the other, or (*b*) the maintenance of what is potential by the agency of what is actual and already like what is acted upon, with such likeness as is compatible with one's being actual and the other potential. For what possesses knowledge becomes an actual knower by a transition which is either not an alteration of it at all (being in reality a development into its true self or actuality) or at least an alteration in a quite different sense from the usual meaning.

Hence it is wrong to speak of a wise man as being "altered" when he uses his wisdom, just as it would be absurd to speak of a builder as being altered when he is using his skill in building a house.

What in the case of knowing or understanding leads from potentiality to actuality ought not to be called teaching but something else. That which starting with the power to know learns or acquires knowledge through the agency of one who actually knows and has the power of teaching either (a) ought not to be said "to be acted upon" at all or (b) we must recognize two senses of alteration, viz., (i) the substitution of one quality for another, the first being the contrary of the second, or (ii) the development of an existent quality from potentiality in the direction of fixity or nature.

In the case of what is to possess sense, the first transition is due to the action of the male parent and takes place before birth so that at birth the living thing is, in respect of sensation, at the stage which corresponds to the *possession* of knowledge. Actual sensation corresponds to the stage of the exercise of knowledge. But between the two cases compared there is a difference; the objects that excite the sensory powers to activity, the seen, the heard, etc., are outside. The ground of this difference is that what actual sensation apprehends is individuals, while what knowledge apprehends is universals, and these are in a sense within the soul. That is why a man can exercise his knowledge when he wishes, but his sensation does not depend upon himself—a sensible object must be there. A similar statement must be made about our *knowledge* of what is sensible—on the same ground, viz., that the sensible objects are individual and external.

A later more appropriate occasion may be found thoroughly to clear up all this. At present it must be enough to recognize the distinctions already drawn; a thing may be said to be potential in either of two senses, (a) in the sense in which we might say of a boy that he may become a general or (b) in the sense in which we might say the same of an adult, and there are two corresponding senses of the term "a potential sentient." There are no separate names for the two stages of potentiality; we have pointed out that they are different and how they are different. We cannot help using the incorrect terms "being acted upon or altered" of the two transitions involved. As we have said, what has the power of sensation is potentially like what the perceived object is actually; that is, while at the beginning of the process of its being acted upon the two interacting factors are dissimilar, at the end the one acted upon is assimilated to the other and is identical in quality with it.

6. [*The different kinds of sensible object.*] In dealing with each of the senses we shall have first to speak of the objects which are perceptible by each. The term "object of sense" covers three kinds of objects, two kinds of which are, in our language, directly perceptible, while the remaining one is only incidentally perceptible. Of the first two kinds one (a) consists of what is perceptible by a single sense, the other (b) of what is perceptible by any and all of the senses. I call by the name of special object of this or that sense that which cannot be perceived by any other sense than that one and in respect of which no error is possible; in this sense colour is the special object of sight, sound of hearing, flavour of taste. Touch, indeed, discriminates more than one set of different qualities. Each sense has one kind of object which it discerns, and never errs in reporting that what is before it is colour or sound (though it may err as to what it is that is coloured or where that is, or what it is that is sounding or where that is). Such objects are what we propose to call the special objects of this or that sense.

"Common sensibles" are movement, rest, number, figure, magnitude; these are not peculiar to any one sense, but are common to all. There are at any rate certain kinds of movement which are perceptible both by touch and by sight.

We speak of an incidental object of sense where, e. g., the white object which we see is the son of Diares; here because "being the son of Diares" is incidental to the directly visible white patch we speak of the son of Diares as being (incidentally) perceived or seen by us. Because this is only incidentally an object of sense, it in no way as such affects the senses. Of the two former kinds, both of which are in their own nature perceptible by sense, the first kind—that of special objects of the several senses—constitute *the* objects of sense in the strictest sense of the term and it is to them that in the nature of things the structure of each several sense is adapted.

* * *

12. [*General characteristics of the external senses.*] The following results applying to any and every sense may now be formulated.

(A) By a "sense" is meant what has the power of receiving into itself the sensible forms of things without the matter. This must be conceived of as taking place in the way in which a piece of wax takes on the impress of a signet ring without the iron or gold; we say that what produces the impression is a signet of bronze or gold, but its particular metallic constitution makes no difference; in a similar way the sense is affected by what is coloured or flavoured or sounding, but it is indifferent what in each case the *substance* is; what alone matters is what *quality* it has, i. e., in what *ratio* its constituents are combined.

(B) By "an organ of sense" is meant that in which ultimately such a power is seated.

The sense and its organ are the same in fact, but their essence is not the same. What perceives is, of course, a spatial magnitude, but we must not admit that either the having the power to perceive or the sense itself is a magnitude; what they are is a certain ratio or power *in* a magnitude. This enables us to explain why objects of sense which possess one of two opposite sensible qualities in a degree largely in excess of the other opposite destroy the organs of sense; if the movement set up by an object is too strong for the organ, the equipoise of contrary qualities in the organ, which just *is* its sensory power, is disturbed; it is precisely as concord and tone are destroyed by too violently twanging the strings of a lyre. This explains also why plants cannot perceive, in spite of their having a portion of soul in them and obviously being affected by tangible objects themselves; for undoubtedly their temperature can be lowered or raised. The explanation is that they have no mean of contrary qualities, and so no principle in them capable of taking on the forms of sensible objects without their matter; in the case of plants the affection is an affection by form-and-matter together. The problem might be raised: Can what cannot smell be said to be affected by smells or what cannot see by colours, and so on? It might be said that a smell is just what can be smelt, and if it produces any effect it can only be so as to make something smell it, and it might be argued that what cannot smell cannot be affected by smells and further that what can smell can be affected by it only in so far as it has in it the power to smell (similarly with the proper objects of all the other senses) Indeed that this *is* so is made quite evident as follows. Light or darkness, sounds and smells leave *bodies* quite unaffected; what does affect bodies is not these but the bodies which are their vehicles, e. g., what splits the trunk of a tree is not the sound of the thunder but the air which accompanies thunder. Yes, but, it may be objected, bodies are affected by what is tangible and by flavours. If not, by what are things that are without soul affected, i. e., altered in quality? Must we not, then, admit that the objects of the other senses also may affect them? Is not the true account this, that all bodies *are* capable of being affected by smells and sounds, but that some on being acted upon, having no boundaries of their own, disintegrate, as in the instance of air, which does become odorous, showing that *some* effect is produced on it by what is odorous? But smelling is more than such an affection by what is odorous—*what* more? Is not the answer that, while the air owing

to the momentary duration of the action upon it of what is
odorous does itself become perceptible to the sense of smell,
smelling is an *observing* of the result produced?

&&&&&&&&&&&&&&&&&&&&&&&&&&&&&&&&&&

BOOK III

1. [*The number of the external senses.*] That there is no
sixth sense in addition to the five enumerated—sight, hearing,
smell, taste, touch—may be established by the following considerations:

If we have actually sensation of everything of which touch
can give us sensation (for all the qualities of the tangible *qua*
tangible are perceived by us through touch); and if absence
of a sense necessarily involves absence of a sense organ; and
if (1) all objects that we perceive by immediate contact with
them are perceptible by touch, which sense we actually
possess, and (2) all objects that we perceive through media,
i. e., without immediate contact, are perceptible by or
through the simple elements, e. g., air and water (and this
is so arranged that (*a*) if more than one kind of sensible object is perceivable through a single medium, the possessor of
a sense organ homogeneous with that medium has the power
of perceiving both kinds of objects; for example, if the sense
organ is made of air, and air is a medium both for sound
and for colour; and that (*b*) if more than one medium can
transmit the same kind of sensible objects, as e. g., water as
well as air can transmit colour, both being transparent, then
the possessor of either alone will be able to perceive the kind
of objects transmissible through both); and if of the simple
elements two only, air and water, go to form sense organs
(for the pupil is made of water, the organ of hearing is made

of air, and the organ of smell of one or other of these two, while fire is found either in none or in all—warmth being an essential condition of all sensibility—and earth either in none or, if anywhere, specially mingled with the components of the organ of touch; wherefore it would remain that there can be no sense organ formed of anything except water and air); and if these sense organs are actually found in certain animals; then all the possible senses are possessed by those animals that are not imperfect or mutilated (for even the mole is observed to have eyes beneath its skin); so that, if there is no fifth element and no property other than those which belong to the four elements of our world, no sense can be wanting to such animals.

Further, there cannot be a special sense organ for the common sensibles either, i. e., the objects which we perceive incidentally through this or that special sense, e. g., movement, rest, figure, magnitude, number, unity; for all these we perceive by movement, e. g., magnitude by movement, and therefore also figure (for figure is a species of magnitude), what is at rest by the absence of movement; number is perceived by the negation of continuity, and by the special sensibles; for each sense perceives one class of sensible objects. So that it is clearly impossible that there should be a special sense for any one of the common sensibles, e. g., movement; for, if that were so, our perception of it would be exactly parallel to our present perception of what is sweet by vision. *That* is so because we have a sense for each of the two qualities, in virtue of which when they happen to meet in one sensible object we are aware of both contemporaneously. If it were not like this our perception of the common qualities would always be incidental, i. e., as is the perception of Cleon's son, where we perceive him not as Cleon's son but as white, and the white thing which we really perceive happens to be Cleon's son.

But in the case of the common sensibles there is already in us a general sensibility which enables us to perceive them directly; there is therefore no special sense required for their perception: if there were, our perception of them would have been exactly like what has been above described.

The senses perceive each other's special objects incidentally; not because the percipient sense is this or that special sense, but because all form a unity; this incidental perception takes place whenever sense is directed at one and the same moment to two disparate qualities in one and the same object, e. g., to the bitterness and the yellowness of bile; the assertion of the identity of both cannot be the act of either of the senses; hence the illusion of sense, e. g., the belief that if a thing is yellow it is bile.

It might be asked why we have more senses than one. Is it to prevent a failure to apprehend the common sensibles, e. g., movement, magnitude, and number, which go along with the special sensibles? Had we no sense but sight, and that sense no object but white, they would have tended to escape our notice and everything would have merged for us into an indistinguishable identity because of the concomitance of colour and magnitude. As it is, the fact that the common sensibles are given in the objects of more than one sense reveals their distinction from each and all of the special sensibles.

2. [*Common sense.*] Since it is through sense that we are aware that we are seeing or hearing, it must be either by sight that we are aware of seeing, or by some sense other than sight. But the sense that gives us this new sensation must perceive both sight and its object, viz., colour; so that either (1) there will be two senses both percipient of the same sensible object, or (2) the sense must be percipient of itself. Further, even if the sense which perceives sight were different from sight, we must either fall into an infinite regress, or we must somewhere assume a sense which is aware of itself. If so, we ought to do this in the first case.

This presents a difficulty: if to perceive by sight is just to see, and what is seen is colour (or the coloured), then if we are to *see* that which sees, that which sees originally must be coloured. It is clear therefore that "to perceive by sight" has more than one meaning; for even when we are not *see-ing*, it is by sight that we discriminate darkness from light, though not in the same way as we distinguish one colour from another. Further, in a sense even that which sees *is* coloured; for in each case the sense organ is capable of receiving the sensible object without its matter. That is why even when the sensible objects are gone the sensings and imaginings continue to exist in the sense organs.

The activity of the sensible object and that of the percipient sense is one and the same activity, and yet the distinction between their being remains. Take as illustration actual sound and actual hearing: a man may have hearing and yet not be hearing, and that which has a sound is not always sounding. But when that which can hear is actively hearing and that which can sound is sounding, then the actual hearing and the actual sound are merged in one (these one might call respectively hearkening and sounding).

If it is true that the movement, both the acting and the being acted upon, is to be found in that which is acted upon, both the sound and the hearing so far as it is actual must be found in that which has the faculty of hearing; for it is in the passive factor that the actuality of the active or motive factor is realized; that is why that which causes movement may be at rest. Now the actuality of that which can sound is just sound or sounding, and the actuality of that which can hear is hearing or hearkening; "sound" and "hearing" are both ambiguous. The same account applies to the other senses and their objects. For as the-acting-and-being-acted-upon is to be found in the passive, not in the active factor, so also the actuality of the sensible object and that of the sensitive subject are both realized in the latter. But while in some cases each aspect of the total actuality has a distinct name, e. g., sounding and hearkening, in some one or other is nameless, e. g., the actuality of sight is called seeing, but the actuality of colour has no name; the actuality of the faculty of taste is called tasting, but the actuality of flavour has no name. Since the actualities of the sensible object and of the sensitive faculty are *one* actuality in spite of the difference between their modes of being, actual hearing and actual sounding appear and disappear from existence at one and the same moment, and so actual savour and actual tasting, etc., while as potentialities one of them may exist without the other. The earlier students of nature were mistaken in their view that without sight there was no white or black, without taste no savour. This statement of theirs is partly true, partly false; "sense" and "the sensible object" are ambiguous terms, i. e., may denote either potentialities or actualities; the statement is true of the latter, false of the former. This ambiguity they wholly failed to notice.

If voice always implies a concord, and if the voice and the hearing of it are in one sense one and the same, and if concord always implies a ratio, hearing as well as what is heard must be a ratio. That is why the excess of either the sharp or the flat destroys the hearing. (So also in the case of savours excess destroys the sense of taste, and in the case of colours excessive brightness or darkness destroys the sight, and in the case of smell excess of strength whether in the direction of sweetness or bitterness is destructive.) This shows that the sense is a ratio.

That is also why the objects of sense are (1) pleasant when the sensible extremes such as acid or sweet or salt being pure and unmixed are brought into the proper ratio; then they are pleasant; and in general what is blended is more pleasant than the sharp or the flat alone; or, to touch, that which is capable of being either warmed or chilled; the sense and the ratio are identical; while (2) in excess the sensible extremes are painful or destructive.

Each sense then is relative to its particular group of sensible qualities; it is found in a sense organ as such and discriminates the differences which exist within that group; e. g., sight discriminates white and black, taste sweet and bitter, and so in all cases. Since we also discriminate white from sweet, and indeed each sensible quality from every other, with what do we perceive that they are different? It must be by sense; for what is before us is sensible objects. (Hence it is also obvious that the flesh cannot be the ultimate sense organ; if it were, the discriminating power could not do its work without immediate contact with the object.)

Therefore (1) discrimination between white and sweet cannot be effected by two agencies which remain separate; both the qualities discriminated must be present to something that is one and single. On any other supposition even if I perceived sweet and you perceived white, the difference between them would be apparent. What says that two things are different must be one; for sweet is different from white. Therefore what asserts this difference must be self-identical, and as what asserts, so also what thinks or perceives. That it is not possible by means of two agencies which remain separate to discriminate two objects which are separate is therefore obvious; and that (2) it is not possible to do this in separate moments of time may be seen if we look at it as follows. For as what asserts the difference between the good and the bad is one and the same, so also the time at which it asserts the one to be different and the other to be different is not accidental to the assertion (as it is for instance when I now assert a difference but do not assert that there is now a difference); it asserts thus—both now and that the objects are different now; the objects therefore must be present at one and the same moment. Both the discriminating power and the time of its exercise must be one and undivided.

But, it may be objected, it is impossible that what is self-identical should be moved at one and the same time with contrary movements in so far as it is undivided, and in an undivided moment of time. For if what is sweet be the quality perceived, it moves the sense or thought in this determinate way, while what is bitter moves it in a contrary way, and what is white in a different way. Is it the case then that what discriminates, though both numerically one and indivisible, is at the same time divided in its being? In one sense, it is what is divided that perceives two separate objects at once, but in another sense it does so *qua* undivided; for it is divisible in its being, but spatially and numerically undivided.

But is not this impossible? For while it is true that what is self-identical and undivided may be both contraries at once *potentially*, it cannot be self-identical in its being—it must lose its unity by being put into activity. It is not possible to be at once white and black, and therefore it must also be impossible for a thing to be affected at one and the same moment by the forms of both, assuming it to be the case that sensation and thinking are properly so described.

The answer is that just as what is called a "point" is, as being at once one and two, properly said to be divisible, so here, that which discriminates is *qua* undivided one, and active in a single moment of time, while so far forth as it is divisible it twice over uses the same dot at one and the same time. So far forth then as it takes the limit as two, it discriminates two separate objects with what in a sense is divided: while so far as it takes it as one, it does so with what is one and occupies in its activity a single moment of time.

About the principle in virtue of which we say that animals are percipient, let this discussion suffice.

3. [*Thinking, perceiving, and imagining.*] There are two distinctive peculiarities by reference to which we characterize the soul: (1) local movement and (2) thinking, discriminating, and perceiving. Thinking, both speculative and practical, is regarded as akin to a form of perceiving; for in the one as well as the other the soul discriminates and is cognizant of something which *is*. Indeed the ancients go so far as to identify thinking and perceiving; e. g., Empedocles says "For 'tis in respect of what is present that man's wit is increased," and again "whence it befalls them from time to time to think diverse thoughts," and Homer's phrase "For suchlike is man's mind" means the same. They all look upon thinking as a bodily process like perceiving, and hold that like is *known* as well as *perceived* by like, as I explained at the beginning of our discussion. Yet they ought at the same time to have accounted for error also; for it is more intimately connected with animal existence and the soul continues longer in the state of error than in that of truth. They cannot escape the dilemma: either (1) whatever seems is true (and there are

some who accept this) or (2) error is contact with the un-like; for that is the opposite of the knowing of like by like.

But it is a received principle that error as well as knowledge in respect to contraries is one and the same.

That perceiving and practical thinking are not identical is therefore obvious; for the former is universal in the animal world, the latter is found in only a small division of it. Further, speculative thinking is also distinct from perceiving—I mean that in which we find rightness and wrongness—rightness in prudence, knowledge, true opinion, wrongness in their opposites; for perception of the special objects of sense is always free from error, and is found in all animals, while it is possible to think falsely as well as truly, and thought is found only where there is discourse of reason as well as sensibility. For imagination is different from either perceiving or discursive thinking, though it is not found without sensation, or judgement without it. That this activity is not the same kind of thinking as judgement is obvious. For imagining lies within our own power whenever we wish (e. g., we can call up a picture, as in the practice of mnemonics by the use of mental images), but in forming opinions we are not free; we cannot escape the alternative of falsehood or truth. Further, when we think something to be fearful or threatening, emotion is immediately produced, and so too with what is encouraging; but when we merely imagine we remain as unaffected as persons who are looking at a painting of some dreadful or encouraging scene. Again within the field of judgement itself we find varieties—knowledge, opinion, prudence, and their opposites; of the differences between these I must speak elsewhere.

Thinking is different from perceiving and is held to be in part imagination, in part judgement: we must therefore first mark off the sphere of imagination and then speak of judgement. If then imagination is that in virtue of which an image arises for us, excluding metaphorical uses of the term, is it a single faculty or disposition relative to images, in virtue of which we discriminate and are either in error or not? The faculties in virtue of which we do this are sense, opinion, science, intelligence.

That imagination is not sense is clear from the following considerations: (1) Sense is either a faculty or an activity, e. g., sight or seeing; imagination takes place in the absence of both, as e. g., in dreams. (2) Again, sense is always present, imagination not. If actual imagination and actual sensation were the same, imagination would be found in all the brutes; this is held not to be the case; e. g., it is not found in ants or bees or grubs. (3) Again, sensations are always true, imaginations are for the most part false. (4) Once more, even in ordinary speech, we do not, when sense functions precisely with regard to its object, say that we imagine it to be a man, but rather when there is some failure of accuracy in its exercise. And (5), as we were saying before, visions appear to us even when our eyes are shut. Neither is imagination *any* of the things that are never in error; e. g., knowledge or intelligence; for imagination may be false.

It remains therefore to see if it is opinion, for opinion may be either true or false.

But opinion involves belief (for without belief in what we opine we cannot have an opinion), and in the brutes though we often find imagination we never find belief. Further, every opinion is accompanied by belief, belief by conviction, and conviction by discourse of reason; while there are some of the brutes in which we find imagination, without discourse of reason. It is clear then that imagination cannot, again, be (1) opinion *plus* sensation, or (2) opinion mediated by sensation, or (3) a blend of opinion and sensation; this is impossible both for these reasons and because the content of the supposed opinion cannot be different from that of the sensation (I mean that imagination must be the blending of the perception of white with the opinion that it is white; it could scarcely be a blend of the opinion that it is good with the perception that it is white); to imagine is therefore (on this view) identical with the thinking of exactly the same as what one in the strictest sense perceives. But what we imagine is sometimes false though our contemporaneous judgement about it is true; e. g., we imagine the sun to be a foot in diameter though we are convinced that it is larger than the inhabited part of the earth, and the following dilemma presents itself. Either (a) while the fact has not changed and the observer has neither forgotten nor lost belief in the true opinion which he had, that opinion has disappeared, or (b) if he retains it then his opinion is at once true and false. A true opinion, however, becomes false only when the fact alters without being noticed.

Imagination is therefore neither any one of the states enumerated, nor compounded out of them.

But since when one thing has been set in motion another thing may be moved by it, and imagination is held to be a movement and to be impossible without sensation, i. e., to occur in beings that are percipient and to have for its content what can be perceived, and since movement may be produced by actual sensation and that movement is necessarily similar in character to the sensation itself, this movement must be (1) necessarily (a) incapable of existing apart from sensation, (b) incapable of existing except when we perceive, (2) such that in virtue of its possession that in which it is found may present various phenomena both active and passive, and (3) such that it may be either true or false.

The reason of the last characteristic is as follows. Perception (1) of the special objects of sense is never in error or admits the least possible amount of falsehood. (2) That of the concomitance of the objects concomitant with the sensible qualities comes next; in this case certainly we may be deceived; for while the perception that there is white before us cannot be false, the perception that what is white is this or that may be false. (3) Third comes the perception of the universal attributes which accompany the concomitant objects to which the special sensibles attach (I mean, e. g., of movement and magnitude); it is in respect of these that the greatest amount of sense illusion is possible.

The motion which is due to the activity of sense in these three modes of its exercise will differ from the activity of sense; (1) the first kind of derived motion is free from error while the sensation is present; (2) and (3) the others may be erroneous whether it is present or absent, especially when the object of perception is far off. If then imagination presents no other features than those enumerated and is what we have described, then imagination must be a movement resulting from an actual exercise of a power of sense.

As sight is the most highly developed sense, the name *phantasia* (imagination) has been formed from *phaos* (light) because it is not possible to see without light.

And because imaginations remain in the organs of sense and resemble sensations, animals in their actions are largely guided by them, some (i. e., the brutes) because of the non-existence in them of mind, others (i. e., men) because of the temporary eclipse in them of mind by feeling or disease or sleep.

About imagination, what it is and why it exists, let so much suffice.

4. [*Passive mind.*] Turning now to the part of the soul with which the soul knows and thinks (whether this is separable from the others in definition only, or spatially as well) we have to inquire (1) what differentiates this part, and (2) how thinking can take place.

If thinking is like perceiving, it must be either a process in which the soul is acted upon by what is capable of being thought, or a process different from but analogous to that. The thinking part of the soul must therefore be, while impassible, capable of receiving the form of an object; that is, must be potentially identical in character with its object without being the object. Mind must be related to what is thinkable, as sense is to what is sensible.

Therefore, since everything is a possible object of thought, mind in order, as Anaxagoras says, to dominate, that is, to know, must be pure from all admixtures; for the co-presence of what is alien to its nature is a hindrance and a block; it follows that it too, like the sensitive part, can have no nature of its own, other than that of having a certain capacity. Thus that in the soul which is called mind (by mind I mean that whereby the soul thinks and judges) is, before it thinks, not actually any real thing. For this reason it cannot reasonably be regarded as blended with the body; if so, it would acquire some quality, e. g., warmth or cold, or even have an organ like the sensitive faculty; as it is, it has none. It was a good idea to call the soul "the place of forms," though (1) this description holds only of the intellective soul, and (2) even this is the forms only potentially, not actually.

Observation of the sense organs and their employment reveals a distinction between the impassibility of the sensitive and that of the intellective faculty. After strong stimulation of a sense we are less able to exercise it than before, as, e. g., in the case of a loud sound we cannot hear easily immediately after, or in the case of a bright colour or a powerful odour we cannot see or smell, but in the case of mind, thought about an object that is highly intelligible renders it more and not less able afterwards to think objects that are less intelligible; the reason is that while the faculty of sensation is dependent upon the body, mind is separable from it.

Once the mind has become each set of its possible objects, as a man of science has, when this phrase is used of one who is actually a man of science (this happens when he is now able to exercise the power on his own initiative), its condition is still one of potentiality, but in a different sense from the potentiality which preceded the acquisition of knowledge by learning or discovery; the mind too is then able to think *itself*.

Since we can distinguish between a spatial magnitude and what it is to be such, and between water and what it is to be water, and so in many other cases (though not in all; for in certain cases the thing and its form are identical), flesh and what it is to be flesh are discriminated either by different faculties, or by the same faculty in two different states; for flesh necessarily involves matter and is like what is snubnosed, a *this* in a *this*. Now it is by means of the sensitive faculty that we discriminate the hot and the cold, i. e., the factors which combined in a certain ratio constitute flesh; the essential character of flesh is apprehended by something different either wholly separate from the sensitive faculty or related to it as a bent line to the same line when it has been straightened out.

Again in the case of abstract objects what is straight is analogous to what is snub-nosed; for it necessarily implies a continuum as its matter; its constitutive essence is different, if we may distinguish between straightness and what is straight; let us take it to be twoness. It must be apprehended, therefore, by a different power or by the same power in a different state. To sum up, in so far as the realities it knows are capable of being separated from their matter, so it is also with the powers of mind.

The problem might be suggested: if thinking is a passive affection, then if mind is simple and impassible and has nothing in common with anything else, as Anaxagoras says, how can it come to think at all? For interaction between two factors is held to require a precedent community of nature between the factors. Again it might be asked, is mind a possible object of thought to itself? For if mind is thinkable *per se* and what is thinkable is in kind one and the same, then either (*a*) mind will belong to everything, or (*b*) mind will contain some element common to it with all other realities which makes them all thinkable.

(1) Have not we already disposed of the difficulty about interaction involving a common element, when we said that mind is in a sense potentially whatever is thinkable, though actually it is nothing until it has thought? What it thinks must be in it just as characters may be said to be on a writing tablet on which as yet nothing actually stands written; this is exactly what happens with mind.

(2) Mind is itself thinkable in exactly the same way as its objects are. For (*a*) in the case of objects which involve no matter, what thinks and what is thought are identical; for speculative knowledge and its object are identical. (Why mind is not always thinking we must consider later.) (*b*) In the case of those which contain matter each of the objects of thought is only potentially present. It follows that while *they* will not have mind in them (for mind is a potentiality

of them only in so far as they are capable of being disengaged from matter) mind may yet be thinkable.

5. [*Active mind.*] Since in every class of things, as in nature as a whole, we find two factors involved, (1) a matter which is potentially all the particulars included in the class, (2) a cause which is productive in the sense that it makes them all (the latter standing to the former, as, e. g., an art to its material), these distinct elements must likewise be found within the soul.

And in fact mind as we have described it is what it is by virtue of becoming all things, while there is another which is what it is by virtue of making all things: this is a sort of positive state like light; for in a sense light makes potential colours into actual colours.

Mind in this sense of it is separable, impassible, unmixed, since it is in its essential nature activity (for always the active is superior to the passive factor, the originating force to the matter which it forms).

Actual knowledge is identical with its object; in the individual, potential knowledge is in time prior to actual knowledge, but in the universe as a whole it is not prior even in time. Mind is not at one time knowing and at another not. When mind is set free from its present conditions it appears as just what it is and nothing more; this alone is immortal and eternal (we do not, however, remember its former activity because, while mind in this sense is impassible, mind as passive is destructible), and without it nothing thinks.

6. [*The double operation of mind.*] The thinking then of the simple objects of thought is found in those cases where falsehood is impossible; where the alternative of true or false applies, there we always find a putting together of objects of thought in a quasi-unity. As Empedocles said that "where heads of many a creature sprouted without necks" they afterwards by Love's power were combined, so here too objects of thought which were given separate are combined, e. g., "incommensurate" and "diagonal"; if the combination be of

objects past or future the combination of thought includes in its content the date. For falsehood always involves a synthesis; for even if you assert that what is white is not white you have included not-white in a synthesis. It is possible also to call all these cases division as well as combination. However that may be, there is not only the true or false assertion that Cleon is white but also the true or false assertion that he *was* or *will be* white. In each and every case that which unifies is mind.

Since the word "simple" has two senses, i. e., may mean either (a) "not capable of being divided" or (b) "not actually divided," there is nothing to prevent mind from knowing what is undivided, e. g., when it apprehends a length (which is actually undivided) and that in an undivided time; for the time is divided or undivided in the same manner as the line. It is not possible, then, to tell what part of the line it was apprehending in each half of the time; the object has no actual parts until it has been divided; if in thought you think each half separately, then by the same act you divide the time also, the half-lines becoming as it were new wholes of length. But if you think it as a whole consisting of these two possible parts, then also you think it in a time which corresponds to both parts together. (But what is not quantitatively but qualitatively simple is thought in a simple time and by a simple act of the soul.)

But that which mind thinks and the time in which it thinks are in this case divisible only incidentally and not as such. For in them too there is something indivisible (though, it may be, not isolable) which gives unity to the time and the whole of length; and this is found equally in every continuum whether temporal or spatial.

Points and similar instances of things that divide, themselves being indivisible, are realized in consciousness in the same manner as privations.

A similar account may be given of all other cases, e. g., how evil or black is cognized; they are cognized, in a sense, by means of their contraries. That which cognizes must have an element of potentiality in its being, and one of the contraries must be in it. But if there is anything that has no contrary, then it knows itself and is actually and possesses independent existence.

Assertion is the saying of something concerning something, e. g., affirmation, and is in every case either true or false; this is not always the case with mind; the thinking of the definition in the sense of the constitutive essence is never in error nor is it the assertion of something concerning something, but, just as while the seeing of the special object of sight can never be in error, the belief that the white object seen is a man may be mistaken, so too in the case of objects which are without matter.

7. [*The practical mind and the contemplative mind.*] Actual knowledge is identical with its object; potential knowledge in the individual is in time prior to actual knowledge but in the universe it has no priority even in time; for all things that come into being arise from what actually is. In the case of sense clearly the sensitive faculty already was potentially what the object makes it to be actually; the faculty is not affected or altered. This must therefore be a different kind from movement; for movement is, as we saw, an activity of what is imperfect, activity in the unqualified sense, i. e., that of what has been perfected, is different from movement.

To perceive then is like bare asserting or knowing; but when the object is pleasant or painful, the soul makes a quasi-affirmation or negation, and pursues or avoids the object. To feel pleasure or pain is to act with the sensitive mean towards what is good or bad as such. Both avoidance and appetite when actual are identical with this; the faculty of appetite and avoidance are not different, either from one another or from the faculty of sense perception; but their being *is* different.

To the thinking soul images serve as if they were contents of perception (and when it asserts or denies them to be good or bad it avoids or pursues them). That is why the soul never thinks without an image. The process is like that in which the air modifies the pupil in this or that way and the pupil transmits the modification to some third thing (and similarly in hearing), while the ultimate point of arrival is one, a single mean, with different manners of being.

With what part of itself the soul discriminates sweet from hot I have explained before and must now describe again as follows: That with which it does so is a sort of unity, but in the way just mentioned, i. e., as a connecting term. And the two faculties it connects, being one by analogy and numerically, are each to each as the qualities discerned are to one another (for what difference does it make whether we raise the problem of discrimination between disparates or between contraries, e. g., white and black?). Let then *C* be to *D* as *A* is to *B*: it follows *alternando* that $C:A::D:B$. If then *C* and *D* belong to one subject, the case will be the same with them as with *A* and *B*; *A* and *B* form a single identity with different modes of being; so too will the former pair. The same reasoning holds if *A* be sweet and *B* white.

The faculty of thinking then thinks the forms in the images, and as in the former case what is to be pursued or avoided is marked out for it, so where there is no sensation and it is engaged upon the images it is moved to pursuit or avoidance. E. g., perceiving by sense that the beacon is fire, it recognizes in virtue of the general faculty of sense that it signifies an enemy, because it sees it moving; but sometimes by means of the images or thoughts which are within the soul, just as if it were seeing, it calculates and deliberates what is to come by reference to what is present; and when it makes a pronouncement, as in the case of sensation it pronounces the object to be pleasant or painful, in this case it avoids or pursues; and so generally in cases of action.

That too which involves no action, i. e., that which is true or false, is in the same province with what is good or bad; yet they differ in this, that the one set imply and the other do not a reference to a particular person.

The so-called abstract objects the mind thinks just as, if one had thought of the snub-nosed not as snub-nosed but as hollow, one would have thought of an actuality without the flesh in which it is embodied; it is thus that the mind when it is thinking the objects of Mathematics thinks as separate, elements which do not exist separate. In every case the mind which is actively thinking is the objects which it thinks. Whether it is possible for it while not existing separate from spatial conditions to think anything that is separate, or not, we must consider later.

8. [*Comparison of mind with sense and imagination.*] Let us now summarize our results about soul, and repeat that the soul is in a way all existing things; for existing things are either sensible or thinkable, and knowledge is in a way what is knowable, and sensation is in a way what is sensible; in *what* way we must inquire.

Knowledge and sensation are divided to correspond with the realities, potential knowledge and sensation answering to potentialities, actual knowledge and sensation to actualities. Within the soul the faculties of knowledge and sensation are *potentially* these objects, the one what is knowable, the other what is sensible. They must be either the things themselves or their forms. The former alternative is of course impossible; it is not the stone which is present in the soul but its form.

It follows that the soul is analogous to the hand; for as the hand is a tool of tools,* so the mind is the form of forms and sense the form of sensible things.

Since according to common agreement there is nothing outside and separate in existence from sensible spatial magnitudes, the objects of thought are in the sensible forms, viz., both the abstract objects and all the states and affections of sensible things. Hence (1) no one can learn or understand anything in the absence of sense, and (2) when the mind is actively aware of anything it is necessarily aware of it along with an image; for images are like sensuous contents except in that they contain no matter.

Imagination is different from assertion and denial; for what is true or false involves a synthesis of concepts. In what will

---

*i. e., a tool for using tools.

the primary concepts differ from images? Must we not say that neither these nor even our other concepts are images, though they necessarily involve them?

9. [*Problems of the motive faculty.*] The soul of animals is characterized by two faculties, (*a*) the faculty of discrimination which is the work of thought and sense, and (*b*) the faculty of originating local movement. Sense and mind we have now sufficiently examined. Let us next consider what it is in the soul which originates movement. Is it a single part of the soul separate either spatially or in definition? Or is it the soul as a whole? If it is a part, is that part different from those usually distinguished or already mentioned by us, or is it one of them? The problem at once presents itself, in what sense we are to speak of parts of the soul, or how many we should distinguish. For in a sense there is an infinity of parts; it is not enough to distinguish, with some thinkers, the calculative, the passionate, and the desiderative, or with others the rational and the irrational; for if we take the dividing lines followed by these thinkers we shall find parts far more distinctly separated from one another than these, namely those we have just mentioned: (1) the nutritive, which belongs both to plants and to all animals, and (2) the sensitive, which cannot easily be classed as either irrational or rational; further (3) the imaginative, which is, in its being, different from all, while it is very hard to say with which of the others it is the same or not the same, supposing we determine to posit *separate* parts in the soul; and lastly (4) the appetitive, which would seem to be distinct both in definition and in power from all hitherto enumerated.

It is absurd to break up the last-mentioned faculty, as these thinkers do, for wish is found in the calculative part and desire and passion in the irrational; and if the soul is tripartite appetite will be found in all three parts. Turning our attention to the present object of discussion, let us ask what that is which originates local movement of the animal.

The movement of growth and decay, being found in all living things, must be attributed to the faculty of reproduction and nutrition, which is common to all; inspiration and expiration, sleep and waking, we must consider later—these too present much difficulty; at present we must consider local movement, asking what it is that originates forward movement in the animal.

That it is not the nutritive faculty is obvious; for this kind of movement is always for an end and is accompanied either by imagination or by appetite; for no animal moves except by compulsion unless it has an impulse towards or away from an object. Further, if it were the nutritive faculty, even plants would have been capable of originating such movement and would have possessed the organs necessary to carry it out. Similarly it cannot be the sensitive faculty either; for there are many animals which have sensibility but remain fast and immovable throughout their lives.

If then Nature never makes anything without a purpose and never leaves out what is necessary (except in the case of mutilated or imperfect growths; and that here we have neither mutilation nor imperfection may be argued from the facts that such animals (a) can reproduce their species and (b) rise to completeness of nature and decay to an end), it follows that, had they been capable of originating forward movement, they would have possessed the organs necessary for that purpose. Further, neither can the calculative faculty or what is called "mind" be the cause of such movement; for mind as speculative never thinks what is practicable, it never says anything about an object to be avoided or pursued, while this movement is always in something which is avoiding or pursuing an object. No, not even when it is aware of such an object does it at once enjoin pursuit or avoidance of it; e. g., the mind often thinks of something terrifying or pleasant without enjoining the emotion of fear. It is the heart that is moved (or in the case of a pleasant object some other part). Further, even when the mind does command and thought bids us pursue or avoid something, sometimes no movement is produced; we act in accordance with desire, as in the case of moral weakness. And, generally, we observe that the possessor of medical knowledge is not necessarily healing, which

shows that something else is required to produce action in
accordance with knowledge; the knowledge alone is not the
cause. Lastly, appetite too is incompetent to account fully
for movement; for those who successfully resist temptation
have appetite and desire and yet follow mind and refuse to
enact that for which they have appetite.

10. [*The cause of movement of living things.*] These two at
all events appear to be sources of movement: appetite and
mind (if one may venture to regard imagination as a kind of
thinking; for many men follow their imaginations contrary to
knowledge, and in all animals other than man there is no
thinking or calculation but only imagination).

Both of these then are capable of originating local movement, mind and appetite: (1) mind, that is, which calculates
means to an end, i. e., mind practical (it differs from mind
speculative in the character of its end); while (2) appetite is
in every form of it relative to an end, for that which is the
object of appetite is the stimulant of mind practical; and
that which is last in the process of thinking is the beginning
of the action. It follows that there is a justification for regarding these two as the sources of movement, i. e., appetite
and practical thought; for the object of appetite starts a movement and as a result of that thought gives rise to movement,
the object of appetite being to it a source of stimulation. So
too when imagination originates movement, it necessarily
involves appetite.

That which moves therefore is a single faculty and the
faculty of appetite; for if there had been two sources of
movement—mind and appetite—they would have produced
movement in virtue of some common character. As it is,
mind is never found producing movement without appetite
(for wish is a form of appetite; and when movement is produced according to calculation it is also according to wish),
but appetite can originate movement contrary to calculation,
for desire is a form of appetite. Now mind is always right, but
appetite and imagination may be either right or wrong. That
is why, though in any case it is the object of appetite which

originates movement, this object may be either the real or the apparent good. To produce movement the object must be more than this: it must be good that can be brought into being by action; and only what can be otherwise than as it is can thus be brought into being. That then such a power in the soul as has been described, i. e., that called appetite, originates movement is clear. Those who distinguish parts in the soul, if they distinguish and divide in accordance with differences of power, find themselves with a very large number of parts, a nutritive, a sensitive, an intellective, a deliberative, and now an appetitive part; for these are more different from one another than the faculties of desire and passion.

Since appetites run counter to one another, which happens when a principle of reason and a desire are contrary and is possible only in beings with a sense of time (for while mind bids us hold back because of what is future, desire is influenced by what is just at hand; a pleasant object which is just at hand presents itself as both pleasant and good, without condition in either case, because of want of foresight into what is farther away in time), it follows that while that which originates movement must be specifically one, viz., the faculty of appetite as such (or rather farthest back of all the object of that faculty; for it is it that itself remaining unmoved originates the movement by being apprehended in thought or imagination), the things that originate movement are numerically many.

All movement involves three factors, (1) that which originates the movement, (2) that by means of which it originates it, and (3) that which is moved. The expression "that which originates the movement" is ambiguous: it may mean either (a) something which itself is unmoved or (b) that which at once moves and is moved. Here that which moves without itself being moved is the realizable good, that which at once moves and is moved is the faculty of appetite (for that which is influenced by appetite so far as it is actually so influenced is set in movement, and appetite in the sense of actual appetite *is* a kind of movement), while that which is in motion is the animal. The instrument which appetite employs to produce movement is no longer psychical but bodily; hence the examination of it falls within the province of the functions common to body and soul. To state the matter summarily at present, that which is the instrument in the production of movement is to be found where a beginning and an end coincide as, e. g., in a ball and socket joint; for there the convex and the concave sides are respectively an end and a beginning (that is why while the one remains at rest, the other is moved); they are separate in definition but not separable spatially. For everything is moved by pushing and pulling. Hence just as in the case of a wheel, so here there must be a point which remains at rest, and from that point the movement must originate.

To sum up, then, and repeat what I have said, inasmuch as an animal is capable of appetite it is capable of self-movement; it is not capable of appetite without possessing imagination; and all imagination is either (1) calculative or (2) sensitive. In the latter all animals, and not only man, partake.

* * *

METAPHYSICS

Translated by W. D. Ross

The name of this work, and of an entire branch of inquiry into first principles, is the result of an accident. An early editor used the title "Metaphysics" to designate a group of works which came after (hence the prefix *meta*) the treatise on Physics; both the title and the sequence remained in subsequent editions.

"First Philosophy," "Wisdom," "Theology": these are some of the other titles that can be used interchangeably for this work. "All men by nature desire to know," Aristotle announces at the beginning of Book I. The special kind of knowledge he attempts to define in the Metaphysics is that of first causes, the knowledge which both underlies and transcends all other sciences and which leads to the ultimate source of motion and life.

In Book I, Aristotle analyzes the grounds and objects of First Philosophy, the study of those causes and principles "the knowledge of which is Wisdom." He points out the inadequacies of other philosophies, including that of Plato, and he concludes that his own doctrine of the four causes (which he had developed in the Physics) is sufficient to support a science of first principles.

In Book XII, he embarks on a majestically and intricately logical search for the source of all motion, for that which causes the heavens to move in perpetual circular motion and which is itself not moved. This is the prime or unmoved mover—"the object of the world's desire"—which is pure being, pure actuality, total knowledge which has itself for an object This Aristotelian Prime Mover, whose sole object of contemplation is itself, is radically different from the Christian notion of a God involved in the fortunes of men, a good shepherd. It was the task of St. Thomas Aquinas and Duns Scotus to reconcile and resolve, although not with entire success, these two ideas of God and to attempt to absorb Aristotle into the Christian tradition.

METAPHYSICS

∽∽∽∽∽∽∽∽∽∽∽∽∽∽∽∽∽∽∽∽∽∽∽∽∽∽∽∽∽

BOOK I

1. [*The advance from sensation, through memory, experience, and art, to theoretical knowledge.*] All men by nature desire to know. An indication of this is the delight we take in our senses; for even apart from their usefulness they are loved for themselves; and above all others the sense of sight. For not only with a view to action, but even when we are not going to do anything, we prefer seeing (one might say) to everything else. The reason is that this, most of all the senses, makes us know and brings to light many differences between things.

By nature animals are born with the faculty of sensation, and from sensation memory is produced in some of them, though not in others. And therefore the former are more intelligent and apt at learning than those which cannot remember; those which are incapable of hearing sounds are intelligent though they cannot be taught, e. g., the bee, and any other race of animals that may be like it; and those which besides memory have this sense of hearing can be taught.

The animals other than man live by appearances and memories, and have but little of connected experience; but the human race lives also by art and reasonings. Now from memory experience is produced in men; for the several memories of the same thing produce finally the capacity for a single experience. And experience seems pretty much like science and art, but really science and art come to men *through* experience; for "experience made art," as Polus says, "but inexperience luck." Now art arises when from many notions gained by experience one universal judgement about a class of objects is produced. For to have a judgement that when Callias was ill of this disease this did him good, and similarly in the case of Socrates and in many individual cases, is a matter of experience; but to judge that it has done good to all persons of a certain constitution, marked off in one class, when they were ill of this disease, e. g., to phlegmatic or bilious people when burning with fever—this is a matter of art.

With a view to action experience seems in no respect inferior to art, and men of experience succeed even better than those who have theory without experience. (The reason is that experience is knowledge of individuals, art of universals, and actions and productions are all concerned with the individual; for the physician does not cure *man*, except in an incidental way, but Callias or Socrates or some other called by some such individual name, who happens to be a man. If, then, a man has the theory without the experience, and recognizes the universal but does not know the individual included in this, he will often fail to cure; for it is the individual that is to be cured.) But yet we think that *knowledge* and *understanding* belong to art rather than to experience, and we suppose artists to be wiser than men of experience (which implies that Wisdom depends in all cases rather on knowledge); and this because the former know the cause, but the latter do not. For men of experience know that the thing is so, but do not know why, while the others know the "why" and the cause. Hence we think also that the master workers in each craft are more honourable and know in a truer sense and are wiser than the manual workers, because they know the causes of the things that are done (we think the manual workers are like certain lifeless things which act indeed, but act without knowing what they do, as fire burns—but while the lifeless things perform each of their functions by a natural tendency, the labourers perform them through habit); thus we view them as being wiser not in virtue of being able to act, but of having the theory for themselves and knowing the causes. And in general it is a sign of the man who knows and of the man who does not know, that the former can teach, and therefore we think art more truly knowledge than experience is; for artists can teach, and men of mere experience cannot.

Again, we do not regard any of the senses as Wisdom; yet surely these give the most authoritative knowledge of particulars. But they do not tell us the "why" of anything—e. g., why fire is hot; they only say *that* it is hot.

At first he who invented any art whatever that went beyond the common perceptions of man was naturally admired by men, not only because there was something useful in the inventions, but because he was thought wise and superior to the rest. But as more arts were invented, and some were directed to the necessities of life, others to recreation, the inventors of the latter were naturally always regarded as wiser than the inventors of the former, because their branches of knowledge did not aim at utility. Hence when all such inventions were already established, the sciences which do not aim at giving pleasure or at the necessities of life were discovered, and first in the places where men first began to have leisure. This is why the mathematical arts were founded in Egypt; for there the priestly caste was allowed to be at leisure.

We have said in the *Ethics* what the difference is between art and science and the other kindred faculties; but the point of our present discussion is this, that all men suppose what is called Wisdom to deal with the first causes and the principles of things; so that, as has been said before, the man of experience is thought to be wiser than the possessors of any sense perception whatever, the artist wiser than the men of experience, the master worker than the mechanic, and the theoretical kinds of knowledge to be more of the nature of Wisdom than the productive. Clearly then Wisdom is knowledge about certain principles and causes.

2. [*Characteristics of "Wisdom" (philosophy)*.] Since we are seeking this knowledge, we must inquire of what kind are the causes and the principles, the knowledge of which is Wisdom. If one were to take the notions we have about the wise man, this might perhaps make the answer more evident. We suppose first, then, that the wise man knows all things, as far as possible, although he has not knowledge of each of them in detail; secondly, that he who can learn things that are difficult, and not easy for man to know, is wise (sense perception is common to all, and therefore easy and no mark of Wisdom); again, that he who is more exact and more capable of teaching the causes is wiser, in every branch of knowledge; and that of the sciences, also, that which is desirable on its own account and for the sake of knowing it is more of the nature of Wisdom than that which is desirable on account of its results, and the superior science is more of the nature of Wisdom than the ancillary; for the wise man must not be ordered but must order, and he must not obey another, but the less wise must obey *him*.

Such and so many are the notions, then, which we have about Wisdom and the wise. Now of these characteristics that of knowing all things must belong to him who has in the highest degree universal knowledge; for he knows in a sense all the instances that fall under the universal. And these things, the most universal, are on the whole the hardest for men to know; for they are farthest from the senses. And the most exact of the sciences are those which deal most with first principles; for those which involve fewer principles are more exact than those which involve additional principles, e. g., arithmetic than geometry. But the science which investigates causes is also *instructive*, in a higher degree, for the people who instruct us are those who tell the causes of each thing. And understanding and knowledge pursued for their own sake are found most in the knowledge of that which is most knowable (for he who chooses to know for the sake of knowing will choose most readily that which is most truly knowledge, and such is the knowledge of that which is most knowable); and the first principles and the causes are most knowable; for by reason of these, and from these, all other things come to be known, and not these by means of the things subordinate to them. And the science which knows to what end each thing must be done is the most authoritative of the sciences, and more authoritative than any ancillary science; and this end is the good of that thing, and in general the supreme good in the whole of nature. Judged by all the tests we have mentioned, then, the name in question falls to the same science; this must be a science that investigates the first principles and causes; for the good, i. e., the end, is one of the causes.

That it is not a science of production is clear even from the history of the earliest philosophers. For it is owing to their wonder that men both now begin and at first began to philosophize; they wondered originally at the obvious difficulties, then advanced little by little and stated difficulties about the greater matters, e. g., about the phenomena of the moon and those of the sun and of the stars, and about the genesis of the universe. And a man who is puzzled and wonders thinks himself ignorant (whence even the lover of myth is in a sense a lover of Wisdom, for the myth is composed of wonders); therefore since they philosophized in order to escape from ignorance, evidently they were pursuing science in order to know, and not for any utilitarian end. And this is confirmed by the facts; for it was when almost all the necessities of life and the things that make for comfort and recreation had been secured, that such knowledge began to be sought. Evidently then we do not seek it for the sake of any other advantage; but as the man is free, we say, who exists for his own sake and not for another's, so we pursue this as the only free science, for it alone exists for its own sake.

Hence also the possession of it might be justly regarded as beyond human power; for in many ways human nature is in bondage, so that, according to Simonides, "God alone can have this privilege," and it is unfitting that man should not be content to seek the knowledge that is suited to him. If, then, there is something in what the poets say, and jealousy is natural to the divine power, it would probably occur in this case above all, and all who excelled in this knowledge would be unfortunate. But the divine power cannot be jealous (nay, according to the proverb, "bards tell many a lie"), nor should any other science be thought more honourable than one of this sort. For the most divine science is also most honourable; and this science alone must be, in two ways, most divine. For the science which it would be most meet for God to have is a divine science, and so is any science that deals with divine objects; and this science alone has both these qualities; for (1) God is thought to be among the causes of all things and to be a first principle, and (2) such a science either God alone can have, or God above all others. All the sciences, indeed, are more necessary than this, but none is better.

Yet the acquisition of it must in a sense end in something which is the opposite of our original inquiries. For all men begin, as we said, by wondering that things are as they are, as they do about self-moving marionettes, or about the solstices or the incommensurability of the diagonal of a square with the side; for it seems wonderful to all who have not yet seen the reason, that there is a thing which cannot be measured even by the smallest unit. But we must end in the contrary and, according to the proverb, the better state, as is the case in these instances too when men learn the cause; for there is nothing which would surprise a geometer so much as if the diagonal turned out to be commensurable.

We have stated, then, what is the nature of the science we are searching for, and what is the mark which our search and our whole investigation must reach.

3. [*The successive recognition by earlier philosophers of the material, efficient, and final causes.*] Evidently we have to acquire knowledge of the original causes (for we say we know each thing only when we think we recognize its first cause), and causes are spoken of in four senses. In one of these we mean the substance, i. e., the essence (for the "why" is reducible finally to the definition, and the ulti-

mate "why" is a cause and principle); in another the matter or substratum, in a third the source of the change, and in a fourth the cause opposed to this, the purpose and the good (for this is the end of all generation and change). We have studied these causes sufficiently in our work on nature, but yet let us call to our aid those who have attacked the investigation of being and philosophized about reality before us. For obviously they too speak of certain principles and causes; to go over their views, then, will be of profit to the present inquiry, for we shall either find another kind of cause, or be more convinced of the correctness of those which we now maintain.

Of the first philosophers, then, most thought the principles which were of the nature of matter were the only principles of all things. That of which all things that are consist, the first from which they come to be, the last into which they are resolved (the substance remaining, but changing in its modifications), this they say is the element and this the principle of things, and therefore they think nothing is either generated or destroyed, since this sort of entity is always conserved, as we say Socrates neither comes to be absolutely when he comes to be beautiful or musical, nor ceases to be when he loses these characteristics, because the substratum, Socrates himself, remains. Just so they say nothing else comes to be or ceases to be; for there must be some entity—either one or more than one—from which all other things come to be, it being conserved.

Yet they do not all agree as to the number and the nature of these principles. Thales, the founder of this type of philosophy, says the principle is water (for which reason he declared that the earth rests on water), getting the notion perhaps from seeing that the nutriment of all things is moist, and that heat itself is generated from the moist and kept alive by it (and that from which they come to be is a principle of all things). He got his notion from this fact, and from the fact that the seeds of all things have a moist nature, and that water is the origin of the nature of moist things.

Some think that even the ancients who lived long before the present generation, and first framed accounts of the gods, had a similar view of nature; for they made Ocean and Tethys the parents of creation, and described the oath of the gods as being by water, to which they give the name of Styx; for what is oldest is most honourable, and the most honourable thing is that by which one swears. It may perhaps be uncertain whether this opinion about nature is primitive and ancient, but Thales at any rate is said to have declared himself thus about the first cause. Hippo no one would think fit to include among these thinkers, because of the paltriness of his thought.

Anaximenes and Diogenes make air prior to water, and the most primary of the simple bodies, while Hippasus of Metapontium and Heraclitus of Ephesus say this of fire, and Empedocles says it of the four elements (adding a fourth—earth—to those which have been named); for these, he says, always remain and do not come to be, except that they come to be more or fewer, being aggregated into one and segregated out of one.

Anaxagoras of Clazomenae, who, though older than Empedocles, was later in his philosophical activity, says the principles are infinite in number; for he says almost all the things that are made of parts like themselves, in the manner of water or fire, are generated and destroyed in this way, only by aggregation and segregation, and are not in any other sense generated or destroyed, but remain eternally.

From these facts one might think that the only cause is the so-called material cause; but as men thus advanced, the very facts opened the way for them and joined in forcing them to investigate the subject. However true it may be that all generation and destruction proceed from some one or (for that matter) from more elements, why does this happen and what is the cause? For at least the substratum itself does not make itself change; e. g., neither the wood nor the bronze causes the change of either of them, nor does the wood manufacture a bed and the bronze a statue, but something else is the cause of the change. And to seek this is to seek the second cause, as *we* should say—that from which comes the beginning of the movement. Now those who at the very beginning set themselves to this kind of inquiry, and said the substratum was one, were not at all dissatisfied with themselves; but some at least of those who maintain it to be one— as though defeated by this search for the second cause—say the one and nature as a whole is unchangeable not only in respect of generation and destruction (for this is a primitive belief, and all agreed in it), but also of all other change; and this view is peculiar to them. Of those who said the universe was one, then, none succeeded in discovering a cause of this sort, except perhaps Parmenides, and he only inasmuch as he supposes that there is not only one but also in some sense two causes. But for those who make more elements it is more possible to state the second cause, e. g., for those who make hot and cold, or fire and earth, the elements; for they treat fire as having a nature which fits it to move things, and water and earth and such things they treat in the contrary way.

When these men and the principles of this kind had had their day, as the latter were found inadequate to generate the nature of things men were again forced by the truth itself, as we said, to inquire into the next kind of cause. For it is not likely either that fire or earth or any such element should be the reason why things manifest goodness and beauty both in their being and in their coming to be, or that those thinkers should have supposed it was; nor again could it be right to entrust so great a matter to spontaneity and chance. When one man said, then, that reason was present—as in animals, so throughout nature—as the cause of order and of all arrangement, he seemed like a sober man in contrast with the random talk of his predecessors. We know that Anaxagoras certainly adopted these views, but Hermotimus of Clazomenae is credited with expressing them earlier. Those who thought thus stated that there is a principle of things which is at the same time the cause of beauty, and that sort of cause from which things acquire movement.

4. [*Inadequacy of the treatment of these causes.*] One might suspect that Hesiod was the first to look for such a thing—or some one else who put love or desire among existing things as a principle, as Parmenides, too, does; for he, in constructing the genesis of the universe, says:

> Love first of all the Gods she planned.

And Hesiod says:

> First of all things was chaos made, and then
> Broad-breasted earth, . . .
> And love, 'mid all the gods pre-eminent,

which implies that among existing things there must be from the first a cause which will move things and bring them together. How these thinkers should be arranged with regard to priority of discovery let us be allowed to decide later; but since the contraries of the various forms of good were also perceived to be present in nature—not only order and the beautiful, but also disorder and the ugly, and bad things in greater number than good, and ignoble things than beautiful —therefore another thinker introduced friendship and strife, each of the two the cause of one of these two sets of qualities. For if we were to follow out the view of Empedocles, and interpret it according to its meaning and not to its lisping expression, we should find that friendship is the cause of good things, and strife of bad. Therefore, if we said that Empedocles in a sense both mentions, and is the first to mention, the bad and the good as principles, we should perhaps be right, since the cause of all goods is the good itself.

These thinkers, as we say, evidently grasped, and to this extent, two of the causes which we distinguished in our work on nature—the matter and the source of the movement— vaguely, however, and with no clearness, but as untrained men behave in fights; for they go round their opponents and often strike fine blows, but they do not fight on scientific principles, and so too these thinkers do not seem to know what they say; for it is evident that, as a rule, they make no use of their causes except to a small extent. For Anaxagoras uses reason as a *deus ex machina* for the making of the world, and when he is at a loss to tell from what cause something necessarily is, then he drags reason in, but in all other cases ascribes events to anything rather than to reason. And Empedocles, though he uses the causes to a greater extent than this, neither does so sufficiently nor attains consistency in their use. At least, in many cases he makes love segregate things, and strife aggregate them. For whenever the universe is dissolved into its elements by strife, fire is aggregated into one, and so is each of the other elements; but whenever again under the influence of love they come together into one, the parts must again be segregated out of each element.

Empedocles, then, in contrast with his predecessors, was the first to introduce the dividing of this cause, not positing one source of movement, but different and contrary sources. Again, he was the first to speak of four material elements; yet he does not *use* four, but treats them as two only; he treats fire by itself, and its opposites—earth, air, and water—as one kind of thing. We may learn this by study of his verses.

This philosopher then, as we say, has spoken of the principles in this way, and made them of this number. Leucippus and his associate Democritus say that the full and the empty are the elements, calling the one being and the other non-being—the full and solid being being, the empty non-being (whence they say being no more is than non-being, because the solid no more is than the empty); and they make these the material causes of things. And as those who make the underlying substance one generate all other things by its modifications, supposing the rare and the dense to be the sources of the modifications, in the same way these philosophers say the differences in the elements are the causes of all other qualities. These differences, they say, are three—shape and order and position. For they say the real is differentiated only by "rhythm" and "inter-contact" and "turning"; and of these rhythm is shape, inter-contact is order, and turning is position; for A differs from N in shape, AN from NA in order, ⨾ from H in position. The question of movement— whence or how it is to belong to things—these thinkers, like the others, lazily neglected.

Regarding the two causes, then, as we say, the inquiry seems to have been pushed thus far by the early philosophers.

5. [*The Pythagorean and Eleatic schools.*] Contemporaneously with these philosophers and before them, the so-called Pythagoreans, who were the first to take up mathematics, not only advanced this study, but also having been brought up in it they thought its principles were the principles of all things. Since of these principles numbers are by nature the first, and in numbers they seemed to see many resemblances to the things that exist and come into being—more than in fire and earth and water (such and such a modification of numbers being justice, another being soul and reason, another being opportunity—and similarly almost all other things being numerically expressible); since, again, they saw that the modifications and the ratios of the musical scales were expressible in numbers; since, then, all other things seemed in their whole nature to be modelled on numbers, and numbers seemed to be the first things in the whole of nature, they supposed the elements of numbers to be the elements of all things, and the whole heaven to be a musical scale and a number. And all the properties of numbers and scales which they could show to agree with the attributes and parts and the whole arrangement of the heavens, they collected and fitted into their scheme; and if there was a gap anywhere, they readily made additions so as to make their whole theory coherent. E. g., as the number 10 is thought to be perfect and to comprise the whole nature of numbers, they say that the bodies which move through the heavens are ten, but as the visible bodies are only nine, to meet this they invent a tenth—the "counter-earth." We have discussed these matters more exactly elsewhere.

But the object of our review is that we may learn from these philosophers also what they suppose to be the principles and how these fall under the causes we have named. Evidently, then, these thinkers also consider that number is the principle both as matter for things and as forming both their modifications and their permanent states, and hold that the elements of number are the even and the odd, and that of these the latter is limited, and the former unlimited; and that the One proceeds from both of these (for it is both even and odd), and number from the One; and that the whole heaven, as has been said, is numbers.

Other members of this same school say there are ten principles, which they arrange in two columns of cognates—limit and unlimited, odd and even, one and plurality, right and left, male and female, resting and moving, straight and curved, light and darkness, good and bad, square and oblong. In this way Alcmaeon of Croton seems also to have conceived the matter, and either he got this view from them or they got it from him; for he expressed himself similarly to them. For he says most human affairs go in pairs, meaning not definite contrarieties such as the Pythagoreans speak of, but any chance contrarieties, e. g., white and black, sweet and bitter, good and bad, great and small. He threw out indefinite suggestions about the other contrarieties, but the Pythagoreans declared both how many and which their contrarieties are.

From both these schools, then, we can learn this much, that the contraries are the principles of things; and how many these principles are and which they are, we can learn from one of the two schools. But how these principles can be brought together under the causes we have named has not been clearly and articulately stated by them; they seem, however, to range the elements under the head of matter; for out of these as immanent parts they say substance is composed and moulded.

From these facts we may sufficiently perceive the meaning of the ancients who said the elements of nature were more than one; but there are some who spoke of the universe as if it were one entity, though they were not all alike either in the excellence of their statement or in its conformity to the

facts of nature. The discussion of them is in no way appropriate to our present investigation of causes, for they do not,
like some of the natural philosophers, assume being to be
one and yet generate it out of the one as out of matter, but
they speak in another way; those others add change, since
they generate the universe, but these thinkers say the universe is unchangeable. Yet *this* much is germane to the present inquiry: Parmenides seems to fasten on that which is one
in definition, Melissus on that which is one in matter, for
which reason the former says that it is limited, the latter that
it is unlimited; while Xenophanes, the first of these partisans
of the One (for Parmenides is said to have been his pupil),
gave no clear statement, nor does he seem to have grasped
the nature of either of these causes, but with reference to the
whole material universe he says the One is God. Now these
thinkers, as we said, must be neglected for the purposes of
the present inquiry—two of them entirely, as being a little
too naïve, viz., Xenophanes and Melissus; but Parmenides
seems in places to speak with more insight. For, claiming
that, besides the existent, nothing nonexistent exists, he thinks
that of necessity one thing exists, viz., the existent and nothing else (on this we have spoken more clearly in our work
on nature), but being forced to follow the observed facts,
and supposing the existence of that which is one in definition,
but more than one according to our sensations, he now posits
two causes and two principles, calling them hot and cold,
i. e., fire and earth; and of these he ranges the hot with the
existent, and the other with the nonexistent.

From what has been said, then, and from the wise men
who have now sat in council with us, we have got thus much
—on the one hand from the earliest philosophers, who regard the first principle as corporeal (for water and fire and
such things are bodies), and of whom some suppose that
there is one corporeal principle, others that there are more
than one, but both put these under the head of matter; and
on the other hand from some who posit both this cause and
besides this the source of movement, which we have got from
some as single and from others as twofold.

Down to the Italian school, then, and apart from it, philosophers have treated these subjects rather obscurely, except that, as we said, they have in fact used two kinds of cause, and one of these—the source of movement—some treat as one and others as two. But the Pythagoreans have said in the same way that there are two principles, but added this much, which is peculiar to them, that they thought that finitude and infinity were not attributes of certain other things, e. g., of fire or earth or anything else of this kind, but that infinity itself and unity itself were the substance of the things of which they are predicated. This is why number was the substance of all things. On this subject, then, they expressed themselves thus; and regarding the question of essence they began to make statements and definitions, but treated the matter too simply. For they both defined superficially and thought that the first subject of which a given definition was predicable was the substance of the thing defined, as if one supposed that "double" and "2" were the same, because 2 is the first thing of which "double" is predicable. But surely to be double and to be 2 are not the same; if they are, one thing will be many—a consequence which they actually drew. From the earlier philosophers, then, and from their successors we can learn thus much.

6. [*The Platonic philosophy.*] After the systems we have named came the philosophy of Plato, which in most respects followed these thinkers, but had peculiarities that distinguished it from the philosophy of the Italians. For, having in his youth first become familiar with Cratylus and with the Heraclitean doctrines (that all sensible things are ever in a state of flux and there is no knowledge about them), these views he held even in later years. Socrates, however, was busying himself about ethical matters and neglecting the world of nature as a whole but seeking the universal in these ethical matters, and fixed thought for the first time on definitions; Plato accepted his teaching, but held that the problem applied not to sensible things but to entities of another kind—for this reason, that the common definition could not

be a definition of any sensible thing, as they were always changing. Things of this other sort, then, he called Ideas, and sensible things, he said, were all named after these, and in virtue of a relation to these; for the many existed by participation in the Ideas that have the same name as they. Only the name "participation" was new; for the Pythagoreans say that things exist by "imitation" of numbers, and Plato says they exist by participation, changing the name. But what the participation or the imitation of the Forms could be they left an open question.

Further, besides sensible things and Forms he says there are the objects of mathematics, which occupy an intermediate position, differing from sensible things in being eternal and unchangeable, from Forms in that there are many alike, while the Form itself is in each case unique.

Since the Forms were the causes of all other things, he thought their elements were the elements of all things. As matter, the great and the small were principles; as essential reality, the One; for from the great and the small, by participation in the One, come the Numbers.

But he agreed with the Pythagoreans in saying that the One is substance and not a predicate of something else; and in saying that the Numbers are the causes of the reality of other things he agreed with them; but positing a dyad and constructing the infinite out of great and small, instead of treating the infinite as one, is peculiar to him; and so is his view that the Numbers exist apart from sensible things, while *they* say that the things themselves are Numbers, and do not place the objects of mathematics between Forms and sensible things. His divergence from the Pythagoreans in making the One and the Numbers separate from things, and his introduction of the Forms, were due to his inquiries in the region of definitions (for the earlier thinkers had no tincture of dialectic), and his making the other entity besides the One a dyad was due to the belief that the numbers, except those which were prime, could be neatly produced out of the dyad as out of some plastic material.

Yet what *happens* is the contrary; the theory is not a

reasonable one. For they make many things out of the matter, and the form generates only once, but what we observe is that one table is made from one matter, while the man who applies the form, though he is one, makes many tables. And the relation of the male to the female is similar; for the latter is impregnated by one copulation, but the male impregnates many females; yet these are analogues of those first principles.

Plato, then, declared himself thus on the points in question; it is evident from what has been said that he has used only two causes, that of the essence and the material cause (for the Forms are the causes of the essence of all other things, and the One is the cause of the essence of the Forms); and it is evident what the underlying matter is, of which the Forms are predicated in the case of sensible things, and the One in the case of Forms, viz., that this is a dyad, the great and the small. Further, he has assigned the cause of good and that of evil to the elements, one to each of the two, as we say some of his predecessors sought to do, e. g., Empedocles and Anaxagoras.

7. [*The relation of the various systems to the four causes.*] Our review of those who have spoken about first principles and reality and of the way in which they have spoken, has been concise and summary; but yet we have learnt *this* much from them, that of those who speak about "principle" and "cause" no one has mentioned any principle except those which have been distinguished in our work on nature, but all evidently have some inkling of *them*, though only vaguely. For some speak of the first principle as matter, whether they suppose one or more first principles, and whether they suppose this to be a body or to be incorporeal; e. g., Plato spoke of the great and the small, the Italians of the infinite, Empedocles of fire, earth, water, and air, Anaxagoras of the infinity of things composed of similar parts. These, then, have all had a notion of this kind of cause, and so have all who speak of air or fire or water, or something denser than

fire and rarer than air; for some have said the prime element is of this kind.

These thinkers grasped this cause only; but certain others have mentioned the source of movement, e. g., those who make friendship and strife, or reason, or love, a principle.

The essence, i. e., the substantial reality, no one has expressed distinctly. It is hinted at chiefly by those who believe in the Forms; for they do not suppose either that the Forms are the matter of sensible things, and the One the matter of the Forms, or that they are the source of movement (for they say these are causes rather of immobility and of being at rest), but they furnish the Forms as the essence of every other thing, and the One as the essence of the Forms.

That for whose sake actions and changes and movements take place, they assert to be a cause in a way, but not in this way, i. e., not in the way in which it is its *nature* to be a cause. For those who speak of reason or friendship class these causes as goods; they do not speak, however, as if anything that exists either existed or came into being for the sake of these, but as if movements started from these. In the same way those who say the One or the existent is the good, say that it is the cause of substance, but not that substance either is or comes to be for the sake of this. Therefore it turns out that in a sense they both say and do not say the good is a cause; for they do not call it a cause *qua* good but only incidentally.

All these thinkers, then, as they cannot pitch on another cause, seem to testify that we have determined rightly both how many and of what sort the causes are. Besides this it is plain that when the causes are being looked for, either all four must be sought thus or they must be sought in one of these four ways. Let us next discuss the possible difficulties with regard to the way in which each of these thinkers has spoken, and with regard to his situation relatively to the first principles.

8. [*Criticism of the pre-Platonic philosophers.*] Those, then, who say the universe is one and posit one kind of thing as

matter, and as corporeal matter which has spatial magnitude, evidently go astray in many ways. For they posit the elements of bodies only, not of incorporeal things, though there are also incorporeal things. And in trying to state the causes of generation and destruction, and in giving a physical account of all things, they do away with the cause of movement. Further, they err in not positing the substance, i. e., the essence, as the cause of anything, and besides this in lightly calling any of the simple bodies except earth the first principle, without inquiring how they are produced out of one another,—I mean fire, water, earth, and air. For some things are produced out of each other by combination, others by separation, and this makes the greatest difference to their priority and posteriority. For (1) in a way the property of being most elementary of all would seem to belong to the first thing from which they are produced by combination, and *this* property would belong to the most fine-grained and subtle of bodies. For this reason those who make fire the principle would be most in agreement with this argument. But each of the other thinkers agrees that the element of corporeal things is of this sort. At least none of those who named one element claimed that earth was the element, evidently because of the coarseness of its grain. (Of the other three elements each has found some judge on its side; for some maintain that fire, others that water, others that air is the element. Yet why, after all, do they not name earth also, as most men do? For people say all things are earth. And Hesiod says earth was produced first of corporeal things; so primitive and popular has the opinion been.) According to this argument, then, no one would be right who either says the first principle is any of the elements other than fire, or supposes it to be denser than air but rarer than water. But (2) if that which is later in generation is prior in nature, and that which is concocted and compounded is later in generation, the contrary of what we have been saying must be true—water must be prior to air, and earth to water.

So much, then, for those who posit one cause such as we mentioned; but the same is true if one supposes more of these, as Empedocles says the matter of things is four bodies. For he too is confronted by consequences some of which are the same as have been mentioned, while others are peculiar to him. For we see these bodies produced from one another, which implies that the same body does not always remain fire or earth (we have spoken about this in our works on nature); and regarding the cause of movement and the question whether we must posit one or two, he must be thought to have spoken neither correctly nor altogether plausibly. And in general, change of quality is necessarily done away with for those who speak thus, for on their view cold will not come from hot nor hot from cold. For if it did there would be something that accepted the contraries themselves, and there would be some one entity that became fire and water, which Empedocles denies.

As regards Anaxagoras, if one were to suppose that he said there were two elements, the supposition would accord thoroughly with an argument which Anaxagoras himself did not state articulately, but which he must have accepted if any one had led him on to it. True, to say that in the beginning all things were mixed is absurd both on other grounds and because it follows that they must have existed before in an unmixed form, and because nature does not allow any chance thing to be mixed with any chance thing, and also because on this view modifications and accidents could be separated from substances (for the same things which are mixed can be separated); yet if one were to follow him up, piecing together what he means, he would perhaps be seen to be somewhat modern in his views. For when nothing was separated out, evidently nothing could be truly asserted of the substance that then existed. I mean, e. g., that it was neither white nor black, nor grey nor any other colour, but of necessity colourless; for if it had been coloured, it would have had one of these colours. And similarly, by this same argument, it was flavourless, nor had it any similar attribute; for it could not be either of any quality or of any size, nor could it be any definite kind of thing. For if it were, one of the particular forms would have belonged to it, and this is impossible, since all were mixed together; for the particular form would necessarily have been already separated out, but he says all were mixed except reason, and this alone was unmixed and pure. From this it follows, then, that he must say the principles are the One (for this is simple and unmixed) and the Other, which is of such a nature as we suppose the indefinite to be before it is defined and partakes of some form. Therefore, while expressing himself neither rightly nor clearly, he means something like what the later thinkers say and what is now more clearly seen to be the case.

But these thinkers are, after all, at home only in arguments about generation and destruction and movement; for it is practically only of this sort of substance that they seek the principles and the causes. But those who extend their vision to all things that exist, and of existing things suppose some to be perceptible and others not perceptible evidently study both classes, which is all the more reason why one should devote some time to seeing what is good in their views and what bad from the standpoint of the inquiry we have now before us.

The "Pythagoreans" treat of principles and elements stranger than those of the physical philosophers (the reason is that they got the principles from non-sensible things, for the objects of mathematics, except those of astronomy, are of the class of things without movement); yet their discussions and investigations are all about nature; for they generate the heavens, and with regard to their parts and attributes and functions they observe the phenomena, and use up the principles and the causes in explaining these, which implies that they agree with the others, the physical philosophers, that the *real* is just all that which is perceptible and contained by the so-called "heavens." But the causes and the principles which they mention are, as we said, sufficient to act as steps even up to the higher realms of reality, and are more suited to these than to theories about nature. They do not tell us at all, however, how there can be movement if limit and unlimited and odd and even are the only things assumed, or how without movement and change there can be generation and destruction, or the bodies that move through the heavens can do what they do.

Further, if one either granted them that spatial magnitude consists of these elements, or this were proved, still how would some bodies be light and others have weight? To judge from what they assume and maintain they are speaking no more of mathematical bodies than of perceptible; hence they have said nothing whatever about fire or earth or the other bodies of this sort, I suppose because they have nothing to say which applies *peculiarly* to perceptible things.

Further, how are we to combine the beliefs that the attributes of number, and number itself, are causes of what exists and happens in the heavens both from the beginning and now, and that there is no other number than this number out of which the world is composed? When in one particular region they place opinion and opportunity, and, a little above or below, injustice and decision or mixture, and allege, as proof, that each of these is a number, and that there happens to be already in this place a plurality of the extended bodies composed of numbers, because these attributes of number attach to the various places—this being so, is this number, which we must suppose each of these abstractions to be, the same number which is exhibited in the material universe, or is it another than this? Plato says it is different; yet even he thinks that both these bodies and their causes are numbers, but that the *intelligible* numbers are causes, while the others are *sensible*.

9. [*Criticism of the doctrine of Ideas.*] Let us leave the Pythagoreans for the present; for it is enough to have touched on them as much as we have done. But as for those who posit the Ideas as causes, firstly, in seeking to grasp the causes of the things around us, they introduced others equal in number to these, as if a man who wanted to count things thought he would not be able to do it while they were few, but tried to count them when he had added to their number. For the Forms are practically equal to—or not fewer than—the things, in trying to explain which these thinkers pro-

ceeded from them to the Forms. For to each thing there answers an entity which has the same name and exists apart from the substances, and so also in the case of all other groups there is a one over many, whether the many are in this world or are eternal.

Further, of the ways in which we prove that the Forms exist, none is convincing; for from some no inference necessarily follows, and from some arise Forms even of things of which we think there are no Forms. For according to the arguments from the existence of the sciences there will be Forms of all things of which there are sciences, and according to the "one over many" argument there will be Forms even of negations, and according to the argument that there is an object for thought even when the thing has perished, there will be Forms of perishable things; for we have an image of these. Further, of the more accurate arguments, some lead to Ideas of relations, of which we say there is no independent class, and others introduce the "third man."

And in general the arguments for the Forms destroy the things for whose existence we are more zealous than for the existence of the Ideas; for it follows that not the dyad but number is first, i. e., that the relative is prior to the absolute— besides all the other points on which certain people by following out the opinions held about the Ideas have come into conflict with the principles of the theory.

Further, according to the assumption on which our belief in the Ideas rests, there will be Forms not only of substances but also of many other things (for the concept is single not only in the case of substances but also in the other cases, and there are sciences not only of substance but also of other things, and a thousand other such difficulties confront them). But according to the necessities of the case and the opinions held about the Forms, if Forms can be shared in there must be Ideas of substances only. For they are not shared in incidentally, but a thing must share in its Form as in something not predicated of a subject (by "being shared in incidentally" I mean that, e. g., if a thing shares in "double itself," it shares also in "eternal," but incidentally; for "eternal" happens to be predicable of the "double"). Therefore the Forms will be substance; but the same terms indicate substance in this and in the ideal world (or what will be the meaning of saying that there is something apart from the particulars—the one over many?). And if the Ideas and the particulars that share in them have the same form, there will be something common to these; for why should "2" be one and the same in the perishable 2's or in those which are many but eternal, and not the same in the "2 itself" as in the particular 2? But if they have not the same form, they must have only the name in common, and it is as if one were to call both Callias and a wooden image a "man," without observing any community between them.

Above all one might discuss the question what on earth the Forms contribute to sensible things, either to those that are eternal or to those that come into being and cease to be. For they cause neither movement nor any change in them. But again they help in no wise either towards the knowledge of the other things (for they are not even the substance of these, else they would have been in them), or towards their being, if they are not *in* the particulars which share in them; though if they were, they might be thought to be causes, as white causes whiteness in a white object by entering into its composition. But this argument, which first Anaxagoras and later Eudoxus and certain others used, is very easily upset; for it is not difficult to collect many insuperable objections to such a view.

But, further, all other things cannot come from the Forms in any of the usual senses of "from." And to say that they are patterns and the other things share in them is to use empty words and poetical metaphors. For what is it that works, looking to the Ideas? And anything can either be, or become, like another without being copied from it, so that whether Socrates exists or not a man like Socrates might come to be; and evidently this might be so even if Socrates were eternal. And there will be several patterns of the same thing, and therefore several Forms; e. g., "animal" and "two-footed" and also "man himself" will be Forms of man. Again, the Forms are patterns not only of sensible things, but of Forms themselves also; i. e., the genus, as genus of various species, will be so; therefore the same thing will be pattern and copy.

Again, it would seem impossible that the substance and that of which it is the substance should exist apart; how, therefore, could the Ideas, being the substances of things, exist apart? In the *Phaedo*, the case is stated in this way—that the Forms are causes both of being and of becoming; yet when the Forms exist, still the things that share in them do not come into being, unless there is something to originate movement; and many other things come into being (e. g., a house or a ring) of which we say there are no Forms. Clearly, therefore, even the other things can both be and come into being owing to such causes as produce the things just mentioned.

Again, if the Forms are numbers, how can they be causes? Is it because existing things are other numbers, e. g., one number is man, another is Socrates, another Callias? Why then are the one set of numbers causes of the other set? It will not make any difference even if the former are eternal and the latter are not. But if it is because things in this sensible world (e. g., harmony) are ratios of numbers, evidently the things between which they are ratios are some one class of things. If, then, this—the matter—is some definite thing, evidently the numbers themselves too will be ratios of something to something else. E. g., if Callias is a numerical ratio between fire and earth and water and air, his Idea also will be a number of certain other underlying things; and man-himself, whether it is a number in a sense or not, will still be a numerical ratio of certain things and not a number proper, nor will it be a kind of number merely because it is a numerical ratio.

Again, from many numbers one number is produced, but how can one Form come from many Forms? And if the number comes not from the many numbers themselves but from the units in them, e. g., in 10,000, how is it with the units? If they are specifically alike, numerous absurdities will follow, and also if they are not alike (neither the units in one number being themselves like one another nor those in other numbers being all like to all); for in what will they differ, as they are without quality? This is not a plausible view, nor is it consistent with our thought on the matter.

Further, they must set up a second kind of number (with which arithmetic deals), and all the objects which are called "intermediate" by some thinkers; and how do these exist or from what principles do they proceed? Or why must they be intermediate between the things in this sensible world and the things-themselves?

Further, the units in 2 must each come from a prior 2; but this is impossible.

Further, why is a number, when taken all together, one?

Again, besides what has been said, if the units are *diverse* the Platonists should have spoken like those who say there are four, or two, elements; for each of these thinkers gives the name of element not to that which is common, e. g., to body, but to fire and earth, whether there is something common to them, viz., body, or not. But in fact the Platonists speak as if the One were *homogeneous* like fire or water; and if this is so, the numbers will not be substances. Evidently, if there is a One-itself and this is a first principle, "one" is being used in more than one sense; for otherwise the theory is impossible.

When we wish to reduce substances to their principles, we state that lines come from the short and long (i. e., from a kind of small and great), and the plane from the broad and narrow, and body from the deep and shallow. Yet how then can either the plane contain a line, or the solid a line or a plane? For the broad and narrow is a different class from the deep and shallow. Therefore, just as number is not present in these, because the many and few are different from these, evidently no other of the higher classes will be present in the lower. But again the broad is not a genus which includes the deep, for then the solid would have been a species of plane. Further, from what principle will the presence of the *points* in the line be derived? Plato even used to object to this class of things as being a geometrical fiction. He gave the name of principle of the line—and this he often posited—to the indivisible lines. Yet these must have a limit; therefore the argument from which the existence of the line follows proves also the existence of the point.

In general, though philosophy seeks the cause of perceptible things, we have given this up (for we say nothing of the cause from which change takes its start), but while we fancy we are stating the substance of perceptible things, we assert the existence of a second class of substances, while our account of the way in which they are the substances of perceptible things is empty talk; for "sharing," as we said before, means nothing.

Nor have the Forms any connexion with what we see to be the cause in the case of the arts, that for whose sake both all mind and the whole of nature are operative—with this cause which we assert to be one of the first principles; but mathematics has come to be identical with philosophy for modern thinkers, though they say that it should be studied for the sake of other things.

Further, one might suppose that the substance which according to them underlies as matter is too mathematical, and is a predicate and differentia of the substance, i. e., of the matter, rather than the matter itself; i. e., the great and the small are like the rare and the dense which the physical philosophers speak of, calling these the primary differentiae of the substratum; for these are a kind of excess and defect. And regarding movement, if the great and the small are to *be* movement, evidently the Forms will be moved; but if they are not to be movement, whence did movement come? The whole study of nature has been annihilated.

And what is thought to be easy—to show that all things are one—is not done; for what is proved by the method of setting out instances is not that all things are one but that there is a One-itself—if we grant all the assumptions. And not even this follows, if we do not grant that the universal is a genus; and this in some cases it cannot be.

Nor can it be explained either how the lines and planes

and solids that come after the numbers exist or can exist, or what significance they have; for these can neither be Forms (for they are not numbers), nor the intermediates (for those are the objects of mathematics), nor the perishable things. This is evidently a distinct fourth class.

In general, if we search for the elements of existing things without distinguishing the many senses in which things are said to exist, we cannot find them, especially if the search for the elements of which things are made is conducted in this manner. For it is surely impossible to discover what "acting" or "being acted on," or "the straight," is made of, but if elements can be discovered at all, it is only the elements of substances; therefore either to seek the elements of all existing things or to think one has them is incorrect.

And how could we *learn* the elements of all things? Evidently we cannot start by knowing anything before. For as he who is learning geometry, though he may know other things before, knows none of the things with which the science deals and about which he is to learn, so is it in all other cases. Therefore if there is a science of all things, such as some assert to exist, he who is learning this will know nothing before. Yet all learning is by means of premises which are (either all or some of them) known before— whether the learning be by demonstration or by definitions; for the elements of the definition must be known before and be familiar; and learning by induction proceeds similarly. But again, if the science were actually innate, it were strange that we are unaware of our possession of the greatest of sciences.

Again, how is one to *come to know* what all things are made of, and how is this to be made *evident?* This also affords a difficulty; for there might be a conflict of opinion, as there is about certain syllables; some say *za* is made out of *s* and *d* and *a*, while others say it is a distinct sound and none of those that are familiar.

Further, how could we know the objects of sense without having the sense in question? Yet we ought to, if the elements of which all things consist, as complex sounds consist of the elements proper to sound, are the same.

10. [*The history of philosophy reveals no causes other than the four.*] It is evident, then, even from what we have said before, that all men seem to seek the causes named in the *Physics*, and that we cannot name any beyond these; but they seek these vaguely; and though in a sense they have all been described before, in a sense they have not been described at all. For the earliest philosophy is, on all subjects, like one who lisps, since it is young and in its beginnings. For even Empedocles says bone exists by virtue of the ratio in it. Now this is the essence and the substance of the thing. But it is similarly necessary that flesh and each of the other tissues should be the ratio of its elements, or that not one of them should; for it is on account of this that both flesh and bone and everything else will exist, and not on account of the matter, which *he* names—fire and earth and water and air. But while he would necessarily have agreed if another had said this, he has not said it clearly.

On these questions our views have been expressed before; but let us return to enumerate the difficulties that might be raised on these same points; for perhaps we may get from them some help towards our later difficulties.

* * *

＠＠＠＠＠＠＠＠＠＠＠＠＠＠＠＠＠＠＠＠＠＠＠＠＠＠＠

BOOK XII

1. [*Substance the primary subject of inquiry.*] The subject of our inquiry is substance; for the principles and the causes we are seeking are those of substances. For if the universe is of the

nature of a whole, substance is its first part; and if it coheres merely by virtue of serial succession, on this view also substance is first, and is succeeded by quality, and then by quantity. At the same time these latter are not even being in the full sense, but are qualities and movements of it—or else even the not-white and the not-straight would be being; at least we say even these *are*, e. g., "there is a not-white." Further, none of the categories other than substance can exist apart. And the early philosophers also in practice testify to the primacy of substance; for it was of substance that they sought the principles and elements and causes. The thinkers of the present day tend to rank universals as substances (for genera are universals, and these they tend to describe as principles and substances, owing to the abstract nature of their inquiry); but the thinkers of old ranked particular things as substances, e. g., fire and earth, not what is common to both, body.

There are three kinds of substance—one that is sensible (of which one subdivision is eternal and another is perishable; the latter is recognized by all men, and includes, e. g., plants and animals), of which we must grasp the elements, whether one or many; and another that is immovable, and this certain thinkers assert to be capable of existing apart, some dividing it into two, others identifying the Forms and the objects of mathematics, and others positing, of these two, only the objects of mathematics. The former two kinds of substance are the subject of physics (for they imply movement); but the third kind belongs to another science, if there is no principle common to it and to the other kinds.

2. [*Change implies not only form and privation but matter.*] Sensible substance is changeable. Now if change proceeds from opposites or from intermediates, and not from all opposites (for the voice is not-white [but it does not therefore change to white]), but from the contrary, there must be something underlying which changes into the contrary state; for the *contraries* do not change. Further, something persists, but the contrary does not persist; there is, then, some third thing besides the contraries, viz., the matter. Now since

changes are of four kinds—either in respect of the "what" or of the quality or of the quantity or of the place, and change in respect of "thisness" is simple generation and destruction, and change in quantity is increase and diminution, and change in respect of an affection is alteration, and change of place is motion, changes will be from given states into those contrary to them in these several respects. The matter, then, which changes must be capable of both states. And since that which "is" has two senses, we must say that everything changes from that which is potentially to that which is actually, e. g., from potentially white to actually white, and similarly in the case of increase and diminution. Therefore not only can a thing come to be, incidentally, out of that which is not, but also all things come to be out of that which is, but is potentially, and is not actually. And this is the "One" of Anaxagoras; for instead of "all things were together"—and the "Mixture" of Empedocles and Anaximander and the account given by Democritus—it is better to say "all things were together potentially but not actually." Therefore these thinkers seem to have had some notion of matter. Now all things that change have matter, but different matter; and of eternal things those which are not generable but are movable in space have matter—not matter for generation, however, but for motion from one place to another.

One might raise the question from what sort of non-being generation proceeds; for "non-being" has three senses. If, then, one form of non-being exists potentially, still it is not by virtue of a potentiality for any and every thing, but different things come from different things; nor is it satisfactory to say that "all things were together"; for they differ in their matter, since otherwise why did an infinity of things come to be, and not one thing? For "reason" is one, so that if matter also were one, that must have come to be in actuality which the matter was in potency. The causes and the principles, then, are three, two being the pair of contraries of which one is definition and form and the other is privation, and the third being the matter.

3. [*Neither matter nor form comes into being.*] Note, next, that neither the matter nor the form comes to be—and I mean the last matter and form. For everything that changes is something and is changed by something and into something. That by which it is changed is the immediate mover; that which is changed, the matter; that into which it is changed, the form. The process, then, will go on to infinity, if not only the bronze comes to be round but also the round or the bronze comes to be; therefore there must be a stop.

Note, next, that each substance comes into being out of something that shares its name. (Natural objects and other things both rank as substances.) For things come into being either by art or by nature or by luck or by spontaneity. Now art is a principle of movement in something other than the thing moved, nature is a principle in the thing itself (for man begets man), and the other causes are privations of these two.

There are three kinds of substance—the matter, which is a "this" in appearance (for all things that are characterized by contact and not by organic unity are matter and substratum, e. g., fire, flesh, head; for these are all matter, and the last matter is the matter of that which is in the full sense substance); the nature, which is a "this" or positive state towards which movement takes place; and again, thirdly, the particular substance which is composed of these two, e. g., Socrates or Callias. Now in some cases the "this" does not exist apart from the composite substance, e. g., the form of house does not so exist, unless the art of building exists apart (nor is there generation and destruction of these forms, but it is in another way that the house apart from its matter, and health, and all ideals of art, exist and do not exist); but if the "this" exists apart from the concrete thing, it is only in the case of natural objects. And so Plato was not far wrong when he said that there are as many Forms as there are kinds of natural object (if there *are* Forms distinct from the things of this earth). The moving causes exist as things preceding the effects, but causes in the sense of definitions are simultaneous with their effects. For when a man is healthy, then

health also exists; and the shape of a bronze sphere exists at
the same time as the bronze sphere. (But we must examine
whether any form also survives afterwards. For in some cases
there is nothing to prevent this; e. g., the soul may be of this
sort—not all soul but the reason; for presumably it is impossible that *all* soul should survive.) Evidently then there is no
necessity, on this ground at least, for the existence of the
Ideas. For man is begotten by man, a given man by an individual father; and similarly in the arts; for the medical art
is the formal cause of health.

4. [*Different things have elements numerically different but
the same in kind.*] The causes and the principles of different
things are in a sense different, but in a sense, if one speaks
universally and analogically, they are the same for all. For
one might raise the question whether the principles and elements are different or the same for substances and for relative
terms, and similarly in the case of each of the categories. But
it would be paradoxical if they were the same for all. For then
from the same elements will proceed relative terms and substances. What then will this common element be? For (1)
(*a*) there is nothing common to and distinct from substance
and the other categories, viz., those which are predicated;
but an element is prior to the things of which it is an element.
But again (*b*) substance is not an element in relative terms,
nor is any of these an element in substance. Further, (2) how
can all things have the same elements? For none of the
elements can be the same as that which is composed of elements, e. g., *b* or *a* cannot be the same as *ba*. (None, therefore, of the intelligibles, e. g., being or unity, is an element;
for these are predicable of each of the compounds as well.)
None of the elements, then, will be either a substance or a
relative term; but it must be one or other. All things, then,
have not the same elements.

Or, as we are wont to put it, in a sense they have and in a
sense they have not; e. g., perhaps the elements of perceptible
bodies are, as *form*, the hot, and in another sense the cold,
which is the *privation*; and, as *matter*, that which directly

and of itself potentially has these attributes; and substances comprise both these and the things composed of these, of which these are the principles, or any unity which is produced out of the hot and the cold, e. g., flesh or bone; for the product must be different from the elements. These things then have the same elements and principles (though specifically different things have specifically different elements); but *all* things have not the same elements in this sense, but only analogically: i. e., one might say that there are three principles—the form, the privation, and the matter. But each of these is different for each class; e. g., in colour they are white, black, and surface, and in day and night they are light, darkness, and air.

Since not only the elements present in a thing are causes, but also something external, i. e., the moving cause, clearly while "principle" and "element" are different both are causes, and "principle" is divided into these two kinds and that which acts as producing movement or rest is a principle and a substance. Therefore analogically there are three elements, and four causes and principles; but the elements are different in different things, and the proximate moving cause is different for different things. Health, disease, body; the moving cause is the medical art. Form, disorder of a particular kind, bricks; the moving cause is the building art. And since the moving cause in the case of natural things is—for man, for instance, man, and in the products of thought the form or its contrary, there will be in a sense three causes, while in a sense there are four. For the medical art is in some sense health, and the building art is the form of the house, and man begets man; further, besides these there is that which as first of all things moves all things.

5. [*Actuality and potency are principles common to all things.*] Some things can exist apart and some cannot, and it is the former that are substances. And therefore all things have the same causes, because, without substances, modifications and movements do not exist. Further, these causes will probably be soul and body, or reason and desire and body.

And in yet another way, analogically identical things are principles, i. e., actuality and potency; but these also are not only different for different things but also apply in different ways to them. For in some cases the same thing exists at one time actually and at another potentially, e. g., wine or flesh or man does so. (And these two fall under the above-named causes. For the form exists actually, if it can exist apart, and so does the complex of form and matter, and the privation, e. g., darkness or disease; but the matter exists potentially; for this is that which can become qualified either by the form or by the privation.) But the distinction of actuality and potentiality applies in another way to cases where the matter of cause and of effect is not the same, in some of which cases the form is not the same but different; e. g., the cause of man is (1) the elements in man (viz., fire and earth as matter, and the peculiar form), and further (2) something else outside, i. e., the father, and (3) besides these the sun and its oblique course, which are neither matter nor form nor privation of man nor of the same species with him, but moving causes.

Further, one must observe that some causes can be expressed in universal terms, and some cannot. The proximate principles of all things are the "this" which is proximate in actuality, and another which is proximate in potentiality. The universal causes, then, of which we spoke do not *exist*. For it is the individual that is the originative principle of the individuals. For while man is the originative principle of man universally, there *is* no universal man, but Peleus is the originative principle of Achilles, and your father of you, and this particular *b* of this particular *ba*, though *b* in general is the originative principle of *ba* taken without qualification.

Further, if the causes of substances are the causes of all things, yet different things have different causes and elements, as was said; the causes of things that are not in the same class, e. g., of colours and sounds, of substances and quantities, are different except in an analogical sense; and those of things in the same species are different, not in species, but in the sense that the causes of different individuals are different, your matter and form and moving cause being different from mine, while in their universal definition they are the same. And if we inquire what are the principles or elements of substances and relations and qualities—whether they are the same or different—clearly when the names of the causes are used in several senses the causes of each are the same, but when the senses are distinguished the causes are not the same but different, except that in the following senses the causes of all are the same. They are (1) the same or analogous in this sense, that matter, form, privation, and the moving cause are common to all things; and (2) the causes of substances may be treated as causes of all things in this sense, that when substances are removed all things are removed; further, (3) that which is first in respect of complete reality is the cause of all things. But in another sense there are different first causes, viz., all the contraries which are neither generic nor ambiguous terms; and, further, the matters of different things are different. We have stated, then, what are the principles of sensible things and how many they are, and in what sense they are the same and in what sense different.

6. [*Since movement must be eternal, there must be an eternal mover.*] Since there were three kinds of substance, two of them physical and one unmovable, regarding the latter we must assert that it is necessary that there should be an eternal unmovable substance. For substances are the first of existing things, and if they are all destructible, all things are destructible. But it is impossible that movement should either have come into being or cease to be (for it must always have existed), or that time should. For there could not be a before and an after if time did not exist. Movement also is continuous, then, in the sense in which time is; for time is either the same thing as movement or an attribute of movement. And there is no continuous movement except movement in place, and of this only that which is circular is continuous.

But if there is something which is capable of moving things or acting on them, but is not actually doing so, there will not necessarily be movement; for that which has a potency need not exercise it. Nothing, then, is gained even if we suppose eternal substances, as the believers in the Forms do, unless there is to be in them some principle which can cause change; nay, even this is not enough, nor is another substance besides the Forms enough; for if it is not to *act*, there will be no movement. Further, even if it acts, this will not be enough, if its essence is potency; for there will not be *eternal* movement, since that which is potentially may possibly not be. There must, then, be such a principle, whose very essence is actuality. Further, then, these substances must be without matter; for they must be eternal, if *anything* is eternal. Therefore they must be actuality.

Yet there is a difficulty; for it is thought that everything that acts is able to act, but that not everything that is able to act acts, so that the potency is prior. But if this is so, nothing that is need be; for it is possible for all things to be capable of existing but not yet to exist.

Yet if we follow the theologians who generate the world from night, or the natural philosophers who say that "all things were together," the same impossible result ensues. For how will there be movement, if there is no actually existing cause? Wood will surely not move itself—the carpenter's art must act on it; nor will the menstrual blood nor the earth set themselves in motion, but the seeds must act on the earth and the semen on the menstrual blood.

This is why some suppose eternal actuality, e. g., Leucippus and Plato; for they say there is always movement. But why and what this movement is they do not say, nor, if the world moves in this way or that, do they tell us the cause of its doing so. Now nothing is moved at random, but there must always be something present to move it; e. g., as a matter of fact a thing moves in one way by nature, and in another by force or through the influence of reason or something else. (Further, what sort of movement is primary? This makes a vast difference.) But again for Plato, at least, it is not permissible to name here that which he sometimes supposes to be the source of movement—that which moves itself; for the soul is later, and coeval with the heavens, according to his account. To suppose potency prior to actuality, then, is in a sense right, and in a sense not; and we have specified these senses. That actuality is prior is testified by Anaxagoras (for his "reason" is actuality) and by Empedocles in his doctrine of love and strife, and by those who say that there is always movement, e. g., Leucippus. Therefore chaos or night did not exist for an infinite time, but the same things have always existed (either passing through a cycle of changes or obeying some other law), since actuality is prior to potency. If, then, there is a constant cycle, something must always remain, acting in the same way. And if there is to be generation and destruction, there must be something else which is always acting in different ways. This must, then, act in one way in virtue of itself, and in another in virtue of something else— either of a third agent, therefore, or of the first. Now it must be in virtue of the first. For otherwise this again causes the motion both of the second agent and of the third. Therefore it is better to say "the first." For it was the cause of eternal uniformity; and something else is the cause of variety, and evidently both together are the cause of eternal variety. This, accordingly, is the character which the motions actually exhibit. What need then is there to seek for other principles?

7. [*The eternal mover originates motion by being the primary object of desire.*] Since (1) this is a possible account of the matter, and (2) if it were not true, the world would have proceeded out of night and "all things together" and out of non-being, these difficulties may be taken as solved. There is, then, something which is always moved with an unceasing motion, which is motion in a circle; and this is plain not in theory only but in fact. Therefore the first heaven must be eternal. There is therefore also something which moves it. And since that which is moved and moves is intermediate, there is something which moves without being moved, being eternal, substance, and actuality. And the object of desire and the object of thought move in this way; they move without being moved. The primary objects of desire and of thought

are the same. For the apparent good is the object of appetite, and the real good is the primary object of rational wish. But desire is consequent on opinion rather than opinion on desire; for the thinking is the starting point. And thought is moved by the object of thought, and one of the two columns of opposites is in itself the object of thought; and in this, substance is first, and in substance, that which is simple and exists actually. (The one and the simple are not the same; for "one" means a measure, but "simple" means that the thing itself has a certain nature.) But the beautiful, also, and that which is in itself desirable are in the same column; and the first in any class is always best, or analogous to the best.

That a final cause may exist among unchangeable entities is shown by the distinction of its meanings. For the final cause is (a) some being for whose good an action is done, and (b) something at which the action aims; and of these the latter exists among unchangeable entities though the former does not. The final cause, then, produces motion as being loved, but all other things move by being moved.

Now if something is moved it is capable of being otherwise than as it is. Therefore if its actuality is the primary form of spatial motion, then in so far as it is subject to change, in *this* respect it is capable of being otherwise—in place, even if not in substance. But since there is something which moves while itself unmoved, existing actually, this can in no way be otherwise than as it is. For motion in space is the first of the kinds of change, and motion in a circle the first kind of spatial motion; and this the first mover *produces*. The first mover, then, exists of necessity; and in so far as it exists by necessity, its mode of being is good, and it is in this sense a first principle. For the necessary has all these senses—that which is necessary perforce because it is contrary to the natural impulse, that without which the good is impossible, and that which cannot be otherwise but can exist only in a single way.

On such a principle, then, depend the heavens and the world of nature. And it is a life such as the best which we enjoy, and enjoy for but a short time (for it is ever in this state, which we cannot be), since its actuality is also pleasure.

(And for this reason are waking, perception, and thinking most pleasant, and hopes and memories are so on account of these.) And thinking in itself deals with that which is best in itself, and that which is thinking in the fullest sense with that which is best in the fullest sense. And thought thinks on itself because it shares the nature of the object of thought; for it becomes an object of thought in coming into contact with and thinking its objects, so that thought and object of thought are the same. For that which is *capable* of receiving the object of thought, i. e., the essence, is thought. But it is *active* when it *possesses* this object. Therefore the possession rather than the receptivity is the divine element which thought seems to contain, and the act of contemplation is what is most pleasant and best. If, then, God is always in that good state in which we sometimes are, this compels our wonder; and if in a better this compels it yet more. And God *is* in a better state. And life also belongs to God; for the actuality of thought is life, and God is that actuality; and God's self-dependent actuality is life most good and eternal. We say therefore that God is a living being, eternal, most good, so that life and duration continuous and eternal belong to God; for this *is* God.

Those who suppose, as the Pythagoreans and Speusippus do, that supreme beauty and goodness are not present in the beginning, because the beginnings both of plants and of animals are *causes*, but beauty and completeness are in the *effects* of these, are wrong in their opinion. For the seed comes from other individuals which are prior and complete, and the first thing is not seed but the complete being; e. g., we must say that before the seed there is a man—not the man produced from the seed, but another from whom the seed comes.

It is clear then from what has been said that there is a substance which is eternal and unmovable and separate from sensible things. It has been shown also that this substance cannot have any magnitude, but is without parts and indivisible (for it produces movement through infinite time, but nothing finite has infinite power; and, while every magnitude is either infinite or finite, it cannot, for the above reason, have finite magnitude, and it cannot have infinite magnitude because there is no infinite magnitude at all). But it has also been shown that it is impassive and unalterable; for all the other changes are posterior to change of place.

8. [*Besides the first mover there must be other unmoved movers.*] It is clear, then, why these things are as they are. But we must not ignore the question whether we have to suppose one such substance or more than one, and if the latter, how many; we must also mention, regarding the opinions expressed by others, that they have said nothing about the number of the substances that can even be clearly stated. For the theory of Ideas has no special discussion of the subject; for those who speak of Ideas say the Ideas are numbers, and they speak of numbers now as unlimited, now as limited by the number 10; but as for the reason why there should be just so many numbers, nothing is said with any demonstrative exactness. We however must discuss the subject, starting from the presuppositions and distinctions we have mentioned. The first principle or primary being is not movable either in itself or accidentally, but produces the primary eternal and single movement. But since that which is moved must be moved by something, and the first mover must be in itself unmovable, and eternal movement must be produced by something eternal and a single movement by a single thing, and since we see that besides the simple spatial movement of the universe, which we say the first and unmovable substance produces, there are other spatial movements—those of the planets—which are eternal (for a body which moves in a circle is eternal and unresting; we have proved these points in the physical treatises), each of *these* movements also must be caused by a substance both unmovable in itself and eternal. For the nature of the stars is eternal just because it is a certain kind of substance, and the mover is eternal and prior to the moved, and that which is prior to a substance must be a substance. Evidently, then, there must be substances which are of the same number as the move-

ments of the stars, and in their nature eternal, and in themselves unmovable, and without magnitude, for the reason before mentioned.

That the movers are substances, then, and that one of these is first and another second according to the same order as the movements of the stars, is evident. But in the number of the movements we reach a problem which must be treated from the standpoint of that one of the mathematical sciences which is most akin to philosophy—viz., of astronomy; for this science speculates about substance which is perceptible but eternal, but the other mathematical sciences, i. e., arithmetic and geometry, treat of no substance. That the movements are more numerous than the bodies that are moved is evident to those who have given even moderate attention to the matter; for each of the planets has more than one movement. But as to the actual number of these movements, we now—to give some notion of the subject—quote what some of the mathematicians say, that our thought may have some definite number to grasp; but, for the rest, we must partly investigate for ourselves, partly learn from other investigators, and if those who study this subject form an opinion contrary to what we have now stated, we must esteem both parties indeed, but follow the more accurate.

Eudoxus supposed that the motion of the sun or of the moon involves, in either case, three spheres, of which the first is the sphere of the fixed stars, and the second moves in the circle which runs along the middle of the zodiac, and the third in the circle which is inclined across the breadth of the zodiac; but the circle in which the moon moves is inclined at a greater angle than that in which the sun moves. And the motion of the planets involves, in each case, four spheres, and of these also the first and second are the same as the first two mentioned above (for the sphere of the fixed stars is that which moves all the other spheres, and that which is placed beneath this and has its movement in the circle which bisects the zodiac is common to all), but the *poles* of the third sphere of each planet are in the circle which bisects the zodiac, and the motion of the fourth sphere is in the circle which is inclined at an angle to the equator of the third sphere; and the poles of the third sphere are different for each of the other planets, but those of Venus and Mercury are the same.

Callippus made the position of the spheres the same as Eudoxus did, but while he assigned the same number as Eudoxus did to Jupiter and to Saturn, he thought two more spheres should be added to the sun and two to the moon, if one is to explain the observed facts; and one more to each of the other planets.

But it is necessary, if all the spheres combined are to explain the observed facts, that for each of the planets there should be other spheres (one fewer than those hitherto assigned) which counteract those already mentioned and bring back to the same position the outermost sphere of the star which in each case is situated below the star in question; for only thus can all the forces at work produce the observed motion of the planets. Since, then, the spheres involved in the movement of the planets themselves are—eight for Saturn and Jupiter and twenty-five for the others, and of these only those involved in the movement of the lowest-situated planet need not be counteracted, the spheres which counteract those of the outermost two planets will be six in number, and the spheres which counteract those of the next four planets will be sixteen; therefore the number of all the spheres—both those which move the planets and those which counteract these—will be fifty-five. And if one were not to add to the moon and to the sun the movements we mentioned, the whole set of spheres will be forty-seven in number.

Let this, then, be taken as the number of the spheres, so that the unmovable substances and principles also may probably be taken as just so many; the assertion of *necessity* must be left to more powerful thinkers. But if there can be no spatial movement which does not conduce to the moving of a star, and if further every being and every substance which is immune from change and in virtue of itself has attained to the best must be considered an end, there can be no other being apart from these we have named, but this must be the number of the substances. For if there are others, they will cause change as being a final cause of movement; but there cannot *be* other movements besides those mentioned. And it is reasonable to infer this from a consideration of the bodies that are moved; for if everything that moves is for the sake of that which is moved, and every movement belongs to something that is moved, no movement can be for the sake of itself or of another movement, but all the movements must be for the sake of the stars. For if there is to be a movement for the sake of a movement, this latter also will have to be for the sake of something else; so that since there cannot be an infinite regress, the end of every movement will be one of the divine bodies which move through the heaven.

(Evidently there is but one heaven. For if there are many heavens as there are many men, the moving principles, of which each heaven will have one, will be one in form but in *number* many. But all things that are many in number have matter; for one and the same definition, e. g., that of man, applies to many things, while Socrates is one. But the primary essence has not matter; for it is complete reality. So the unmovable first mover is one both in definition and in number; so too, therefore, is that which is moved always and continuously; therefore there is one heaven alone.)

Our forefathers in the most remote ages have handed down to their posterity a tradition, in the form of a myth, that these bodies are gods and that the divine encloses the whole of nature. The rest of the tradition has been added later in mythical form with a view to the persuasion of the multitude and to its legal and utilitarian expediency; they say these gods are in the form of men or like some of the other animals, and they say other things consequent on and similar to these which we have mentioned. But if one were to separate the first point from these additions and take it alone—that they thought the first substances to be gods, one must regard this as an inspired utterance, and reflect that, while probably each art and each science has often been developed as far as possible and has again perished, these opinions, with others, have been preserved until the present like relics of the ancient treasure. Only thus far, then, is the opinion of our ancestors and of our earliest predecessors clear to us.

9. [*The divine thought must be concerned with the most divine object, which is itself.*] The nature of the divine thought involves certain problems; for while thought is held to be the most divine of things observed by us, the question how it must be situated in order to have that character involves difficulties. For if it thinks of nothing, what is there here of dignity? It is just like one who sleeps. And if it thinks, but this depends on something else, then (since that which is its substance is not the act of thinking, but a potency) it cannot be the best substance; for it is through thinking that its value belongs to it. Further, whether its substance is the faculty of thought or the act of thinking, what does it think of? Either of itself or of something else; and if of something else, either of the same thing always or of something different. Does it matter, then, or not, whether it thinks of the good or of any chance thing? Are there not some things about which it is incredible that it should think? Evidently, then, it thinks of that which is most divine and precious, and it does not change; for change would be change for the worse, and this would be already a movement. First, then, if "thought" is not the act of thinking but a potency, it would be reasonable to suppose that the continuity of its thinking is wearisome to it. Secondly, there would evidently be something else more precious than thought, viz., that which is thought of. For both thinking and the act of thought will belong even to one who thinks of the worst thing in the world, so that if this ought to be avoided (and it ought, for there are even some things which it is better not to see than to see), the act of thinking cannot be the best of things. Therefore it must be of itself that the divine thought thinks (since it is the most excellent of things), and its thinking is a thinking on thinking.

But evidently knowledge and perception and opinion and understanding have always something else as their object, and themselves only by the way. Further, if thinking and being thought of are different, in respect of which does goodness belong to thought? For to *be* an act of thinking and to *be* an object of thought are not the same thing. We answer that in some cases the knowledge is the object. In the productive sciences it is the substance or essence of the object, matter omitted, and in the theoretical sciences the definition or the act of thinking is the object. Since, then, thought and the object of thought are not different in the case of things that have not matter, the divine thought and its object will be the same, i. e., the thinking will be one with the object of its thought.

A further question is left—whether the object of the divine thought is composite; for if it were, thought would change in passing from part to part of the whole. We answer that everything which has not matter is indivisible—as human thought, or rather the thought of composite beings, is in a certain period of time (for it does not possess the good at this moment or at that, but its best, being something *different* from it, is attained only in a whole period of time), so throughout eternity is the thought which has *itself* for its object.

10. [*How the good is present in the universe both as the order of the parts and as their ruler.*] We must consider also in which of two ways the nature of the universe contains the good and the highest good, whether as something separate and by itself, or as the order of the parts. Probably in both ways, as an army does; for its good is found both in its order and in its leader, and more in the latter; for he does not depend on the order but it depends on him. And all things are ordered together somehow, but not all alike—both fishes and fowls and plants; and the world is not such that one thing has nothing to do with another, but they are connected. For all are ordered together to one end, but it is as in a house, where the freemen are least at liberty to act at random, but all things or most things are already ordained for them, while the slaves and the animals do little for the common good, and for the most part live at random; for this is the sort of prin-

ciple that constitutes the nature of each. I mean, for instance, that all must at least come to be dissolved into their elements, and there are other functions similarly in which all share for the good of the whole.

We must not fail to observe how many impossible or paradoxical results confront those who hold different views from our own, and what are the views of the subtler thinkers, and which views are attended by fewest difficulties. All make all things out of contraries. But neither "all things" nor "out of contraries" is right; nor do these thinkers tell us how all the things in which the contraries are present can be made out of the contraries; for contraries are not affected by one another. Now for us this difficulty is solved naturally by the fact that there is a third element. These thinkers however make one of the two contraries matter; this is done for instance by those who make the unequal matter for the equal, or the many matter for the one. But this also is refuted in the same way; for the one matter which underlies any pair of contraries is contrary to nothing. Further, all things, except the one, will, on the view we are criticizing, partake of evil; for the bad itself is one of the two elements. But the other school does not treat the good and the bad even as principles; yet in all things the good is in the highest degree a principle. The school we first mentioned is right in saying that it is a principle, but *how* the good is a principle they do not say—whether as end or as mover or as form.

Empedocles also has a paradoxical view; for he identifies the good with love, but this is a principle both as mover (for it brings things together) and as matter (for it is part of the mixture). Now even if it happens that the same thing is a principle both as matter and as mover, still the being, at least, of the two is not the same. In which respect then is love a principle? It is paradoxical also that strife should be imperishable; the nature of his "evil" is just strife.

Anaxagoras makes the good a motive principle; for his "reason" moves things. But it moves them for an end, which must be something other than it, except according to *our* way of stating the case; for, on our view, the medical art is in a sense health. It is paradoxical also not to suppose a contrary to the good, i. e., to reason. But all who speak of the contraries make no use of the contraries, unless we bring their views into shape. And why some things are perishable and others imperishable, no one tells us; for they make all existing things out of the same principles. Further, some make existing things out of the nonexistent; and others to avoid the necessity of this make all things one.

Further, why should there always be becoming, and what is the cause of becoming?—this no one tells us. And those who suppose two principles must suppose another, a superior principle, and so must those who believe in the Forms; for why did things come to participate, or why do they participate, in the Forms? And all other thinkers are confronted by the necessary consequence that there is something contrary to Wisdom, i. e., to the highest knowledge; but *we* are not. For there is nothing contrary to that which is primary; for all contraries have matter, and things that have matter exist only potentially; and the ignorance which is contrary to any knowledge leads to an object contrary to the object of the knowledge; but what is primary has no contrary.

Again, if besides sensible things no others exist, there will be no first principle, no order, no becoming, no heavenly bodies, but each principle will have a principle before it, as in the accounts of the theologians and all the natural philosophers. But if the Forms or the numbers are to exist, they will be causes of nothing; or if not that, at least not of movement. Further, how is extension, i. e., a *continuum*, to be produced out of unextended parts? For number will not, either as mover or as form, produce a *continuum*. But again there cannot be any *contrary* that is also essentially a productive or moving principle; or it would be possible not to be. Or at least its action would be posterior to its potency. The world, then, would not be eternal. But it is; one of the premisses, then, must be denied. And we have said how this must be done. Further, in virtue of what the numbers, or the soul and the body, or in general the form and the thing, are one—of this no one tells us anything; nor can any one tell, unless he says, as we do, that the mover makes them one. And those who say mathematical number is first and go on to generate one kind of substance after another and give different principles for each, make the substance of the universe a mere series of episodes (for one substance has no influence on another by its existence or nonexistence), and they give us many governing principles; but the world refuses to be governed badly.

"The rule of many is not good; one ruler let there be" [Homer].

NICOMACHEAN ETHICS

Translated by W. D. Ross

Aristotelian ethics is a practical science; its object is not only to know but to act in the light of knowledge. It is an approximate science, because its data can be modified by opinion, and Aristotle warns us not to expect precise formulations. It is eventually a political science, in that the goals of the state reflect the goals of the individual citizens. Because he deals with ethics primarily in social and political terms, Aristotle is concerned with practical, achievable ends. He stresses common sense, moderation, and orthodoxy, and, since he is writing explicitly within the assumptions of the society he knew, his bias is fundamentally aristocratic: he insists that the highest virtue is reserved for the very few and that the purely contemplative life is best.

The good that all men seek is happiness, Aristotle declares, and he defines happiness as the result of a life governed by reason, as "an activity of the soul in accordance with perfect virtue." He devotes six books to characterizing the two broad classes of the moral and intellectual virtues. It is in the course of this discussion that he presents his celebrated doctrine of the golden mean, a doctrine in which some have felt that moderation has been carried to the point of excess. If a virtue can be neither an excess nor a deficiency of a particular quality or activity, then courage, for example, must be a mean between rashness and cowardice, temperance a mean between self-indulgence and "insensibility," and pride (or "magnanimity") a mean between vanity and humility.

Aristotle devotes two books to the study of friendship, which he sees both as necessary and noble, and as the binding principle of states and societies. In his analysis of pleasure and happiness at the end of the NICOMACHEAN ETHICS, he touches on problems of legislation and education which he will explore in full in the POLITICS.

NICOMACHEAN ETHICS

~~~~~~

BOOK I

1. [*All human activities aim at some good.*] Every art and every inquiry, and similarly every action and pursuit, is thought to aim at some good; and for this reason the good has rightly been declared to be that at which all things aim. But a certain difference is found among ends; some are activities, others are products apart from the activities that produce them. Where there are ends apart from the actions, it is the nature of the products to be better than the activities. Now, as there are many actions, arts, and sciences, their ends also are many; the end of the medical art is health, that of shipbuilding a vessel, that of strategy victory, that of economics wealth. But where such arts fall under a single capacity—as bridle-making and the other arts concerned with the equipment of horses fall under the art of riding, and this and every military action under strategy, in the same way other arts fall under yet others—in all of these the ends of the master arts are to be preferred to all the subordinate ends; for it is for the sake of the former that the latter are pursued. It makes no difference whether the activities themselves are the ends of the actions, or something else apart from the activities, as in the case of the sciences just mentioned.

2. [*The science of the good for man in politics.*] If, then, there is some end of the things we do, which we desire

for its own sake (everything else being desired for the sake of this), and if we do not choose everything for the sake of something else (for at that rate the process would go on to infinity, so that our desire would be empty and vain), clearly this must be the good and the chief good. Will not the knowledge of it, then, have a great influence on life? Shall we not, like archers who have a mark to aim at, be more likely to hit upon what is right? If so, we must try, in outline at least, to determine what it is, and of which of the sciences or capacities it is the object. It would seem to belong to the most authoritative art and that which is most truly the master art. And politics appears to be of this nature; for it is this that ordains which of the sciences should be studied in a state, and which each class of citizens should learn and up to what point they should learn them; and we see even the most highly esteemed of capacities to fall under this, e. g., strategy, economics, rhetoric; now, since politics uses the rest of the sciences, and since, again, it legislates as to what we are to do and what we are to abstain from, the end of this science must include those of the others, so that this end must be the good for man. For even if the end is the same for a single man and for a state, that of the state seems at all events something greater and more complete whether to attain or to preserve; though it is worth while to attain the end merely for one man, it is finer and more godlike to attain it for a nation or for city-states. These, then, are the ends at which our inquiry aims, since it is political science, in one sense of that term.

3. [*We must not expect more precision than the subject matter admits.*] Our discussion will be adequate if it has as much clearness as the subject matter admits of, for precision is not to be sought for alike in all discussions, any more than in all the products of the crafts. Now fine and just actions, which political science investigates, admit of much variety and fluctuation of opinion, so that they may be thought to exist only by convention, and not by nature. And goods also

give rise to a similar fluctuation because they bring harm to many people; for before now men have been undone by reason of their wealth, and others by reason of their courage. We must be content, then, in speaking of such subjects and with such premises to indicate the truth roughly and in outline, and in speaking about things which are only for the most part true and with premises of the same kind to reach conclusions that are no better. In the same spirit, therefore, should each type of statement be *received*; for it is the mark of an educated man to look for precision in each class of things just so far as the nature of the subject admits; it is evidently equally foolish to accept probable reasoning from a mathematician and to demand from a rhetorician scientific proofs.

Now each man judges well the things he knows, and of these he is a good judge. And so the man who has been educated in a subject is a good judge of that subject, and the man who has received an all-round education is a good judge in general. Hence a young man is not a proper hearer of lectures on political science; for he is inexperienced in the actions that occur in life, but its discussions start from these and are about these; and, further, since he tends to follow his passions, his study will be vain and unprofitable, because the end aimed at is not knowledge but action. And it makes no difference whether he is young in years or youthful in character; the defect does not depend on time, but on his living, and pursuing each successive object, as passion directs. For to such persons, as to the incontinent, knowledge brings no profit; but to those who desire and act in accordance with a rational principle knowledge about such matters will be of great benefit.

These remarks about the student, the sort of treatment to be expected, and the purpose of the inquiry, may be taken as our preface.

4. [*The good for man is generally agreed to be happiness.*] Let us resume our inquiry and state, in view of the fact that all knowledge and every pursuit aims at some good, what it

is that we say political science aims at and what is the highest of all goods achievable by action. Verbally there is very general agreement; for both the general run of men and people of superior refinement say that it is happiness, and identify living well and doing well with being happy; but with regard to what happiness is they differ, and the many do not give the same account as the wise. For the former think it is some plain and obvious thing, like pleasure, wealth, or honour; they differ, however, from one another—and often even the same man identifies it with different things, with health when he is ill, with wealth when he is poor; but, conscious of their ignorance, they admire those who proclaim some great ideal that is above their comprehension. Now some thought that apart from these many goods there is another which is self-subsistent and causes the goodness of all these as well. To examine all the opinions that have been held were perhaps somewhat fruitless; enough to examine those that are most prevalent or that seem to be arguable.

Let us not fail to notice, however, that there is a difference between arguments from and those to the first principles. For Plato, too, was right in raising this question and asking, as he used to do, "Are we on the way from or to the first principles?" There is a difference, as there is in a racecourse between the course from the judges to the turning point and the way back. For, while we must begin with what is known, things are objects of knowledge in two senses—some to us, some without qualification. Presumably, then, *we* must begin with things known to *us*. Hence any one who is to listen intelligently to lectures about what is noble and just and, generally, about the subjects of political science must have been brought up in good habits. For the fact is the starting point, and if this is sufficiently plain to him, he will not at the start need the reason as well; and the man who has been well brought up has or can easily get starting points. And as for him who neither has nor can get them, let him hear the words of Hesiod:

Far best is he who knows all things himself;
Good, he that hearkens when men counsel right;
But he who neither knows, nor lays to heart
Another's wisdom, is a useless wight.

5. [*The popular views that the good is pleasure, honour, wealth.*] Let us, however, resume our discussion from the point at which we digressed. To judge from the lives that men lead, most men, and men of the most vulgar type, seem (not without some ground) to identify the good, or happiness, with pleasure; which is the reason why they love the life of enjoyment. For there are, we may say, three prominent types of life—that just mentioned, the political, and thirdly the contemplative life. Now the mass of mankind are evidently quite slavish in their tastes, preferring a life suitable to beasts, but they get some ground for their view from the fact that many of those in high places share the tastes of Sardanapallus. A consideration of the prominent types of life shows that people of superior refinement and of active disposition identify happiness with honour; for this is, roughly speaking, the end of the political life. But it seems too superficial to be what we are looking for, since it is thought to depend on those who bestow honour rather than on him who receives it, but the good we divine to be something proper to a man and not easily taken from him. Further, men seem to pursue honour in order that they may be assured of their goodness; at least it is by men of practical wisdom that they seek to be honoured, and among those who know them, and on the ground of their virtue; clearly, then, according to them, at any rate, virtue is better. And perhaps one might even suppose this to be, rather than honour, the end of the political life. But even this appears somewhat incomplete; for possession of virtue seems actually compatible with being asleep, or with lifelong inactivity, and, further, with the greatest sufferings and misfortunes; but a man who was living so no one would call happy, unless he were maintaining a thesis at all costs. But enough of this; for the subject has been sufficient-

ly treated even in the current discussions. Third comes the contemplative life, which we shall consider later.

The life of money-making is one undertaken under compulsion, and wealth is evidently not the good we are seeking; for it is merely useful and for the sake of something else. And so one might rather take the aforenamed objects to be ends; for they are loved for themselves. But it is evident that not even these are ends; yet many arguments have been thrown away in support of them. Let us leave this subject, then.

6. [*The Idea of good.*] We had perhaps better consider the universal good and discuss thoroughly what is meant by it, although such an inquiry is made an uphill one by the fact that the Forms have been introduced by friends of our own. Yet it would perhaps be thought to be better, indeed to be our duty, for the sake of maintaining the truth even to destroy what touches us closely, especially as we are philosophers or lovers of wisdom; for, while both are dear, piety requires us to honour truth above our friends.

The men who introduced this doctrine did not posit Ideas of classes within which they recognized priority and posteriority (which is the reason why they did not maintain the existence of an Idea embracing all numbers); but the term "good" is used both in the category of substance and in that of quality and in that of relation, and that which is *per se,* i. e., substance, is prior in nature to the relative (for the latter is like an offshoot and accident of being); so that there could not be a common Idea set over all these goods. Further, since "good" has as many senses as "being" (for it is predicated both in the category of substance, as of God and of reason, and in quality, i. e., of the virtues, and in quantity, i. e., of that which is moderate, and in relation, i. e., of the useful, and in time, i. e., of the right opportunity, and in place, i. e., of the right locality and the like), clearly it cannot be something universally present in all cases and single; for then it could not have been predicated in all the categories but in one only. Further, since of the things answering to one Idea there is one science, there would have been one science of all the goods; but as it is there are many sciences even of the things that fall under one category, e. g., of opportunity, for opportunity in war is studied by strategics and in disease by medicine, and the moderate in food is studied by medicine and in exercise by the science of gymnastics. And one might ask the question, what in the world they *mean* by "a thing itself," if (as is the case) in "man himself" and in a particular man the account of man is one and the same. For in so far as they are man, they will in no respect differ; and if this is so, neither will "good itself" and particular goods, in so far as they are good. But again it will not be good any the more for being eternal, since that which lasts long is no whiter than that which perishes in a day. The Pythagoreans seem to give a more plausible account of the good, when they place the one in the column of goods; and it is they that Speusippus seems to have followed.

But let us discuss these matters elsewhere; an objection to what we have said, however, may be discerned in the fact that the Platonists have not been speaking about *all* goods, and that the goods that are pursued and loved for themselves are called good by reference to a single Form, while those which tend to produce or to preserve these somehow or to prevent their contraries are called so by reference to these, and in a secondary sense. Clearly, then, goods must be spoken of in two ways, and some must be good in themselves, the others by reason of these. Let us separate, then, things good in themselves from things useful, and consider whether the former are called good by reference to a single Idea. What sort of goods would one call good in themselves? Is it those that are pursued even when isolated from others, such as intelligence, sight, and certain pleasures and honours? Certainly, if we pursue these also for the sake of something else, yet one would place them among things good in themselves. Or is nothing other than the Idea of good good in itself? In that case the Form will be empty. But if the things we have named are also things good in themselves, the account of the good will have to appear as something

identical in them all, as that of whiteness is identical in snow
and in white lead. But of honour, wisdom, and pleasure, just
in respect of their goodness, the accounts are distinct and
diverse. The good, therefore, is not some common element
answering to one Idea.

But what then do we mean by the good? It is surely not
like the things that only chance to have the same name. Are
goods one, then, by being derived from one good or by all
contributing to one good, or are they rather one by analogy?
Certainly as sight is in the body, so is reason in the soul,
and so on in other cases. But perhaps these subjects had
better be dismissed for the present; for perfect precision
about them would be more appropriate to another branch of
philosophy. And similarly with regard to the Idea; even if
there is some one good which is universally predicable of
goods or is capable of separate and independent existence,
clearly it could not be achieved or attained by man; but we
are now seeking something attainable. Perhaps, however,
some one might think it worth while to recognize this with a
view to the goods that *are* attainable and achievable; for
having this as a sort of pattern we shall know better the goods
that are good for us, and if we know them shall attain them.
This argument has some plausibility, but seems to clash with
the procedure of the sciences; for all of these, though they
aim at some good and seek to supply the deficiency of it,
leave on one side the knowledge of *the* good. Yet that all
the exponents of the arts should be ignorant of, and should
not even seek, so great an aid is not probable. It is hard, too,
to see how a weaver or a carpenter will be benefited in regard to his own craft by knowing this "good itself," or how
the man who has viewed the Idea itself will be a better doctor or general thereby. For a doctor seems not even to study
health in this way, but the health of man, or perhaps rather
the health of a particular man; it is individuals that he is
healing. But enough of these topics.

7. [*The good must be something final and self-sufficient.*]
Let us again return to the good we are seeking, and ask what

it can be. It seems different in different actions and arts; it is different in medicine, in strategy, and in the other arts likewise. What then is the good of each? Surely that for whose sake everything else is done. In medicine this is health, in strategy victory, in architecture a house, in any other sphere something else, and in every action and pursuit the end; for it is for the sake of this that all men do whatever else they do. Therefore, if there is an end for all that we do, this will be the good achievable by action, and if there are more than one, these will be the goods achievable by action.

So the argument has by a different course reached the same point; but we must try to state this even more clearly. Since there is evidently more than one end, and we choose some of these (e. g., wealth, flutes, and in general instruments) for the sake of something else, clearly not all ends are final ends; but the chief good is evidently something final. Therefore, if there is only one final end, this will be what we are seeking, and if there are more than one, the most final of these will be what we are seeking. Now we call that which is in itself worthy of pursuit more final than that which is worthy of pursuit for the sake of something else, and that which is never desirable for the sake of something else more final than the things that are desirable both in themselves and for the sake of that other thing, and therefore we call final without qualification that which is always desirable in itself and never for the sake of something else.

Now such a thing happiness, above all else, is held to be; for this we choose always for itself and never for the sake of something else, but honour, pleasure, reason, and every virtue we choose indeed for themselves (for if nothing resulted from them we should still choose each of them), but we choose them also for the sake of happiness, judging that by means of them we shall be happy. Happiness, on the other hand, no one chooses for the sake of these, nor, in general, for anything other than itself.

From the point of view of self-sufficiency the same result seems to follow; for the final good is thought to be self-sufficient. Now by self-sufficient we do not mean that which is sufficient for a man by himself, for one who lives a solitary life, but also for parents, children, wife, and in general for his friends and fellow citizens, since man is born for citizenship. But some limit must be set to this; for if we extend our requirement to ancestors and descendants and friends' friends we are in for an infinite series. Let us examine this question, however, on another occasion; the self-sufficient we now define as that which when isolated makes life desirable and lacking in nothing; and such we think happiness to be; and further we think it most desirable of all things, without being counted as one good thing among others—if it were so counted it would clearly be made more desirable by the addition of even the least of goods; for that which is added becomes an excess of goods, and of goods the greater is always more desirable. Happiness, then, is something final and self-sufficient, and is the end of action.

Presumably, however, to say that happiness is the chief good seems a platitude, and a clearer account of what it is is still desired. This might perhaps be given, if we could first ascertain the function of man. For just as for a flute player, a sculptor, or any artist, and, in general, for all things that have a function or activity, the good and the "well" is thought to reside in the function, so would it seem to be for man, if he has a function. Have the carpenter, then, and the tanner certain functions or activities, and has man none? Is he born without a function? Or as eye, hand, foot, and in general each of the parts evidently has a function, may one lay it down that man similarly has a function apart from all these? What then can this be? Life seems to be common even to plants, but we are seeking what is peculiar to man. Let us exclude, therefore, the life of nutrition and growth. Next there would be a life of perception, but *it* also seems to be common even to the horse, the ox, and every animal. There remains, then, an active life of the element that has a rational principle; of this, one part has such a principle in the sense of being obedient to one, the other in the sense of possessing one and exercising thought. And, as "life of the rational element" also has two meanings, we must state that life in the sense of activity is what we mean; for this seems to be the more proper sense of the term. Now if the function of man is an activity of soul which follows or implies a rational principle, and if we say "a so-and-so" and "a good so-and-so" have a function which is the same in kind, e. g., a lyre player and a good lyre player, and so without qualification in all cases, eminence in respect of goodness being added to the name of the function (for the function of a lyre player is to play the lyre, and that of a good lyre player is to do so well); if this is the case [and we state the function of man to be a certain kind of life, and this to be an activity or actions of the soul implying a rational principle, and the function of a good man to be the good and noble performance of these, and if any action is well performed when it is performed in accordance with the appropriate excellence; if this is the case], human good turns out to be activity of soul in accordance with virtue, and if there is more than one virtue, in accordance with the best and most complete.

But we must add "in a complete life." For one swallow does not make a summer, nor does one day; and so too one day, or a short time, does not make a man blessed and happy.

Let this serve as an outline of the good; for we must presumably first sketch it roughly, and then later fill in the details. But it would seem that any one is capable of carrying on and articulating what has once been well outlined, and that time is a good discoverer or partner in such a work; to which facts the advances of the arts are due; for any one can add what is lacking. And we must also remember what has been said before, and not look for precision in all things alike, but in each class of things such precision as accords with the subject matter, and so much as is appropriate to the inquiry. For a carpenter and a geometer investigate the right angle in different ways; the former does so in so far as the right angle is useful for his work, while the latter inquires what it is or what sort of thing it is; for he is a spectator of the truth. We must act in the same way, then, in all other matters as well, that our main task may not be subordinated to minor questions. Nor must we demand the cause in all matters alike; it is enough in some cases that the *fact* be well established, as in the case of the first principles; the fact is the primary thing or first principle. Now of first principles we see some by induction, some by perception, some by a certain habituation, and others too in other ways. But each set of principles we must try to investigate in the natural way, and we must take pains to state them definitely, since they have a great influence on what follows. For the beginning is thought to be more than half of the whole, and many of the questions we ask are cleared up by it.

8. [*Current beliefs about happiness.*] We must consider it, however, in the light not only of our conclusion and our premisses, but also of what is commonly said about it; for with a true view all the data harmonize, but with a false one the facts soon clash. Now goods have been divided into three classes, and some are described as external, others as relating to soul or to body; we call those that relate to soul most properly and truly goods, and psychical actions and activities we class as relating to soul. Therefore our account must be sound, at least according to this view, which is an old one and agreed on by philosophers. It is correct also in that we identify the end with certain actions and activities; for thus it falls among goods of the soul and not among external goods. Another belief which harmonizes with our account is that the happy man lives well and does well; for we have practically defined happiness as a sort of good life and good action. The characteristics that are looked for in happiness seem also, all of them, to belong to what we have defined happiness as being. For some identify happiness with virtue, some with practical wisdom, others with a kind of philosophic wisdom, others with these, or one of these, accompanied by pleasure or not without pleasure; while others include also external prosperity. Now some of these views have been held by many men and men of old, others by a few eminent persons; and it is not probable that either of these should be entirely mistaken, but rather that they should

be right in at least some one respect or even in most respects.

With those who identify happiness with virtue or some one virtue our account is in harmony; for to virtue belongs virtuous activity. But it makes, perhaps, no small difference whether we place the chief good in possession or in use, in state of mind or in activity. For the state of mind may exist without producing any good result, as in a man who is asleep or in some other way quite inactive, but the activity cannot; for one who has the activity will of necessity be acting, and acting well. And as in the Olympic Games it is not the most beautiful and the strongest that are crowned but those who compete (for it is some of these that are victorious), so those who act win, and rightly win, the noble and good things in life.

Their life is also in itself pleasant. For pleasure is a state of *soul*, and to each man that which he is said to be a lover of is pleasant; e. g., not only is a horse pleasant to the lover of horses, and a spectacle to the lover of sights, but also in the same way just acts are pleasant to the lover of justice and in general virtuous acts to the lover of virtue. Now for most men their pleasures are in conflict with one another because these are not by nature pleasant, but the lovers of what is noble find pleasant the things that are by nature pleasant; and virtuous actions are such, so that these are pleasant for such men as well as in their own nature. Their life, therefore, has no further need of pleasure as a sort of adventitious charm, but has its pleasure in itself. For, besides what we have said, the man who does not rejoice in noble actions is not even good; since no one would call a man just who did not enjoy acting justly, nor any man liberal who did not enjoy liberal actions; and similarly in all other cases. If this is so, virtuous actions must be in themselves pleasant. But they are also *good* and *noble*, and have each of these attributes in the highest degree, since the good man judges well about these attributes; his judgement is such as we have described. Happiness then is the best, noblest, and most pleasant thing in the world, and these attributes are not severed as in the inscription at Delos—

> Most noble is that which is justest, and best is health;
> But pleasantest is it to win what we love.

For all these properties belong to the best activities; and these, or one—the best—of these, we identify with happiness.

Yet evidently, as we said, it needs the external goods as well; for it is impossible, or not easy, to do noble acts without the proper equipment. In many actions we use friends and riches and political power as instruments; and there are some things the lack of which takes the lustre from happiness, as good birth, goodly children, beauty; for the man who is very ugly in appearance or ill-born or solitary and childless is not very likely to be happy, and perhaps a man would be still less likely if he had thoroughly bad children or friends or had lost good children or friends by death. As we said, then, happiness seems to need this sort of prosperity in addition; for which reason some identify happiness with good fortune, though others identify it with virtue.

9. [*How happiness is acquired.*] For this reason also the question is asked, whether happiness is to be acquired by learning or by habituation or some other sort of training, or comes in virtue of some divine providence or again by chance. Now if there is *any* gift of the gods to men, it is reasonable that happiness should be god-given, and most surely god-given of all human things inasmuch as it is the best. But this question would perhaps be more appropriate to another inquiry; happiness seems, however, even if it is not god-sent but comes as a result of virtue and some process of learning or training, to be among the most godlike things; for that which is the prize and end of virtue seems to be the best thing in the world, and something godlike and blessed.

It will also on this view be very generally shared; for all who are not maimed as regards their potentiality for virtue may win it by a certain kind of study and care. But if it is better to be happy thus than by chance, it is reasonable that the facts should be so, since everything that depends on the action of nature is by nature as good as it can be, and similarly everything that depends on art or any rational cause, and especially if it depends on the best of all causes. To entrust to chance what is greatest and most noble would be a very defective arrangement.

The answer to the question we are asking is plain also from the definition of happiness; for it has been said to be a virtuous activity of soul, of a certain kind. Of the remaining goods, some must necessarily pre-exist as conditions of happiness, and others are naturally co-operative and useful as instruments. And this will be found to agree with what we said at the outset; for we stated the end of political science to be the best end, and political science spends most of its pains on making the citizens to be of a certain character, viz., good and capable of noble acts.

It is natural, then, that we call neither ox nor horse nor any other of the animals happy; for none of them is capable of sharing in such activity. For this reason also a boy is not happy; for he is not yet capable of such acts, owing to his age; and boys who are called happy are being congratulated by reason of the hopes we have for them. For there is required, as we said, not only complete virtue but also a complete life, since many changes occur in life, and all manner of chances, and the most prosperous may fall into great misfortunes in old age, as is told of Priam in the Trojan Cycle; and one who has experienced such chances and has ended wretchedly no one calls happy.

10. [*Should no man be called happy while he lives?*] Must no one at all, then, be called happy while he lives; must we, as Solon says, see the end? Even if we are to lay down this doctrine, is it also the case that a man *is* happy when he is *dead?* Or is not this quite absurd, especially for us who say that happiness is an activity? But if we do not call the dead man happy, and if Solon does not mean this, but that one can then safely *call* a man blessed as being at last beyond evils and misfortunes, this also affords matter for discussion; for both evil and good are thought to exist for a dead man, as much as for one who is alive but not aware of them;

e. g., honours and dishonours and the good or bad fortunes of children and in general of descendants. And this also presents a problem; for though a man has lived happily up to old age and has had a death worthy of his life, many reverses may befall his descendants—some of them may be good and attain the life they deserve, while with others the opposite may be the case; and clearly too the degrees of relationship between them and their ancestors may vary indefinitely. It would be odd, then, if the dead man were to share in these changes and become at one time happy, at another wretched; while it would also be odd if the fortunes of the descendants did not for *some* time have *some* effect on the happiness of their ancestors.

But we must return to our first difficulty; for perhaps by a consideration of it our present problem might be solved. Now if we must see the end and only then call a man happy, not as being happy but as having been so before, surely this is a paradox, that when he is happy the attribute that belongs to him is not to be truly predicated of him because we do not wish to call living men happy, on account of the changes that may befall them, and because we have assumed happiness to be something permanent and by no means easily changed, while a single man may suffer many turns of fortune's wheel. For clearly if we were to keep pace with his fortunes, we should often call the same man happy and again wretched, making the happy man out to be a "chameleon and insecurely based." Or is this keeping pace with his fortunes quite wrong? Success or failure in life does not depend on these, but human life, as we said, needs these as mere additions, while virtuous activities or their opposites are what constitute happiness or the reverse.

The question we have now discussed confirms our definition. For no function of man has so much permanence as virtuous activities (these are thought to be more durable even than knowledge of the sciences), and of these themselves the most valuable are more durable because those who are happy spend their life most readily and most continuously in these; for this seems to be the reason why we do not forget them. The attribute in question, then, will belong to the happy man, and he will be happy throughout his life; for always, or by preference to everything else, he will be engaged in virtuous action and contemplation, and he will bear the chances of life most nobly and altogether decorously, if he is "truly good" and "foursquare beyond reproach."

Now many events happen by chance, and events differing in importance; small pieces of good fortune or of its opposite clearly do not weigh down the scales of life one way or the other, but a multitude of great events if they turn out well will make life happier (for not only are they themselves such as to add beauty to life, but the way a man deals with them may be noble and good), while if they turn out ill they crush and maim happiness; for they both bring pain with them and hinder many activities. Yet even in these nobility shines through, when a man bears with resignation many great misfortunes, not through insensibility to pain but through nobility and greatness of soul.

If activities are, as we said, what gives life its character, no happy man can become miserable; for he will never do the acts that are hateful and mean. For the man who is truly good and wise, we think, bears all the chances of life becomingly and always makes the best of circumstances, as a good general makes the best military use of the army at his command and a good shoemaker makes the best shoes out of the hides that are given him; and so with all other craftsmen. And if this is the case, the happy man can never become miserable—though he will not reach *blessedness*, if he meet with fortunes like those of Priam.

Nor, again, is he many-coloured and changeable; for neither will he be moved from his happy state easily or by any ordinary misadventures, but only by many great ones, nor, if he has had many great misadventures, will he recover his happiness in a short time, but if at all, only in a long and complete one in which he has attained many splendid successes.

Why then should we not say that he is happy who is active in accordance with complete virtue and is sufficiently equipped with external goods, not for some chance period but throughout a complete life? Or must we add "and who is destined to live thus and die as befits his life"? Certainly the future is obscure to us, while happiness, we claim, is an end and something in every way final. If so, we shall call happy those among living men in whom these conditions are, and are to be, fulfilled—but happy *men*. So much for these questions.

11. [*Do the fortunes of the living affect the dead?*] That the fortunes of descendants and of all a man's friends should not affect his happiness at all seems a very unfriendly doctrine, and one opposed to the opinions men hold; but since the events that happen are numerous and admit of all sorts of difference, and some come more near to us and others less so, it seems a long—nay, an infinite—task to discuss each in detail; a general outline will perhaps suffice. If, then, as some of a man's own misadventures have a certain weight and influence on life while others are, as it were, lighter, so too there are differences among the misadventures of our friends taken as a whole, and it makes a difference whether the various sufferings befall the living or the dead (much more even than whether lawless and terrible deeds are presupposed in a tragedy or done on the stage), this difference also must be taken into account; or rather, perhaps, the fact that doubt is felt whether the dead share in any good or evil. For it seems, from these considerations, that even if anything whether good or evil penetrates to them, it must be something weak and negligible, either in itself or for them, or if not, at least it must be such in degree and kind as not to make happy those who are not happy nor to take away their blessedness from those who are. The good or bad fortunes of friends, then, seem to have some effects on the dead, but effects of such a kind and degree as neither to make the happy unhappy nor to produce any other change of the kind.

12. [*Virtue is praiseworthy, but happiness is above praise.*]
These questions having been definitely answered, let us consider whether happiness is among the things that are praised
or rather among the things that are prized; for clearly it is
not to be placed among *potentialities*. Everything that is
praised seems to be praised because it is of a certain kind and
is related somehow to something else; for we praise the just
or brave man and in general both the good man and virtue
itself because of the actions and functions involved, and we
praise the strong man, the good runner, and so on, because
he is of a certain kind and is related in a certain way to something good and important. This is clear also from the praises
of the gods; for it seems absurd that the gods should be referred to our standard, but this *is* done because praise involves a reference, as we said, to something else. But if
praise is for things such as we have described, clearly what
applies to the best things is not praise, but something greater
and better, as is indeed obvious; for what we do to the gods
and the most godlike of men is to call them blessed and
happy. And so too with good *things;* no one praises happiness as he does justice, but rather calls it blessed, as being
something more divine and better.

Eudoxus also seems to have been right in his method of
advocating the supremacy of pleasure; he thought that the
fact that, though a good, it is not praised indicated it to be
better than the things that are praised, and that this is what
God and the good are; for by reference to these all other
things are judged. *Praise* is appropriate to virtue, for as a
result of virtue men tend to do noble deeds; but *encomia* are
bestowed on acts, whether of the body or of the soul. But
perhaps nicety in these matters is more proper to those who
have made a study of encomia; to us it is clear from what
has been said that happiness is among the things that are
prized and perfect. It seems to be so also from the fact that
it is a first principle; for it is for the sake of this that we all
do all that we do, and the first principle and cause of goods
is, we claim, something prized and divine.

13. [*Intellectual and moral faculties and virtues.*] Since happiness is an activity of soul in accordance with perfect virtue, we must consider the nature of virtue; for perhaps we shall thus see better the nature of happiness. The true student of politics, too, is thought to have studied virtue above all things; for he wishes to make his fellow citizens good and obedient to the laws. As an example of this we have the lawgivers of the Cretans and the Spartans, and any others of the kind that there may have been. And if this inquiry belongs to political science, clearly the pursuit of it will be in accordance with our original plan. But clearly the virtue we must study is human virtue; for the good we were seeking was human good and the happiness human happiness. By human virtue we mean not that of the body but that of the soul; and happiness also we call an activity of soul. But if this is so, clearly the student of politics must know somehow the facts about soul, as the man who is to heal the eyes or the body as a whole must know about the eyes or the body; and all the more since politics is more prized and better than medicine; but even among doctors the best educated spend much labour on acquiring knowledge of the body. The student of politics, then, must study the soul, and must study it with these objects in view, and do so just to the extent which is sufficient for the questions we are discussing; for further precision is perhaps something more laborious than our purposes require.

Some things are said about it, adequately enough, even in the discussions outside our school, and we must use these; e. g., that one element in the soul is irrational and one has a rational principle. Whether these are separated as the parts of the body or of anything divisible are, or are distinct by definition but by nature inseparable, like convex and concave in the circumference of a circle, does not affect the present question.

Of the irrational element one division seems to be widely distributed, and vegetative in its nature, I mean that which causes nutrition and growth; for it is this kind of power of the soul that one must assign to all nurslings and to embryos, and this same power to full-grown creatures; this is more reasonable than to assign some different power to them. Now the excellence of this seems to be common to all species and not specifically human; for this part or faculty seems to function most in sleep, while goodness and badness are least manifest in sleep (whence comes the saying that the happy are no better off than the wretched for half their lives; and this happens naturally enough, since sleep is an inactivity of the soul in that respect in which it is called good or bad), unless perhaps to a small extent some of the movements actually penetrate to the soul, and in this respect the dreams of good men are better than those of ordinary people. Enough of this subject, however; let us leave the nutritive faculty alone, since it has by its nature no share in human excellence.

There seems to be also another irrational element in the soul—one which in a sense, however, shares in a rational principle. For we praise the rational principle of the continent man and of the incontinent, and the part of their soul that has such a principle, since it urges them aright and towards the best objects; but there is found in them also another element naturally opposed to the rational principle, which fights against and resists that principle. For exactly as paralysed limbs when we intend to move them to the right turn on the contrary to the left, so is it with the soul; the impulses of incontinent people move in contrary directions. But while in the body we see that which moves astray, in the soul we do not. No doubt, however, we must none the less suppose that in the soul too there is something contrary to the rational principle, resisting and opposing it. In what sense it is distinct from the other elements does not concern us. Now even this seems to have a share in a rational principle, as we said; at any rate in the continent man it obeys the rational principle—and presumably in the temperate and brave man it is still more obedient; for in him it speaks, on all matters, with the same voice as the rational principle.

Therefore the irrational element also appears to be twofold. For the vegetative element in no way shares in a rational principle, but the appetitive, and in general the de-

siring element in a sense shares in it, in so far as it listens
to and obeys it; this is the sense in which we speak of "taking account" of one's father or one's friends, not that in which
we speak of "accounting" for a mathematical property. That
the irrational element is in some sense persuaded by a rational principle is indicated also by the giving of advice and
by all reproof and exhortation. And if this element also must
be said to have a rational principle, that which has a rational
principle (as well as that which has not) will be twofold,
one subdivision having it in the strict sense and in itself, and
the other having a tendency to obey as one does one's father.

Virtue too is distinguished into kinds in accordance with
this difference; for we say that some of the virtues are intellectual and others moral, philosophic wisdom and understanding and practical wisdom being intellectual, liberality and temperance moral. For in speaking about a man's
character we do not say that he is wise or has understanding
but that he is good-tempered or temperate; yet we praise
the wise man also with respect to his state of mind; and of
states of mind we call those which merit praise virtues.

BOOK II

1. [Moral virtue acquired by practice.] Virtue, then, being
of two kinds, intellectual and moral, intellectual virtue in
the main owes both its birth and its growth to teaching (for
which reason it requires experience and time), while moral
virtue comes about as a result of habit, whence also its
name *ethike* is one that is formed by a slight variation from
the word *ethos* (habit). From this it is also plain that none
of the moral virtues arises in us by nature; for nothing that

exists by nature can form a habit contrary to its nature. For instance the stone which by nature moves downwards cannot be habituated to move upwards, not even if one tries to train it by throwing it up ten thousand times; nor can fire be habituated to move downwards, nor can anything else that by nature behaves in one way be trained to behave in another. Neither by nature, then, nor contrary to nature do the virtues arise in us; rather we are adapted by nature to receive them, and are made perfect by habit.

Again, of all the things that come to us by nature we first acquire the potentiality and later exhibit the activity (this is plain in the case of the senses; for it was not by often seeing or often hearing that we got these senses, but on the contrary we had them before we used them, and did not come to have them by using them); but the virtues we get by first exercising them, as also happens in the case of the arts as well. For the things we have to learn before we can do them, we learn by doing them, e. g., men become builders by building and lyre players by playing the lyre; so too we become just by doing just acts, temperate by doing temperate acts, brave by doing brave acts.

This is confirmed by what happens in states; for legislators make the citizens good by forming habits in them, and this is the wish of every legislator, and those who do not effect it miss their mark, and it is in this that a good constitution differs from a bad one.

Again, it is from the same causes and by the same means that every virtue is both produced and destroyed, and similarly every art; for it is from playing the lyre that both good and bad lyre players are produced. And the corresponding statement is true of builders and of all the rest; men will be good or bad builders as a result of building well or badly. For if this were not so, there would have been no need of a teacher, but all men would have been born good or bad at their craft. This, then, is the case with the virtues also; by doing the acts that we do in our transactions with other men we become just or unjust, and by doing the acts that we do in the presence of danger, and being habituated to feel fear or confidence, we become brave or cowardly. The same is true of appetites and feelings of anger; some men become temperate and good-tempered, others self-indulgent and irascible, by behaving in one way or the other in the appropriate circumstances. Thus, in one word, states of character arise out of like activities. This is why the activities we exhibit must be of a certain kind; it is because the states of character correspond to the differences between these. It makes no small difference, then, whether we form habits of one kind or of another from our very youth; it makes a very great difference, or rather *all* the difference.

2. [*These practices must avoid excess and defect.*] Since, then, the present inquiry does not aim at theoretical knowledge like the others (for we are inquiring not in order to know what virtue is, but in order to become good, since otherwise our inquiry would have been of no use), we must examine the nature of actions, namely how we ought to do them; for these determine also the nature of the states of character that are produced, as we have said. Now, that we must act according to the right rule is a common principle and must be assumed—it will be discussed later, i. e., both what the right rule is, and how it is related to the other virtues. But this must be agreed upon beforehand, that the whole account of matters of conduct must be given in outline and not precisely, as we said at the very beginning that the accounts we demand must be in accordance with the subject matter; matters concerned with conduct and questions of what is good for us have no fixity, any more than matters of health. The general account being of this nature, the account of particular cases is yet more lacking in exactness; for they do not fall under any art or precept but the agents themselves must in each case consider what is appropriate to the occasion, as happens also in the art of medicine or of navigation.

But though our present account is of this nature we must give what help we can. First, then, let us consider this, that it is the nature of such things to be destroyed by defect and excess, as we see in the case of strength and of health (for to gain light on things imperceptible we must use the evidence of sensible things); both excessive and defective exercise destroys the strength, and similarly drink or food which is above or below a certain amount destroys the health, while that which is proportionate both produces and increases and preserves it. So too is it, then, in the case of temperance and courage and the other virtues. For the man who flies from and fears everything and does not stand his ground against anything becomes a coward, and the man who fears nothing at all but goes to meet every danger becomes rash; and similarly the man who indulges in every pleasure and abstains from none becomes self-indulgent, while the man who shuns every pleasure, as boors do, becomes in a way insensible; temperance and courage, then, are destroyed by excess and defect, and preserved by the mean.

But not only are the sources and causes of their origination and growth the same as those of their destruction, but also the sphere of their actualization will be the same; for this is also true of the things which are more evident to sense, e. g., of strength; it is produced by taking much food and undergoing much exertion, and it is the strong man that will be most able to do these things. So too is it with the virtues; by abstaining from pleasures we become temperate, and it is when we have become so that we are most able to abstain from them; and similarly too in the case of courage; for by being habituated to despise things that are terrible and to stand our ground against them we become brave, and it is when we have become so that we shall be most able to stand our ground against them.

3. [*Pleasure in doing virtuous acts.*] We must take as a sign of states of character the pleasure or pain that ensues on acts; for the man who abstains from bodily pleasures and delights in this very fact is temperate, while the man who is annoyed at it is self-indulgent, and he who stands his ground against things that are terrible and delights in this or at least is not pained is brave, while the man who is pained is a coward.

For moral excellence is concerned with pleasures and pains; it is on account of the pleasure that we do bad things, and on account of the pain that we abstain from noble ones. Hence we ought to have been brought up in a particular way from our very youth, as Plato says, so as both to delight in and to be pained by the things that we ought; for this is the right education.

Again, if the virtues are concerned with actions and passions, and every passion and every action is accompanied by pleasure and pain, for this reason also virtue will be concerned with pleasures and pains. This is indicated also by the fact that punishment is inflicted by these means; for it is a kind of cure, and it is the nature of cures to be effected by contraries.

Again, as we said but lately, every state of soul has a nature relative to and concerned with the kind of things by which it tends to be made worse or better; but it is by reason of pleasures and pains that men become bad, by pursuing and avoiding these—either the pleasures and pains they ought not or when they ought not or as they ought not, or by going wrong in one of the other similar ways that may be distinguished. Hence men even define the virtues as certain states of impassivity and rest; not well, however, because they speak absolutely, and do not say "as one ought" and "as one ought not" and "when one ought or ought not," and the other things that may be added. We assume, then, that this kind of excellence tends to do what is best with regard to pleasures and pains, and vice does the contrary.

The following facts also may show us that virtue and vice are concerned with these same things. There being three objects of choice and three of avoidance, the noble, the advantageous, the pleasant, and their contraries, the base, the injurious, the painful, about all of these the good man tends to go right and the bad man to go wrong, and especially about pleasure; for this is common to the animals, and also it accompanies all objects of choice; for even the noble and the advantageous appear pleasant.

Again, it has grown up with us all from our infancy; this

is why it is difficult to rub off this passion, engrained as it is in our life. And we measure even our actions, some of us more and others less, by the rule of pleasure and pain. For this reason, then, our whole inquiry must be about these; for to feel delight and pain rightly or wrongly has no small effect on our actions.

Again, it is harder to fight with pleasure than with anger, to use Heraclitus' phrase, but both art and virtue are always concerned with what is harder; for even the good is better when it is harder. Therefore for this reason also the whole concern both of virtue and of political science is with pleasures and pains; for the man who uses these well will be good, he who uses them badly bad.

That virtue, then, is concerned with pleasures and pains, and that by the acts from which it arises it is both increased and, if they are done differently, destroyed, and that the acts from which it arose are those in which it actualizes itself— let this be taken as said.

4. [*Actions that produce moral virtue.*] The question might be asked, what we mean by saying that we must become just by doing just acts, and temperate by doing temperate acts; for if men do just and temperate acts, they are already just and temperate, exactly as, if they do what is in accordance with the laws of grammar and of music, they are grammarians and musicians.

Or is this not true even of the arts? It is possible to do something that is in accordance with the laws of grammar, either by chance or at the suggestion of another. A man will be a grammarian, then, only when he has both done something grammatical and done it grammatically; and this means doing it in accordance with the grammatical knowledge in himself.

Again, the case of the arts and that of the virtues are not similar; for the products of the arts have their goodness in themselves; so that it is enough that they should have a certain character, but if the acts that are in accordance with the virtues have themselves a certain character it does not follow that they are done justly or temperately. The agent also must be in a certain condition when he does them; in the first place he must have knowledge, secondly he must choose the acts, and choose them for their own sakes, and thirdly his action must proceed from a firm and unchangeable character. These are not reckoned in as conditions of the possession of the arts, except the bare knowledge; but as a condition of the possession of the virtues knowledge has little or no weight, while the other conditions count not for a little but for everything, i. e., the very conditions which result from often doing just and temperate acts.

Actions, then, are called just and temperate when they are such as the just or the temperate man would do; but it is not the man who does these that is just and temperate, but the man who also does them *as* just and temperate men do them. It is well said, then, that it is by doing just acts that the just man is produced, and by doing temperate acts the temperate man; without doing these no one would have even a prospect of becoming good.

But most people do not do these, but take refuge in theory and think they are being philosophers and will become good in this way, behaving somewhat like patients who listen attentively to their doctors, but do none of the things they are ordered to do. As the latter will not be made well in body by such a course of treatment, the former will not be made well in soul by such a course of philosophy.

5. [*Moral virtue is a state of character.*] Next we must consider what virtue is. Since things that are found in the soul are of three kinds—passions, faculties, states of character, virtue must be one of these. By passions I mean appetite, anger, fear, confidence, envy, joy, friendly feeling, hatred, longing, emulation, pity, and in general the feelings that are accompanied by pleasure or pain; by faculties the things in virtue of which we are said to be capable of feeling these, e. g., of becoming angry or being pained or feeling pity; by states of character the things in virtue of which we stand well or badly with reference to the passions, e. g., with refer-

ence to anger we stand badly if we feel it violently or too weakly, and well if we feel it moderately; and similarly with reference to the other passions.

Now neither the virtues nor the vices are *passions,* because we are not called good or bad on the ground of our passions, but are so called on the ground of our virtues and our vices, and because we are neither praised nor blamed for our passions (for the man who feels fear or anger is not praised, nor is the man who simply feels anger blamed, but the man who feels it in a certain way), but for our virtues and our vices we *are* praised or blamed.

Again, we feel anger and fear without choice, but the virtues are modes of choice or involve choice. Further, in respect of the passions we are said to be moved, but in respect of the virtues and the vices we are said not to be moved but to be disposed in a particular way.

For these reasons also they are not *faculties;* for we are neither called good nor bad, nor praised nor blamed, for the simple capacity of feeling the passions; again, we have the faculties by nature, but we are not made good or bad by nature; we have spoken of this before.

If, then, the virtues are neither passions nor faculties, all that remains is that they should be *states of character*.

Thus we have stated what virtue is in respect of its genus.

6. [*Moral virtue is a disposition to choose the mean.*] We must, however, not only describe virtue as a state of character, but also say what sort of state it is. We may remark, then, that every virtue or excellence both brings into good condition the thing of which it is the excellence and makes the work of that thing be done well; e. g., the excellence of the eye makes both the eye and its work good; for it is by the excellence of the eye that we see well. Similarly the excellence of the horse makes a horse both good in itself and good at running and at carrying its rider and at awaiting the attack of the enemy. Therefore, if this is true in every case, the virtue of man also will be the state of character which

makes a man good and which makes him do his own work well.

How this is to happen we have stated already, but it will be made plain also by the following consideration of the specific nature of virtue. In everything that is continuous and divisible it is possible to take more, less, or an equal amount, and that either in terms of the thing itself or relatively to us; and the equal is an intermediate between excess and defect. By the intermediate in the object I mean that which is equidistant from each of the extremes, which is one and the same for all men; by the intermediate relatively to us that which is neither too much nor too little—and this is not one, nor the same for all. For instance, if ten is many and two is few, six is the intermediate, taken in terms of the object; for it exceeds and is exceeded by an equal amount; this is intermediate according to arithmetical proportion. But the intermediate relatively to us is not to be taken so; if ten pounds are too much for a particular person to eat and two too little, it does not follow that the trainer will order six pounds; for this also is perhaps too much for the person who is to take it, or too little—too little for Milo, too much for the beginner in athletic exercises. The same is true of running and wrestling. Thus a master of any art avoids excess and defect, but seeks the intermediate and chooses this—the intermediate not in the object but relatively to us.

If it is thus, then, that every art does its work well—by looking to the intermediate and judging its works by this standard (so that we often say of good works of art that it is not possible either to take away or to add anything, implying that excess and defect destroy the goodness of works of art, while the mean preserves it; and good artists, as we say, look to this in their work), and if, further, virtue is more exact and better than any art, as nature also is, then virtue must have the quality of aiming at the intermediate. I mean moral virtue; for it is this that is concerned with passions and actions, and in these there is excess, defect, and the intermediate. For instance, both fear and confidence and appetite and anger and pity and in general pleasure and pain may be felt both too much and too little, and in both cases not well; but to feel them at the right times, with reference to the right objects, towards the right people, with the right motive, and in the right way, is what is both intermediate and best, and this is characteristic of virtue. Similarly with regard to actions also there is excess, defect, and the intermediate. Now virtue is concerned with passions and actions, in which excess is a form of failure, and so is defect, while the intermediate is praised and is a form of success; and being praised and being successful are both characteristics of virtue. Therefore virtue is a kind of mean, since, as we have seen, it aims at what is intermediate.

Again, it is possible to fail in many ways (for evil belongs to the class of the unlimited, as the Pythagoreans conjectured, and good to that of the limited), while to succeed is possible only in one way (for which reason also one is easy and the other difficult—to miss the mark easy, to hit it difficult); for these reasons also, then, excess and defect are characteristic of vice, and the mean of virtue;

For men are good in but one way, but bad in many.

Virtue, then, is a state of character concerned with choice, lying in a mean, i. e., the mean relative to us, this being determined by a rational principle, and by that principle by which the man of practical wisdom would determine it. Now it is a mean between two vices, that which depends on excess and that which depends on defect; and again it is a mean because the vices respectively fall short of or exceed what is right in both passions and actions, while virtue both finds and chooses that which is intermediate. Hence in respect of its substance and the definition which states its essence virtue is a mean, with regard to what is best and right an extreme.

But not every action nor every passion admits of a mean; for some have names that already imply badness, e. g., spite, shamelessness, envy, and in the case of actions adultery, theft, murder; for all of these and suchlike things imply by their names that they are themselves bad, and not the excesses or deficiencies of them. It is not possible, then, ever to be right with regard to them; one must always be wrong. Nor does goodness or badness with regard to such things depend on committing adultery with the right woman, at the right time, and in the right way, but simply to do any of them is to go wrong. It would be equally absurd, then, to expect that in unjust, cowardly, and voluptuous action there should be a mean, an excess, and a deficiency; for at that rate there would be a mean of excess and of deficiency, an excess of excess, and a deficiency of deficiency. But as there is no excess and deficiency of temperance and courage because what is intermediate is in a sense an extreme, so too of the actions we have mentioned there is no mean nor any excess and deficiency, but however they are done they are wrong; for in general there is neither a mean of excess and deficiency, nor excess and deficiency of a mean.

7. [*The particular virtues.*] We must, however, not only make this general statement, but also apply it to the individual facts. For among statements about conduct those which are general apply more widely, but those which are particular are more genuine, since conduct has to do with individual cases, and our statements must harmonize with the facts in these cases. We may take these cases from our table. With regard to feelings of fear and confidence courage is the mean; of the people who exceed, he who exceeds in fearlessness has no name (many of the states have no name), while the man who exceeds in confidence is rash, and he who exceeds in fear and falls short in confidence is a coward. With regard to pleasures and pains—not all of them, and not so much with regard to the pains—the mean is temperance, the excess self-indulgence. Persons deficient with regard to the pleasures are not often found; hence such persons also have received no name. But let us call them "insensible."

With regard to giving and taking of money the mean is liberality, the excess and the defect prodigality and meanness. In these actions people exceed and fall short in contrary ways; the prodigal exceeds in spending and falls short in taking, while the mean man exceeds in taking and falls short in spending. (At present we are giving a mere outline or summary, and are satisfied with this; later these states will be more exactly determined.) With regard to money there are also other dispositions—a mean, magnificence (for the magnificent man differs from the liberal man; the former deals with large sums, the latter with small ones), an excess, tastelessness and vulgarity, and a deficiency, niggardliness; these differ from the states opposed to liberality, and the mode of their difference will be stated later.

With regard to honour and dishonour the mean is proper pride, the excess is known as a sort of "empty vanity," and the deficiency is undue humility; and as we said liberality was related to magnificence, differing from it by dealing with small sums, so there is a state similarly related to proper pride, being concerned with small honours while that is concerned with great. For it is possible to desire honour as one ought, and more than one ought, and less, and the man who exceeds in his desires is called ambitious, the man who falls short unambitious, while the intermediate person has no name. The dispositions also are nameless, except that that of the ambitious man is called ambition. Hence the people who are at the extremes lay claim to the middle place; and we ourselves sometimes call the intermediate person ambitious and sometimes unambitious, and sometimes praise the ambitious man and sometimes the unambitious. The reason of our doing this will be stated in what follows; but now let us speak of the remaining states according to the method which has been indicated.

With regard to anger also there is an excess, a deficiency, and a mean. Although they can scarcely be said to have names, yet since we call the intermediate person good-tempered let us call the mean good temper; of the persons at the extremes let the one who exceeds be called irascible, and his vice irascibility, and the man who falls short an inirascible sort of person, and the deficiency inirascibility.

There are also three other means, which have a certain

likeness to one another, but differ from one another; for they are all concerned with intercourse in words and actions, but differ in that one is concerned with truth in this sphere, the other two with pleasantness; and of this one kind is exhibited in giving amusement, the other in all the circumstances of life. We must therefore speak of these too, that we may the better see that in all things the mean is praiseworthy, and the extremes neither praiseworthy nor right, but worthy of blame. Now most of these states also have no names, but we must try, as in the other cases, to invent names ourselves so that we may be clear and easy to follow. With regard to truth, then, the intermediate is a truthful sort of person and the mean may be called truthfulness, while the pretence which exaggerates is boastfulness and the person character- ized by it a boaster, and that which understates is mock mod- esty and the person characterized by it mock-modest. With regard to pleasantness in the giving of amusement the inter- mediate person is ready-witted and the disposition ready wit, the excess is buffoonery and the person characterized by it a buffoon, while the man who falls short is a sort of boor and his state is boorishness. With regard to the remaining kind of pleasantness, that which is exhibited in life in general, the man who is pleasant in the right way is friendly and the mean is friendliness, while the man who exceeds is an ob- sequious person if he has no end in view, a flatterer if he is aiming at his own advantage, and the man who falls short and is unpleasant in all circumstances is a quarrelsome and surly sort of person.

There are also means in the passions and concerned with the passions; since shame is not a virtue, and yet praise is extended to the modest man. For even in these matters one man is said to be intermediate, and another to exceed, as for instance the bashful man who is ashamed of everything; while he who falls short or is not ashamed of anything at all is shameless, and the intermediate person is modest. Right- eous indignation is a mean between envy and spite, and these states are concerned with the pain and pleasures that are felt at the fortunes of our neighbours; the man who is characterized by righteous indignation is pained at undeserved good fortune, the envious man, going beyond him, is pained at all good fortune, and the spiteful man falls so far short of being pained that he even rejoices. But these states there will be an opportunity of describing elsewhere; with regard to justice, since it has not one simple meaning, we shall, after describing the other states, distinguish its two kinds and say how each of them is a mean; and similarly we shall treat also of the rational virtues.

8. [*The extremes are opposed to each other and to the mean.*] There are three kinds of disposition, then, two of them vices, involving excess and deficiency respectively, and one a virtue, viz., the mean, and all are in a sense opposed to all; for the extreme states are contrary both to the intermediate state and to each other, and the intermediate to the extremes; as the equal is greater relatively to the less, less relatively to the greater, so the middle states are excessive relatively to the deficiencies, deficient relatively to the excesses, both in passions and in actions. For the brave man appears rash relatively to the coward, and cowardly relatively to the rash man; and similarly the temperate man appears self-indulgent relatively to the insensible man, insensible relatively to the self-indulgent, and the liberal man prodigal relatively to the mean man, mean relatively to the prodigal. Hence also the people at the extremes push the intermediate man each over to the other, and the brave man is called rash by the coward, cowardly by the rash man, and correspondingly in the other cases.

These states being thus opposed to one another, the greatest contrariety is that of the extremes to each other, rather than to the intermediate; for these are further from each other than from the intermediate, as the great is further from the small and the small from the great than both are from the equal. Again, to the intermediate some extremes show a certain likeness, as that of rashness to courage and that of prodigality to liberality; but the extremes show the greatest unlikeness to each other; now contraries are defined as the things that are furthest from each other, so that things that are further apart are more contrary.

To the mean in some cases the deficiency, in some the excess is more opposed; e. g., it is not rashness, which is an excess, but cowardice, which is a deficiency, that is more opposed to courage, and not insensibility, which is a deficiency, but self-indulgence, which is an excess, that is more opposed to temperance. This happens from two reasons, one being drawn from the thing itself; for because one extreme is nearer and liker to the intermediate, we oppose not this but rather its contrary to the intermediate. E. g., since rashness is thought liker and nearer to courage, and cowardice more unlike, we oppose rather the latter to courage; for things that are further from the intermediate are thought more contrary to it. This, then, is one cause, drawn from the thing itself; another is drawn from ourselves; for the things to which we ourselves more naturally tend seem more contrary to the intermediate. For instance, we ourselves tend more naturally to pleasures, and hence are more easily carried away towards self-indulgence than towards propriety. We describe as contrary to the mean, then, rather the directions in which we more often go to great lengths; and therefore self-indulgence, which is an excess, is the more contrary to temperance.

9. [*The mean is hard to attain.*] That moral virtue is a mean, then, and in what sense it is so, and that it is a mean between two vices, the one involving excess, the other deficiency, and that it is such because its character is to aim at what is intermediate in passions and in actions, has been sufficiently stated. Hence also it is no easy task to be good. For in everything it is no easy task to find the middle, e. g., to find the middle of a circle is not for every one but for him who knows; so, too, any one can get angry—that is easy— or give or spend money; but to do this to the right person, to the right extent, at the right time, with the right motive, and in the right way, *that* is not for every one, nor is it easy; wherefore goodness is both rare and laudable and noble.

Hence he who aims at the intermediate must first depart from what is the more contrary to it, as Calypso advises—

Hold the ship out beyond that surf and spray.

For of the extremes one is more erroneous, one less so; therefore, since to hit the mean is hard in the extreme, we must as a second best, as people say, take the least of the evils; and this will be done best in the way we describe.

But we must consider the things towards which we ourselves also are easily carried away; for some of us tend to one thing, some to another; and this will be recognizable from the pleasure and the pain we feel. We must drag ourselves away to the contrary extreme; for we shall get into the intermediate state by drawing well away from error, as people do in straightening sticks that are bent.

Now in everything the pleasant or pleasure is most to be guarded against; for we do not judge it impartially. We ought, then, to feel towards pleasure as the elders of the people felt towards Helen, and in all circumstances repeat their saying; for if we dismiss pleasure thus we are less likely to go astray. It is by doing this, then (to sum the matter up), that we shall best be able to hit the mean.

But this is no doubt difficult, and especially in individual cases; for it is not easy to determine both how and with whom and on what provocation and how long one should be angry; for we too sometimes praise those who fall short and call them good-tempered, but sometimes we praise those who get angry and call them manly. The man, however, who deviates little from goodness is not blamed, whether he do so in the direction of the more or of the less, but only the man who deviates more widely; for *he* does not fail to be noticed. But up to what point and to what extent a man must deviate before he becomes blameworthy it is not easy to determine by reasoning, any more than anything else that is perceived by the senses; such things depend on particular facts, and the decision rests with perception. So much, then, is plain, that the intermediate state is in all things to be praised, but that we must incline sometimes towards the excess, sometimes towards the deficiency; for so shall we most easily hit the mean and what is right.

BOOK III

1. [*Praise and blame attach to voluntary actions.*] Since virtue is concerned with passions and actions, and on voluntary passions and actions praise and blame are bestowed, on those that are involuntary pardon, and sometimes also pity, to distinguish the voluntary and the involuntary is presumably necessary for those who are studying the nature of virtue, and useful also for legislators with a view to the assigning both of honours and of punishments.

Those things, then, are thought involuntary, which take place under compulsion or owing to ignorance; and that is compulsory of which the moving principle is outside, being a principle in which nothing is contributed by the person who is acting or is feeling the passion, e. g., if he were to be carried somewhere by a wind, or by men who had him in their power.

But with regard to the things that are done from fear of greater evils or for some noble object (e. g., if a tyrant were to order one to do something base, having one's parents and children in his power, and if one did the action they were to be saved, but otherwise would be put to death), it may be debated whether such actions are involuntary or voluntary. Something of the sort happens also with regard to the throwing of goods overboard in a storm; for in the abstract no one throws goods away voluntarily, but on condition of its securing the safety of himself and his crew any sensible man does so. Such actions, then, are mixed, but are more like voluntary actions; for they are worthy of choice at the time when they are done, and the end of an action is relative to the occasion. Both the terms, then, "voluntary" and "involuntary," must be used with reference to the moment of action. Now the man acts voluntarily; for the principle that moves the instrumental parts of the body in such actions is in him, and the things of which the moving principle is in a man himself are in his power to do or not to do. Such actions, therefore, are voluntary, but in the abstract perhaps involuntary; for no one would choose any such act in itself.

For such actions men are sometimes even praised, when they endure something base or painful in return for great and noble objects gained; in the opposite case they are blamed, since to endure the greatest indignities for no noble end or for a trifling end is the mark of an inferior person. On some actions praise indeed is not bestowed, but pardon is, when one does what he ought not under pressure which overstrains human nature and which no one could withstand. But some acts, perhaps, we cannot be forced to do, but ought rather to face death after the most fearful sufferings; for the things that "forced" Euripides' Alcmaeon to slay his mother seem absurd. It is difficult sometimes to determine what should be chosen at what cost, and what should be endured in return for what gain, and yet more difficult to abide by our decisions; for as a rule what is expected is painful, and what we are forced to do is base, whence praise and blame are bestowed on those who have been compelled or have not.

What sort of acts, then, should be called compulsory? We answer that without qualification actions are so when the cause is in the external circumstances and the agent contributes nothing. But the things that in themselves are involuntary, but now and in return for these gains are worthy of choice, and whose moving principle is in the agent, are in themselves involuntary, but now and in return for these gains voluntary. They are more like voluntary acts; for actions are in the class of particulars, and the particular acts here are voluntary. What sort of things are to be chosen, and in return for what, it is not easy to state; for there are many differences in the particular cases.

But if some one were to say that pleasant and noble objects have a compelling power, forcing us from without, all acts would be for him compulsory; for it is for these objects that all men do everything they do. And those who act under compulsion and unwillingly act with pain, but those who do acts for their pleasantness and nobility do them with pleasure; it is absurd to make external circumstances responsible, and not oneself, as being easily caught by such attractions, and to make oneself responsible for noble acts but the pleasant objects responsible for base acts. The compulsory, then, seems to be that whose moving principle is outside, the person compelled contributing nothing.

Everything that is done by reason of ignorance is *not* voluntary; it is only what produces pain and repentance that is *in*voluntary. For the man who has done something owing to ignorance, and feels not the least vexation at his action, has not acted voluntarily, since he did not know what he was doing, nor yet involuntarily, since he is not pained. Of people, then, who act by reason of ignorance he who repents is thought an involuntary agent, and the man who does not repent may, since he is different, be called a not voluntary agent; for, since he differs from the other, it is better that he should have a name of his own.

Acting by reason of ignorance seems also to be different from acting *in* ignorance; for the man who is drunk or in a rage is thought to act as a result not of ignorance but of one of the causes mentioned, yet not knowingly but in ignorance.

Now every wicked man is ignorant of what he ought to do and what he ought to abstain from, and it is by reason of error of this kind that men become unjust and in general bad; but the term "involuntary" tends to be used not if a man is ignorant of what is to his advantage—for it is not mistaken purpose that causes involuntary action (it leads rather to wickedness), nor ignorance of the universal (for *that* men are *blamed*), but ignorance of particulars, i. e., of the circumstances of the action and the objects with which it is concerned. For it is on these that both pity and pardon depend, since the person who is ignorant of any of these acts involuntarily.

Perhaps it is just as well, therefore, to determine their nature and number. A man may be ignorant, then, of who he is, what he is doing, what or whom he is acting on, and sometimes also what (e. g., what instrument) he is doing it with, and to what end (e. g., he may think his act will conduce to some one's safety), and how he is doing it (e. g., whether gently or violently). Now of all of these no one could be ignorant unless he were mad, and evidently also he could not be ignorant of the agent; for how could he not know himself? But of what he is doing a man might be ignorant, as for instance people say "it slipped out of their mouths as they were speaking," or "they did not know it was a secret," as Aeschylus said of the mysteries, or a man might say he "let it go off when he merely wanted to show its working," as the man did with the catapult. Again, one might think one's son was an enemy, as Merope did, or that a pointed spear had a button on it, or that a stone was pumice stone; or one might give a man a draught to save him, and really kill him; or one might want to touch a man, as people do in sparring, and really wound him. The ignorance may relate, then, to any of these things, i.e., of the circumstances of the action, and the man who was ignorant of any of these is thought to have acted involuntarily, and especially if he was ignorant on the most important points; and these are thought to be the circumstances of the action and its end. Further, the doing of an act that is called involuntary in virtue of ignorance of this sort must be painful and involve repentance.

Since that which is done under compulsion or by reason of ignorance is involuntary, the voluntary would seem to be that of which the moving principle is in the agent himself, he being aware of the particular circumstances of the action. Presumably acts done by reason of anger or appetite are not rightly called involuntary. For in the first place, on that showing none of the other animals will act voluntarily, nor will children; and secondly, is it meant that we do not do voluntarily *any* of the acts that are due to appetite or anger, or that we do the noble acts voluntarily and the base acts involuntarily? Is not this absurd, when one and the same thing is the cause? But it would surely be odd to describe as involuntary the things one ought to desire; and we ought both to be angry at certain things and to have an appetite for certain things, e. g., for health and for learning. Also what is involuntary is thought to be painful, but what is in accordance with appetite is thought to be pleasant. Again, what is the difference in respect of involuntariness between errors committed upon calculation and those committed in anger? Both are to be avoided, but the irrational passions are thought not less human than reason is, and therefore also the actions which proceed from anger or appetite are the man's actions. It would be odd, then, to treat them as involuntary.

2. [*Moral virtue implies that the action is done by choice.*] Both the voluntary and the involuntary having been delimited, we must next discuss choice; for it is thought to be most closely bound up with virtue and to discriminate characters better than actions do.

Choice, then, seems to be voluntary, but not the same thing as the voluntary; the latter extends more widely. For both children and the lower animals share in voluntary action, but not in choice, and acts done on the spur of the moment we describe as voluntary, but not as chosen.

Those who say it is appetite or anger or wish or a kind of opinion do not seem to be right. For choice is not common to irrational creatures as well, but appetite and anger are. Again, the incontinent man acts with appetite, but not with choice; while the continent man on the contrary acts with choice, but not with appetite. Again, appetite is contrary to choice, but not appetite to appetite. Again, appetite relates to the pleasant and the painful, choice neither to the painful nor to the pleasant.

Still less is it anger; for acts due to anger are thought to be less than any others objects of choice.

But neither is it wish, though it seems near to it; for choice cannot relate to impossibles, and if any one said he chose them he would be thought silly; but there may be a wish even for impossibles, e. g., for immortality. And wish may relate to things that could in no way be brought about by one's own efforts, e. g., that a particular actor or athlete should win in a competition; but no one chooses such things, but only the things that he thinks could be brought about by his own efforts. Again, wish relates rather to the end, choice to the means; for instance, we wish to be healthy, but we choose the acts which will make us healthy, and we wish to be happy and say we do, but we cannot well say we choose to be so; for, in general, choice seems to relate to the things that are in our own power.

For this reason, too, it cannot be opinion; for opinion is thought to relate to all kinds of things, no less to eternal things and impossible things than to things in our own power; and it is distinguished by its falsity or truth, not by its badness or goodness, while choice is distinguished rather by these.

Now with opinion in general perhaps no one even says it is identical. But it is not identical even with any kind of opinion; for by choosing what is good or bad we are men of a certain character, which we are not by holding certain opinions. And we choose to get or avoid something good or bad, but we have opinions about what a thing is or whom it is good for or how it is good for him; we can hardly be said to opine to get or avoid anything. And choice is praised for being related to the right object rather than for being rightly related to it, opinion for being truly related to its object. And we choose what we best know to be good, but we opine what we do not quite know; and it is not the same people that are thought to make the best choices and to have the best opinions, but some are thought to have fairly good opinions, but by reason of vice to choose what they should not. If opinion precedes choice or accompanies it, that makes no difference;

for it is not this that we are considering, but whether it is *identical* with some kind of opinion.

What, then, or what kind of thing is it, since it is none of the things we have mentioned? It seems to be voluntary, but not all that is voluntary to be an object of choice. Is it, then, what has been decided on by previous deliberation? At any rate choice involves a rational principle and thought. Even the name seems to suggest that it is what is chosen before other things.

3. [*The nature of deliberation and its objects.*] Do we deliberate about everything, and is everything a possible subject of deliberation, or is deliberation impossible about some things? We ought presumably to call not what a fool or a madman would deliberate about, but what a sensible man would deliberate about, a subject of deliberation. Now about eternal things no one deliberates, e. g., about the material universe or the incommensurability of the diagonal and the side of a square. But no more do we deliberate about the things that involve movement but always happen in the same way, whether of necessity or by nature or from any other cause, e. g., the solstices and the risings of the stars; nor about things that happen now in one way, now in another, e. g., droughts and rains; nor about chance events, like the finding of treasure. But we do not deliberate even about all human affairs; for instance, no Spartan deliberates about the best constitution for the Scythians. For none of these things can be brought about by our own efforts.

We deliberate about things that are in our power and can be done; and these are in fact what is left. For nature, necessity, and chance are thought to be causes, and also reason and everything that depends on man. Now every class of men deliberates about the things that can be done by their own efforts. And in the case of exact and self-contained science there is no deliberation, e. g., about the letters of the alphabet (for we have no doubt how they should be written); but the things that are brought about by our own efforts, but not always in the same way, are the things about which we deliberate, e. g., questions of medical treatment or of money-making. And we do so more in the case of the art of navigation than in that of gymnastics, inasmuch as it has been less exactly worked out, and again about other things in the same ratio, and more also in the case of the arts than in that of the sciences; for we have more doubt about the former. Deliberation is concerned with things that happen in a certain way for the most part, but in which the event is obscure, and with things in which it is indeterminate. We call in others to aid us in deliberation on important questions, distrusting ourselves as not being equal to deciding.

We deliberate not about ends but about means. For a doctor does not deliberate whether he shall heal, nor an orator whether he shall persuade, nor a statesman whether he shall produce law and order, nor does any one else deliberate about his end. They assume the end and consider how and by what means it is to be attained; and if it seems to be produced by several means they consider by which it is most easily and best produced, while if it is achieved by one only they consider how it will be achieved by this and by what means *this* will be achieved, till they come to the first cause, which in the order of discovery is last. For the person who deliberates seems to investigate and analyse in the way described as though he were analysing a geometrical construction (not all investigation appears to be deliberation—for instance mathematical investigations—but all deliberation is investigation), and what is last in the order of analysis seems to be first in the order of becoming. And if we come on an impossibility, we give up the search, e. g., if we need money and this cannot be got; but if a thing appears possible we try to do it. By "possible" things I mean things that might be brought about by our own efforts; and these in a sense include things that can be brought about by the efforts of our friends, since the moving principle is in ourselves. The subject of investigation is sometimes the instruments, sometimes the use of them; and similarly in the other cases—sometimes the means, sometimes the mode of using it or the means of bringing it about. It seems, then, as has been said, that man is a moving principle of actions; now deliberation is about the things to be done by the agent himself, and actions are for the sake of things other than themselves. For the end cannot be a subject of deliberation, but only the means; nor indeed can the particular facts be a subject of it, as whether this is bread or has been baked as it should; for these are matters of perception. If we are to be always deliberating, we shall have to go on to infinity.

The same thing is deliberated upon and is chosen, except that the object of choice is already determinate, since it is that which has been decided upon as a result of deliberation that is the object of choice. For every one ceases to inquire how he is to act when he has brought the moving principle back to himself and to the ruling part of himself; for this is what chooses. This is plain also from the ancient constitutions, which Homer represented; for the kings announced their choices to the people. The object of choice being one of the things in our own power which is desired after deliberation, choice will be deliberate desire of things in our own power; for when we have decided as a result of deliberation, we desire in accordance with our deliberation.

We may take it, then, that we have described choice in outline, and stated the nature of its objects and the fact that it is concerned with means.

4. [*The object of rational wish is the good or the apparent good.*] That *wish* is for the end has already been stated; some think it is for the good, others for the apparent good. Now those who say that the good is the object of wish must admit in consequence that that which the man who does not choose aright wishes for is not an object of wish (for if it is to be so, it must also be good; but it was, if it so happened, bad); while those who say the apparent good is the object of wish must admit that there is no natural object of wish, but only what seems good to each man. Now different things appear good to different people, and, if it so happens, even contrary things.

If these consequences are unpleasing, are we to say that absolutely and in truth the good is the object of wish, but for each person the apparent good; that that which is in truth an object of wish is an object of wish to the good man, while any chance thing may be so to the bad man, as in the case of bodies also the things that are in truth wholesome are wholesome for bodies which are in good condition, while for those that are diseased other things are wholesome—or bitter or sweet or hot or heavy, and so on; since the good man judges each class of things rightly, and in each the truth appears to him? For each state of character has its own ideas of the noble and the pleasant, and perhaps the good man differs from others most by seeing the truth in each class of things, being as it were the norm and measure of them. In most things the error seems to be due to pleasure; for it appears a good when it is not. We therefore choose the pleasant as a good, and avoid pain as an evil.

5. [*We are responsible for bad as well as for good actions.*] The end, then, being what we wish for, the means what we deliberate about and choose, actions concerning means must be according to choice and voluntary. Now the exercise of the virtues is concerned with means. Therefore virtue also is in our own power, and so too vice. For where it is in our power to act it is also in our power not to act, and *vice versa;* so that, if to act, where this is noble, is in our power, not to act, which will be base, will also be in our power, and if not to act, where this is noble, is in our power, to act, which will be base, will also be in our power. Now if it is in our power to do noble or base acts, and likewise in our power not to do them, and this was what being good or bad meant, then it is in our power to be virtuous or vicious.

The saying that "no one is voluntarily wicked nor involuntarily happy" seems to be partly false and partly true; for no one is involuntarily happy, but wickedness *is* voluntary. Or else we shall have to dispute what has just been said, at any rate, and deny that man is a moving principle or begetter of his actions as of children. But if these facts are evident and we cannot refer actions to moving principles other than those in ourselves, the acts whose moving principles are in us must themselves also be in our power and voluntary.

Witness seems to be borne to this both by individuals in their private capacity and by legislators themselves; for these punish and take vengeance on those who do wicked acts (unless they have acted under compulsion or as a result of ignorance for which they are not themselves responsible), while they honour those who do noble acts, as though they meant to encourage the latter and deter the former. But no one is encouraged to do the things that are neither in our power nor voluntary; it is assumed that there is no gain in being persuaded not to be hot or in pain or hungry or the like, since we shall experience these feelings none the less. Indeed, we punish a man for his very ignorance, if he is thought responsible for the ignorance, as when penalties are doubled in the case of drunkenness; for the moving principle is in the man himself, since he had the power of not getting drunk and his getting drunk was the cause of his ignorance. And we punish those who are ignorant of anything in the laws that they ought to know and that is not difficult, and so too in the case of anything else that they are thought to be ignorant of through carelessness; we assume that it is in their power not to be ignorant, since they have the power of taking care.

But perhaps a man is the kind of man not to take care. Still they are themselves by their slack lives responsible for becoming men of that kind, and men make themselves responsible for being unjust or self-indulgent, in the one case by cheating and in the other by spending their time in drinking bouts and the like; for it is activities exercised on particular objects that make the corresponding character. This is plain from the case of people training for any contest or action; they practise the activity the whole time. Now not to know that it is from the exercise of activities on particular objects that states of character are produced is the mark of a thoroughly senseless person. Again, it is irrational to suppose that a man who acts unjustly does not wish to be unjust or a man who acts self-indulgently to be self-indulgent. But if *without* being ignorant a man does the things which will make him unjust, he will be unjust voluntarily. Yet it does not follow that if he wishes he will cease to be unjust and will be just. For neither does the man who is ill become well on those terms. We may suppose a case in which he is ill voluntarily, through living incontinently and disobeying his doctors. In that case it was *then* open to him not to be ill, but not now, when he has thrown away his chance, just as when you have let a stone go it is too late to recover it; but yet it was in your power to throw it, since the moving principle was in you. So, too, to the unjust and to the self-indulgent man it was open at the beginning not to become men of this kind, and so they are unjust and self-indulgent voluntarily; but now that they have become so it is not possible for them not to be so.

But not only are the vices of the soul voluntary, but those of the body also for some men, whom we accordingly blame; while no one blames those who are ugly by nature, we blame those who are so owing to want of exercise and care. So it is, too, with respect to weakness and infirmity; no one would reproach a man blind from birth or by disease or from a blow, but rather pity him, while every one would blame a man who was blind from drunkenness or some other form of self-indulgence. Of vices of the body, then, those in our own power are blamed, those not in our power are not. And if this be so, in the other cases also the vices that are blamed must be in our own power.

Now some one may say that all men desire the apparent good, but have no control over the appearance, but the end appears to each man in a form answering to his character. We reply that if each man is somehow responsible for his state of mind, he will also be himself somehow responsible for the appearance; but if not, no one is responsible for his own evildoing, but every one does evil acts through ignorance of the end, thinking that by these he will get what is best, and the aiming at the end is not self-chosen but one must be born with an eye, as it were, by which to judge rightly and choose what is truly good, and he is well endowed by nature who is well endowed with this. For it is what is greatest and most noble, and what we cannot get or learn from another, but must have just such as it was when given us at birth, and to be well and nobly endowed with this will be perfect and true excellence of natural endowment. If this is true, then, how will virtue be more voluntary than vice? To both men alike, the good and the bad, the end appears and is fixed by nature or however it may be, and it is by referring everything else to this that men do whatever they do.

Whether, then, it is not by nature that the end appears to each man such as it does appear, but something also depends on him, or the end is natural but because the good man adopts the means voluntarily virtue is voluntary, vice also will be none the less voluntary; for in the case of the bad man there is equally present that which depends on himself in his actions even if not in his end. If, then, as is asserted, the virtues are voluntary (for we are ourselves somehow partly responsible for our states of character, and it is by being persons of a certain kind that we assume the end to be so and so), the vices also will be voluntary; for the same is true of them.

With regard to the virtues in *general* we have stated their genus in outline, viz., that they are means and that they are states of character, and that they tend, and by their own nature, to the doing of the acts by which they are produced, and that they are in our power and voluntary, and act as the right rule prescribes. But actions and states of character are not voluntary in the same way; for we are masters of our actions from the beginning right to the end, if we know the particular facts, but though we control the beginning of our states of character the gradual progress is not obvious, any more than it is in illnesses; because it was in our power, however, to act in this way or not in this way, therefore the states are voluntary.

* * *

BOOK IV

1. [*Liberality, prodigality, meanness.*] Let us speak next of liberality. It seems to be the mean with regard to wealth; for the liberal man is praised not in respect of military matters, nor of those in respect of which the temperate man is praised, nor of judicial decisions, but with regard to the giving and taking of wealth, and especially in respect of giving. Now by "wealth" we mean all the things whose value is measured by money. Further, prodigality and meanness are excesses and defects with regard to wealth; and meanness we always impute to those who care more than they ought for wealth, but we sometimes apply the word "prodigality" in a complex sense; for we call those men prodigals who are incontinent and spend money on self-indulgence. Hence also they are thought the poorest characters; for they combine more vices than one. Therefore the application of the word to them is not its proper use; for a "prodigal" means a man who has a single evil quality, that of wasting his substance; since a prodigal is one who is being ruined by his own fault, and the wasting of substance is thought to be a sort of ruining of oneself, life being held to depend on possession of substance.

This, then, is the sense in which we take the word "prodigality." Now the things that have a use may be used either well or badly; and riches is a useful thing; and everything is used best by the man who has the virtue concerned with it; riches, therefore, will be used best by the man who has the virtue concerned with wealth; and this is the liberal man. Now spending and giving seem to be the using of wealth; taking and keeping rather the possession of it. Hence it is more the mark of the liberal man to give to the right people than to take from the right sources and not to take from the wrong. For it is more characteristic of virtue to do good than to have good done to one, and more characteristic to do what is noble than not to do what is base; and it is not hard to see that giving implies doing good and doing what is noble, and taking implies having good done to one or not acting basely. And gratitude is felt towards him who gives, not towards him who does not take, and praise also is bestowed more on him. It is easier, also, not to take than to give; for men are apter to give away their own too little than to take what is another's. Givers, too, are called liberal; but those who do not take are not praised for liberality but rather for justice; while those who take are hardly praised at all. And the liberal are almost the most loved of all virtuous characters, since they are useful; and this depends on their giving.

Now virtuous actions are noble and done for the sake of the noble. Therefore the liberal man, like other virtuous men, will give for the sake of the noble, and rightly; for he will give to the right people, the right amounts, and at the right time, with all the other qualifications that accompany right giving; and that too with pleasure or without pain; for that which is virtuous is pleasant or free from pain—least of all will it be painful. But he who gives to the wrong people or not for the sake of the noble but for some other cause, will be called not liberal but by some other name. Nor is he liberal who gives with pain; for he would prefer the wealth to the noble act, and this is not characteristic of a liberal man. But no more will the liberal man take from wrong sources; for such taking is not characteristic of the man who sets no store by wealth. Nor will he be a ready asker; for it is not characteristic of a man who confers benefits to accept them lightly. But he will take from the right sources, e. g., from his own possessions, not as something noble but as a necessity, that he may have something to give. Nor will he neglect his own property, since he wishes by means of this to help others. And he will refrain from giving to anybody and everybody, that he may have something to give to the right people, at the right time, and where it is noble to do so. It is highly characteristic of a liberal man also to go to excess in giving, so that he leaves too little for himself; for it is the nature of a liberal man not to look to himself. The term "liberality" is used relatively to a man's substance; for liberality resides not in the multitude of the gifts but in the state of character of the giver, and this is relative to the giver's substance. There is therefore nothing to prevent the man who gives less from being the more liberal man, if he has less to give. Those are thought to be more liberal who have not made their wealth but inherited it; for in the first place they have no experience of want, and secondly all men are fonder of their own productions, as are parents and poets. It is not easy for the liberal man to be rich, since he is not apt either at taking or at keeping, but at giving away, and does not value wealth for its own sake but as a means to giving. Hence comes the charge that is brought against fortune, that those who deserve riches most get it least. But it is not unreasonable that it should turn out so; for he cannot have wealth, any more than anything else, if he does not take pains to have it. Yet he will not give to the wrong people nor at the wrong time, and so on; for he would no longer be acting in accordance with liberality, and if he spent on these objects he would have nothing to spend on the right objects. For, as has been said, he is liberal who spends according to his substance and on the right objects; and he who exceeds is prodigal. Hence we do not call despots prodigal; for it is thought not easy for them to give and spend beyond the amount of their possessions. Liberality, then, being a mean with regard to giving and taking of wealth, the liberal man will both give and spend the right amounts and on the right objects, alike in small things and in great, and that with pleasure; he will also take the right amounts and from the right sources. For, the virtue being a mean with regard to both, he will do both as he ought; since this sort of taking accompanies proper giving, and that which is not of this sort is contrary to it, and accordingly the giving and taking that accompany each other are present together in the same man, while the contrary kinds evidently are not. But if he happens to spend in a manner contrary to what is right and noble, he will be pained, but moderately and as he ought; for it is the mark of virtue both to be pleased and to be pained at the right objects and in the right way. Further, the liberal man is easy to deal with in money matters; for he can be got the better of, since he sets no store by money, and is more annoyed if he has not spent something that he ought than pained if he has spent something that he ought not, and does not agree with the saying of Simonides.

The prodigal errs in these respects also; for he is neither pleased nor pained at the right things or in the right way; this will be more evident as we go on. We have said that prodigality and meanness are excesses and deficiencies, and in two things, in giving and in taking; for we include spending under giving. Now prodigality exceeds in giving and not taking, and falls short in taking, while meanness falls short in giving, and exceeds in taking, except in small things.

The characteristics of prodigality are not often combined; for it is not easy to give to all if you take from none; private persons soon exhaust their substance with giving, and it is to these that the name of prodigals is applied—though a man of this sort would seem to be in no small degree better than a mean man. For he is easily cured both by age and by poverty, and thus he may move towards the middle state. For he has the characteristics of the liberal man, since he both gives and refrains from taking, though he does neither of these in the right manner or well. Therefore if he were brought to do so by habituation or in some other way, he would be liberal; for he will then give to the right people, and will not take from the wrong sources. This is why he is thought to have not a bad character; it is not the mark of a wicked or ignoble man to go to excess in giving and not taking, but only of a foolish one. The man who is prodigal in this way is thought much better than the mean man both for the aforesaid reasons and because he benefits many while the other benefits no one, not even himself.

But most prodigal people, as has been said, also take from

the wrong sources, and are in this respect mean. They become apt to take because they wish to spend and cannot do this easily; for their possessions soon run short. Thus they are forced to provide means from some other source. At the same time, because they care nothing for honour, they take recklessly and from any source; for they have an appetite for giving, and they do not mind how or from what source. Hence also their giving is not liberal; for it is not noble, nor does it aim at nobility, nor is it done in the right way; sometimes they make rich those who should be poor, and will give nothing to people of respectable character, and much to flatterers or those who provide them with some other pleasure. Hence also most of them are self-indulgent; for they spend lightly and waste money on their indulgences, and incline towards pleasures because they do not live with a view to what is noble.

The prodigal man, then, turns into what we have described if he is left untutored, but if he is treated with care he will arrive at the intermediate and right state. But meanness is both incurable (for old age and every disability is thought to make men mean) and more innate in men than prodigality; for most men are fonder of getting money than of giving. It also extends widely, and is multiform, since there seem to be many kinds of meanness.

For it consists in two things, deficiency in giving and excess in taking, and is not found complete in all men but is sometimes divided; some men go to excess in taking, others fall short in giving. Those who are called by such names as "miserly," "close," "stingy," all fall short in giving, but do not covet the possessions of others nor wish to get them. In some this is due to a sort of honesty and avoidance of what is disgraceful (for some seem, or at least profess, to hoard their money for this reason, that they may not some day be forced to do something disgraceful; to this class belong the cheeseparer and every one of the sort; he is so called from his excess of unwillingness to give anything); while others again keep their hands off the property of others from fear, on the ground that it is not easy, if one takes the property of

others oneself, to avoid having one's own taken by them; they
are therefore content neither to take nor to give.

Others again exceed in respect of taking by taking anything and from any source, e. g., those who ply sordid trades,
pimps and all such people, and those who lend small sums
and at high rates. For all of these take more than they ought
and from wrong sources. What is common to them is evidently sordid love of gain; they all put up with a bad name
for the sake of gain, and little gain at that. For those who
make great gains but from wrong sources, and not the right
gains, e. g., despots when they sack cities and spoil temples,
we do not call mean but rather wicked, impious, and unjust.
But the gamester and the footpad [and the highwayman]
belong to the class of the mean, since they have a sordid love
of gain. For it is for gain that both of them ply their craft
and endure the disgrace of it, and the one faces the greatest
dangers for the sake of the booty, while the other makes
gain from his friends, to whom he ought to be giving. Both,
then, since they are willing to make gain from wrong sources,
are sordid lovers of gain; therefore all such forms of taking
are mean.

And it is natural that meanness is described as the contrary
of liberality; for not only is it a greater evil than prodigality,
but men err more often in this direction than in the way of
prodigality as we have described it.

So much, then, for liberality and the opposed vices.

2. [*Magnificence, vulgarity, niggardliness.*] It would seem
proper to discuss magnificence next. For this also seems to
be a virtue concerned with wealth; but it does not like liberality extend to all the actions that are concerned with wealth,
but only to those that involve expenditure; and in these it
surpasses liberality in scale. For, as the name itself suggests,
it is a fitting expenditure involving largeness of scale. But the
scale is relative; for the expense of equipping a trireme is
not the same as that of heading a sacred embassy. It is what
is fitting, then, in relation to the agent, and to the circumstances and the object. The man who in small or middling

things spends according to the merits of the case is not called magnificent (e. g., the man who can say "many a gift I gave the wanderer"), but only the man who does so in great things. For the magnificent man is liberal, but the liberal man is not necessarily magnificent. The deficiency of this state of character is called niggardliness, the excess vulgarity, lack of taste, and the like, which do not go to excess in the amount spent on right objects, but by showy expenditure in the wrong circumstances and the wrong manner; we shall speak of these vices later.

The magnificent man is like an artist; for he can see what is fitting and spend large sums tastefully. For, as we said at the beginning, a state of character is determined by its activities and by its objects. Now the expenses of the magnificent man are large and fitting. Such, therefore, are also his results; for thus there will be a great expenditure and one that is fitting to its result. Therefore the result should be worthy of the expense, and the expense should be worthy of the result, or should even exceed it. And the magnificent man will spend such sums for honour's sake; for this is common to the virtues. And further he will do so gladly and lavishly; for nice calculation is a niggardly thing. And he will consider how the result can be made most beautiful and most becoming rather than for how much it can be produced and how it can be produced most cheaply. It is necessary, then, that the magnificent man be also liberal. For the liberal man also will spend what he ought and as he ought; and it is in these matters that the greatness implied in the name of the magnificent man—his bigness, as it were—is manifested, since liberality is concerned with these matters; and at an equal expense he will produce a more magnificent work of art. For a possession and a work of art have not the same excellence. The most valuable possession is that which is worth most, e. g., gold, but the most valuable work of art is that which is great and beautiful (for the contemplation of such a work inspires admiration, and so does magnificence); and a work has an excellence—viz., magnificence—which involves magnitude. Magnificence is an attribute of expenditures of the kind which we call honourable, e. g., those connected with the gods—votive offerings, buildings, and sacrifices—and similarly with any form of religious worship, and all those that are proper objects of public-spirited ambition, as when people think they ought to equip a chorus or a trireme, or entertain the city, in a brilliant way. But in all cases, as has been said, we have regard to the agent as well and ask who he is and what means he has; for the expenditure should be worthy of his means, and suit not only the result but also the producer. Hence a poor man cannot be magnificent, since he has not the means with which to spend large sums fittingly; and he who tries is a fool, since he spends beyond what can be expected of him and what is proper, but it is *right* expenditure that is virtuous. But great expenditure is becoming to those who have suitable means to start with, acquired by their own efforts or from ancestors or connexions, and to people of high birth or reputation, and so on; for all these things bring with them greatness and prestige. Primarily, then, the magnificent man is of this sort, and magnificence is shown in expenditures of this sort, as has been said; for these are the greatest and most honourable. Of *private* occasions of expenditure the most suitable are those that take place once for all, e. g., a wedding or anything of the kind, or anything that interests the whole city or the people of position in it, and also the receiving of foreign guests and the sending of them on their way, and gifts and counter-gifts; for the magnificent man spends not on himself but on public objects, and gifts bear some resemblance to votive offerings. A magnificent man will also furnish his house suitably to his wealth (for even a house is a sort of public ornament), and will spend by preference on those works that are lasting (for these are the most beautiful), and on every class of things he will spend what is becoming; for the same things are not suitable for gods and for men, nor in a temple and in a tomb. And since each expenditure may be great of its kind, and what is most magnificent absolutely is great expenditure on a great object, but what is magnificent *here* is what is great in *these* circumstances, and greatness in the work differs from greatness in the expense (for the most beautiful ball or bottle is magnificent as a gift to a child, but the price of it is small and mean)—therefore it is characteristic of the magnificent man, whatever kind of result he is producing, to produce it magnificently (for such a result is not easily surpassed) and to make it worthy of the expenditure.

Such, then, is the magnificent man; the man who goes to excess and is vulgar exceeds, as has been said, by spending beyond what is right. For on small objects of expenditure he spends much and displays a tasteless showiness; e. g., he gives a club dinner on the scale of a wedding banquet, and when he provides the chorus for a comedy he brings them on to the stage in purple, as they do at Megara. And all such things he will do not for honour's sake but to show off his wealth, and because he thinks he is admired for these things, and where he ought to spend much he spends little and where little, much. The niggardly man on the other hand will fall short in everything, and after spending the greatest sums will spoil the beauty of the result for a trifle, and whatever he is doing he will hesitate and consider how he may spend least, and lament even that, and think he is doing everything on a bigger scale than he ought.

These states of character, then, are vices; yet they do not bring *disgrace* because they are neither harmful to one's neighbour nor very unseemly.

3. [*Pride, vanity, humility.*] Pride seems even from its name to be concerned with great things; what sort of great things, is the first question we must try to answer. It makes no difference whether we consider the state of character or the man characterized by it. Now the man is thought to be proud who thinks himself worthy of great things, being worthy of them; for he who does so beyond his deserts is a fool, but no virtuous man is foolish or silly. The proud man, then, is the man we have described. For he who is worthy of little and thinks himself worthy of little is temperate, but not proud; for pride implies greatness, as beauty implies a good-sized

body, and little people may be neat and well-proportioned but cannot be beautiful. On the other hand, he who thinks himself worthy of great things, being unworthy of them, is vain; though not every one who thinks himself worthy of more than he really is worthy of is vain. The man who thinks himself worthy of less than he is really worthy of is unduly humble, whether his deserts be great or moderate, or his deserts be small but his claims yet smaller. And the man whose deserts are great would seem *most* unduly humble; for what would he have done if they had been less? The proud man, then, is an extreme in respect of the greatness of his claims, but a mean in respect of the rightness of them; for he claims what is in accordance with his merits, while the others go to excess or fall short.

If, then, he deserves and claims great things, and above all the greatest things, he will be concerned with one thing in particular. Desert is relative to external goods; and the greatest of these, we should say, is that which we render to the gods, and which people of position most aim at, and which is the prize appointed for the noblest deeds; and this is honour; that is surely the greatest of external goods. Honours and dishonours, therefore, are the objects with respect to which the proud man is as he should be. And even apart from argument it is with honour that proud men appear to be concerned; for it is honour that they chiefly claim, but in accordance with their deserts. The unduly humble man falls short both in comparison with his own merits and in comparison with the proud man's claims. The vain man goes to excess in comparison with his own merits, but does not exceed the proud man's claims.

Now the proud man, since he deserves most, must be good in the highest degree; for the better man always deserves more, and the best man most. Therefore the truly proud man must be good. And greatness in every virtue would seem to be characteristic of a proud man. And it would be most unbecoming for a proud man to fly from danger, swinging his arms by his sides, or to wrong another; for to what end should he do disgraceful acts, he to whom nothing is great?

If we consider him point by point, we shall see the utter absurdity of a proud man who is not good. Nor, again, would he be worthy of honour if he were bad; for honour is the prize of virtue, and it is to the good that it is rendered. Pride, then, seems to be a sort of crown of the virtues; for it makes them greater, and it is not found without them. Therefore it is hard to be truly proud; for it is impossible without nobility and goodness of character. It is chiefly with honours and dishonours, then, that the proud man is concerned; and at honours that are great and conferred by good men he will be moderately pleased, thinking that he is coming by his own or even less than his own; for there can be no honour that is worthy of perfect virtue, yet he will at any rate accept it since they have nothing greater to bestow on him; but honour from casual people and on trifling grounds he will utterly despise, since it is not this that he deserves, and dishonour too, since in his case it cannot be just. In the first place, then, as has been said, the proud man is concerned with honours; yet he will also bear himself with moderation towards wealth and power and all good or evil fortune, whatever may befall him, and will be neither overjoyed by good fortune nor overpained by evil. For not even towards honour does he bear himself as if it were a very great thing. Power and wealth are desirable for the sake of honour (at least those who have them wish to get honour by means of them); and for him to whom even honour is a little thing the others must be so too. Hence proud men are thought to be disdainful.

The goods of fortune also are thought to contribute towards pride. For men who are well born are thought worthy of honour, and so are those who enjoy power or wealth; for they are in a superior position, and everything that has a superiority in something good is held in greater honour. Hence even such things make men prouder; for they are honoured by some for having them; but in truth the good man alone is to be honoured; he, however, who has both advantages is thought the more worthy of honour. But those who without virtue have such goods are neither justified in making great claims nor entitled to the name of "proud"; for these things imply perfect virtue. Disdainful and insolent, however, even those who have such goods become. For without virtue it is not easy to bear gracefully the goods of fortune; and, being unable to bear them, and thinking themselves superior to others, they despise others and themselves do what they please. They imitate the proud man without being like him, and this they do where they can; so they do not act virtuously, but they do despise others. For the proud man despises justly (since he thinks truly), but the many do so at random.

He does not run into trifling dangers, nor is he fond of danger, because he honours few things; but he will face great dangers, and when he is in danger he is unsparing of his life, knowing that there are conditions on which life is not worth having. And he is the sort of man to confer benefits, but he is ashamed of receiving them; for the one is the mark of a superior, the other of an inferior. And he is apt to confer greater benefits in return; for thus the original benefactor besides being paid will incur a debt to him, and will be the gainer by the transaction. They seem also to remember any service they have done, but not those they have received (for he who receives a service is inferior to him who has done it, but the proud man wishes to be superior), and to hear of the former with pleasure, of the latter with displeasure; this, it seems, is why Thetis did not mention to Zeus the services she had done him, and why the Spartans did not recount their services to the Athenians, but those they had received. It is a mark of the proud man also to ask for nothing or scarcely anything, but to give help readily, and to be dignified towards people who enjoy high position and good fortune, but unassuming towards those of the middle class; for it is a difficult and lofty thing to be superior to the former, but easy to be so to the latter, and a lofty bearing over the former is no mark of ill-breeding, but among humble people it is as vulgar as a display of strength against the weak. Again, it is characteristic of the proud man not to aim at the things commonly held in honour, or the things in which others excel; to be sluggish and to hold back except where great honour or a great work is at stake, and to be a man of few deeds, but of great and notable ones. He must also be open in his hate and in his love (for to conceal one's feelings, i. e., to care less for truth than for what people will think, is a coward's part), and must speak and act openly; for he is free of speech because he is contemptuous, and he is given to telling the truth, except when he speaks in irony to the vulgar. He must be unable to make his life revolve round another, unless it be a friend; for this is slavish, and for this reason all flatterers are servile and people lacking in self-respect are flatterers. Nor is he given to admiration; for nothing to him is great. Nor is he mindful of wrongs; for it is not the part of a proud man to have a long memory, especially for wrongs, but rather to overlook them. Nor is he a gossip; for he will speak neither about himself nor about another, since he cares not to be praised nor for others to be blamed; nor again is he given to praise; and for the same reason he is not an evil-speaker, even about his enemies, except from haughtiness. With regard to necessary or small matters he is least of all men given to lamentation or the asking of favours; for it is the part of one who takes such matters seriously to behave so with respect to them. He is one who will possess beautiful and profitless things rather than profitable and useful ones; for this is more proper to a character that suffices to itself.

Further, a slow step is thought proper to the proud man, a deep voice, and a level utterance; for the man who takes few things seriously is not likely to be hurried, nor the man who thinks nothing great to be excited, while a shrill voice and a rapid gait are the results of hurry and excitement.

Such, then, is the proud man; the man who falls short of him is unduly humble, and the man who goes beyond him is vain. Now even these are not thought to be bad (for they are not malicious), but only mistaken. For the unduly humble man, being worthy of good things, robs himself of what he deserves, and seems to have something bad about him from the fact that he does not think himself worthy of good things, and seems also not to know himself; else he would have desired the things he was worthy of, since these were good. Yet such people are not thought to be fools, but rather unduly retiring. Such a reputation, however, seems actually to make them worse; for each class of people aims at what corresponds to its worth, and these people stand back even from noble actions and undertakings, deeming themselves unworthy, and from external goods no less. Vain people, on the other hand, are fools and ignorant of themselves, and that manifestly; for, not being worthy of them, they attempt honourable undertakings, and then are found out; and they adorn themselves with clothing and outward show and such things, and wish their strokes of good fortune to be made public, and speak about them as if they would be honoured for them. But undue humility is more opposed to pride than vanity is; for it is both commoner and worse.

Pride, then, is concerned with honour on the grand scale, as has been said.

* * *

BOOK VI

1. [*Reasons for studying intellectual virtue.*] Since we have previously said that one ought to choose that which is intermediate, not the excess nor the defect, and that the intermediate is determined by the dictates of the right rule, let us discuss the nature of these dictates. In all the states of character we have mentioned, as in all other matters, there is a mark to which the man who has the rule looks, and heightens or relaxes his activity accordingly, and there is a standard which determines the mean states which we say are inter-

mediate between excess and defect, being in accordance
with the right rule. But such a statement, though true, is by
no means clear; for not only here but in all other pursuits
which are objects of knowledge it is indeed true to say that
we must not exert ourselves nor relax our efforts too much
nor too little, but to an intermediate extent and as the right
rule dictates; but if a man had only this knowledge he would
be none the wiser—e. g., we should not know what sort of
medicines to apply to our body if some one were to say "all
those which the medical art prescribes, and which agree with
the practice of one who possesses the art." Hence it is necessary with regard to the states of the soul also not only that
this true statement should be made, but also that it should
be determined what is the right rule and what is the standard that fixes it.

We divided the virtues of the soul and said that some are
virtues of character and others of intellect. Now we have
discussed in detail the moral virtues; with regard to the
others let us express our view as follows, beginning with
some remarks about the soul. We said before that there are
two parts of the soul—that which grasps a rule or rational
principle, and the irrational; let us now draw a similar distinction within the part which grasps a rational principle.
And let it be assumed that there are two parts which grasp
a rational principle—one by which we contemplate the kind
of things whose originative causes are invariable, and one by
which we contemplate variable things; for where objects
differ in kind the part of the soul answering to each of the
two is different in kind, since it is in virtue of a certain likeness and kinship with their objects that they have the knowledge they have. Let one of these parts be called the scientific
and the other the calculative; for to deliberate and to cal-
culate are the same thing, but no one deliberates about the
invariable. Therefore the calculative is one part of the faculty
which grasps a rational principle. We must, then, learn what
is the best state of each of these two parts; for this is the
virtue of each.

2. [*Objects of the contemplative and the calculative intellects.*] The virtue of a thing is relative to its proper work. Now there are three things in the soul which control action and truth—sensation, reason, desire.

Of these sensation originates no action; this is plain from the fact that the lower animals have sensation but no share in action.

What affirmation and negation are in thinking, pursuit and avoidance are in desire; so that since moral virtue is a state of character concerned with choice, and choice is deliberate desire, therefore both the reasoning must be true and the desire right, if the choice is to be good, and the latter must pursue just what the former asserts. Now this kind of intellect and of truth is practical; of the intellect which is contemplative, not practical nor productive, the good and the bad state are truth and falsity respectively (for this is the work of everything intellectual); while of the part which is practical and intellectual the good state is truth in agreement with right desire.

The origin of action—its efficient, not its final cause—is choice, and that of choice is desire and reasoning with a view to an end. This is why choice cannot exist either without reason and intellect or without a moral state; for good action and its opposite cannot exist without a combination of intellect and character. Intellect itself, however, moves nothing, but only the intellect which aims at an end and is practical; for this rules the productive intellect as well, since every one who makes makes for an end, and that which is made is not an end in the unqualified sense (but only an end in a particular relation, and the end of a particular operation)—only that which is *done* is that; for good action is an end, and desire aims at this. Hence choice is either desiderative reason or ratiocinative desire, and such an origin of action is a man. (It is to be noted that nothing that is past is an object of choice, e. g., no one chooses to have sacked Troy; for no one *deliberates* about the past, but about what is future and capable of being otherwise, while what is past is not capable of not having taken place; hence Agathon is right in saying,

> For this alone is lacking even to God,
> To make undone things that have once been done.)

The work of both the intellectual parts, then, is truth. Therefore the states that are most strictly those in respect of which each of these parts will reach truth are the virtues of the two parts.

3. [*Science—demonstrative knowledge of the necessary and eternal.*] Let us begin, then, from the beginning, and discuss these states once more. Let it be assumed that the states by virtue of which the soul possesses truth by way of affirmation or denial are five in number, i. e., art, scientific knowledge, practical wisdom, philosophic wisdom, intuitive reason; we do not include judgement and opinion because in these we may be mistaken.

Now what *scientific knowledge* is, if we are to speak exactly and not follow mere similarities, is plain from what follows. We all suppose that what we know is not even capable of being otherwise; of things capable of being otherwise we do not know, when they have passed outside our observation, whether they exist or not. Therefore the object of scientific knowledge is of necessity. Therefore it is eternal: for things that are of necessity in the unqualified sense are all eternal; and things that are eternal are ungenerated and imperishable. Again, every science is thought to be capable of being taught, and its object of being learned. And all teaching starts from what is already known, as we maintain in the *Analytics* also; for it proceeds sometimes through induction and sometimes by syllogism. Now induction is the starting point which knowledge even of the universal presupposes, while syllogism proceeds *from* universals. There are therefore starting points from which syllogism proceeds, which are not reached by syllogism; it is therefore by induction that they are acquired. Scientific knowledge is, then, a state of capacity to demonstrate, and has the other limiting characteristics which we specify in the *Analytics*; for it is when a man believes in a certain way and the starting points are known to him that he has scientific knowledge, since if they are not better known to him than the conclusion, he will have his knowledge only incidentally.

Let this, then, be taken as our account of scientific knowledge.

4. [*Art—knowledge of how to make things.*] In the variable are included both things made and things done; making and acting are different (for their nature we treat even the discussions outside our school as reliable); so that the reasoned state of capacity to act is different from the reasoned state of capacity to make. Hence too they are not included one in the other; for neither is acting making nor is making acting. Now since architecture is an art and is essentially a reasoned state of capacity to make, and there is neither any art that is not such a state nor any such state that is not an art, *art* is identical with a state of capacity to make, involving a true course of reasoning. All art is concerned with coming into being, i. e., with contriving and considering how something may come into being which is capable of either being or not being, and whose origin is in the maker and not in the thing made; for art is concerned neither with things that are, or come into being, by necessity, nor with things that do so in accordance with nature (since these have their origin in themselves). Making and acting being different, art must be a matter of making, not of acting. And in a sense chance and art are concerned with the same objects; as Agathon says, "art loves chance and chance loves art." Art, then, as has been said, is a state concerned with making, involving a true course of reasoning, and lack of art on the contrary is a state concerned with making, involving a false course of reasoning; both are concerned with the variable.

5. [*Practical wisdom—knowledge of how to secure the ends of human life.*] Regarding *practical wisdom* we shall get at

the truth by considering who are the persons we credit with it. Now it is thought to be the mark of a man of practical wisdom to be able to deliberate well about what is good and expedient for himself, not in some particular respect, e. g., about what sorts of thing conduce to health or to strength, but about what sorts of thing conduce to the good life in general. This is shown by the fact that we credit men with practical wisdom in some particular respect when they have calculated well with a view to some good end which is one of those that are not the object of any art. It follows that in the general sense also the man who is capable of deliberating has practical wisdom. Now no one deliberates about things that are invariable, nor about things that it is impossible for him to do. Therefore, since scientific knowledge involves demonstration, but there is no demonstration of things whose first principles are variable (for all such things might actually be otherwise), and since it is impossible to deliberate about things that are of necessity, practical wisdom cannot be scientific knowledge nor art; not science because that which can be done is capable of being otherwise, not art because action and making are different kinds of thing. The remaining alternative, then, is that it is a true and reasoned state of capacity to act with regard to the things that are good or bad for man. For while making has an end other than itself, action cannot; for good action itself is its end. It is for this reason that we think Pericles and men like him have practical wisdom, viz., because they can see what is good for themselves and what is good for men in general; we consider that those can do this who are good at managing households or states. (This is why we call temperance [*sophrosyne*] by this name; we imply that it preserves one's practical wisdom [*sodsousa ten phronesin*]. Now what it preserves is a judgement of the kind we have described. For it is not any and every judgement that pleasant and painful objects destroy and pervert, e. g., the judgement that the triangle has or has not its angles equal to two right angles, but only judgements about what is to be done. For the originating causes of the things that are done consist in the end at which they are aimed; but the man who has been ruined by pleasure or pain forthwith fails to see any such originating cause—to see that for the sake of this or because of this he ought to choose and do whatever he chooses and does; for vice is destructive of the originating cause of action.)

Practical wisdom, then, must be a reasoned and true state of capacity to act with regard to human goods. But further, while there is such a thing as excellence in art, there is no such thing as excellence in practical wisdom; and in art he who errs willingly is preferable, but in practical wisdom, as in the virtues, he is the reverse. Plainly, then, practical wisdom is a virtue and not an art. There being two parts of the soul that can follow a course of reasoning, it must be the virtue of one of the two, i. e., of that part which forms opinions; for opinion is about the variable and so is practical wisdom. But yet it is not only a reasoned state; this is shown by the fact that a state of that sort may be forgotten but practical wisdom cannot.

6. [*Intuitive reason—knowledge of the principles from which science proceeds.*] Scientific knowledge is judgement about things that are universal and necessary, and the conclusions of demonstration, and all scientific knowledge, follow from first principles (for scientific knowledge involves apprehension of a rational ground). This being so, the first principle from which what is scientifically known follows cannot be an object of scientific knowledge, of art, or of practical wisdom; for that which can be scientifically known can be demonstrated, and art and practical wisdom deal with things that are variable. Nor are these first principles the objects of philosophic wisdom, for it is a mark of the philosopher to have *demonstration* about some things. If, then, the states of mind by which we have truth and are never deceived about things invariable or even variable are scientific knowledge, practical wisdom, philosophic wisdom, and intuitive reason, and it cannot be any of the three (i. e., practical wisdom, scientific knowledge, or philosophic wisdom), the remaining

alternative is that it is *intuitive reason* that grasps the first principles.

7. [*Philosophic wisdom—the union of intuitive reason and science.*] *Wisdom* (1) in the arts we ascribe to their most finished exponents, e. g., to Phidias as a sculptor and to Polyclitus as a maker of portrait statues, and here we mean nothing by wisdom except excellence in art; but (2) we think that some people are wise in general, not in some particular field or in any other limited respect, as Homer says in the *Margites,*

> Him did the gods make neither a digger nor yet a ploughman
> Nor wise in anything else.

Therefore wisdom must plainly be the most finished of the forms of knowledge. It follows that the wise man must not only know what follows from the first principles, but must also possess truth about the first principles. Therefore wisdom must be intuitive reason combined with scientific knowledge—scientific knowledge of the highest objects which has received as it were its proper completion.

Of the highest objects, we say; for it would be strange to think that the art of politics, or practical wisdom, is the best knowledge, since man is not the best thing in the world. Now if what is healthy or good is different for men and for fishes, but what is white or straight is always the same, any one would say that what is wise is the same but what is practically wise is different; for it is to that which observes well the various matters concerning itself that one ascribes practical wisdom, and it is to this that one will entrust such matters. This is why we say that some even of the lower animals have practical wisdom, viz., those which are found to have a power of foresight with regard to their own life. It is evident also that philosophic wisdom and the art of politics cannot be the same; for if the state of mind concerned with a man's own interests is to be called philosophic wisdom, there will be many philosophic wisdoms; there will not be one concerned with the good of all animals (any more than there is one art of medicine for all existing things), but a different philosophic wisdom about the good of each species.

But if the argument be that man is the best of the animals, this makes no difference; for there are other things much more divine in their nature even than man, e. g., most conspicuously, the bodies of which the heavens are framed. From what has been said it is plain, then, that philosophic wisdom is scientific knowledge, combined with intuitive reason, of the things that are highest by nature. This is why we say Anaxagoras, Thales, and men like them have philosophic but not practical wisdom, when we see them ignorant of what is to their own advantage, and why we say that they know things that are remarkable, admirable, difficult, and divine, but useless; viz., because it is not human goods that they seek.

Practical wisdom on the other hand is concerned with things human and things about which it is possible to deliberate; for we say this is above all the work of the man of practical wisdom, to deliberate well, but no one deliberates about things invariable, nor about things which have not an end, and that a good that can be brought about by action. The man who is without qualification good at deliberating is the man who is capable of aiming in accordance with calculation at the best for man of things attainable by action. Nor is practical wisdom concerned with universals only—it must also recognize the particulars; for it is practical, and practice is concerned with particulars. This is why some who do not know, and especially those who have experience, are more practical than others who know; for if a man knew that light meats are digestible and wholesome, but did not know which sorts of meat are light, he would not produce health, but the man who knows that chicken is wholesome is more likely to produce health.

Now practical wisdom is concerned with action; therefore one should have both forms of it, or the latter in preference to the former. But of practical as of philosophic wisdom there must be a controlling kind.

8. [*Relations between practical wisdom and political science.*] Political wisdom and practical wisdom are the same state of mind, but their essence is not the same. Of the wisdom concerned with the city, the practical wisdom which plays a controlling part is legislative wisdom, while that which is related to this as particulars to their universal is known by the general name "political wisdom"; this has to do with action and deliberation, for a decree is a thing to be carried out in the form of an individual act. This is why the exponents of this art are alone said to "take part in politics"; for these alone "do things" as manual labourers "do things."

Practical wisdom also is identified especially with that form of it which is concerned with a man himself—with the individual; and this is known by the general name "practical wisdom"; of the other kinds one is called household management, another legislation, the third politics, and of the latter one part is called deliberative and the other judicial. Now knowing what is good for oneself will be one kind of knowledge, but it is very different from the other kinds; and the man who knows and concerns himself with his own interests is thought to have practical wisdom, while politicians are thought to be busybodies; hence the words of Euripides,

> But how could I be wise, who might at ease,
> Numbered among the army's multitude,
> Have had an equal share? . . .
> For those who aim too high and do too much . . .

Those who think thus seek their own good, and consider that one ought to do so. From this opinion, then, has come the view that such men have practical wisdom; yet perhaps one's own good cannot exist without household management, nor without a form of government. Further, how one should order one's own affairs is not clear and needs inquiry.

What has been said is confirmed by the fact that while

young men become geometricians and mathematicians and wise in matters like these, it is thought that a young man of practical wisdom cannot be found. The cause is that such wisdom is concerned not only with universals but with particulars, which become familiar from experience, but a young man has no experience, for it is length of time that gives experience; indeed one might ask this question too, why a boy may become a mathematician, but not a philosopher or a physicist. Is it because the objects of mathematics exist by abstraction, while the first principles of these other subjects come from experience, and because young men have no conviction about the latter but merely use the proper language, while the essence of mathematical objects is plain enough to them?

Further, error in deliberation may be either about the universal or about the particular; we may fail to know either that all water that weighs heavy is bad, or that this particular water weighs heavy.

That practical wisdom is not scientific knowledge is evident; for it is, as has been said, concerned with the ultimate particular fact, since the thing to be done is of this nature. It is opposed, then, to intuitive reason; for intuitive reason is of the limiting premisses, for which no reason can be given, while practical wisdom is concerned with the ultimate particular, which is the object not of scientific knowledge but of perception—not the perception of qualities peculiar to one sense but a perception akin to that by which we perceive that the particular figure before us is a triangle; for in that direction as well as in that of the major premiss there will be a limit. But this is rather perception than practical wisdom, though it is another kind of perception than that of the qualities peculiar to each sense.

* * *

BOOK VIII

1. [*Friendship both necessary and noble.*] After what we have said, a discussion of friendship would naturally follow, since it is a virtue or implies virtue, and is besides most necessary with a view to living. For without friends no one would choose to live, though he had all other goods; even rich men and those in possession of office and of dominating power are thought to need friends most of all; for what is the use of such prosperity without the opportunity of beneficence, which is exercised chiefly and in its most laudable form towards friends? Or how can prosperity be guarded and preserved without friends? The greater it is, the more exposed is it to risk. And in poverty and in other misfortunes men think friends are the only refuge. It helps the young, too, to keep from error; it aids older people by ministering to their needs and supplementing the activities that are failing from weakness; those in the prime of life it stimulates to noble actions—"two going together"—for with friends men are more able both to think and to act. Again, parent seems by nature to feel it for offspring and offspring for parent, not only among men but among birds and among most animals; it is felt mutually by members of the same race, and especially by men, whence we praise lovers of their fellowmen. We may see even in our travels how near and dear every man is to every other. Friendship seems too to hold states together, and lawgivers to care more for it than for justice; for unanimity seems to be something like friendship, and this they aim at most of all, and expel faction as their worst enemy; and when men are friends they have no need of justice, while when

234

they are just they need friendship as well, and the truest form of justice is thought to be a friendly quality.

But it is not only necessary but also noble; for we praise those who love their friends, and it is thought to be a fine thing to have many friends; and again we think it is the same people that are good men and are friends.

Not a few things about friendship are matters of debate. Some define it as a kind of likeness and say like people are friends, whence come the sayings "like to like," "birds of a feather flock together," and so on; others on the contrary say "two of a trade never agree." On this very question they inquire for deeper and more physical causes, Euripides saying that "parched earth loves the rain, and stately heaven when filled with rain loves to fall to earth," and Heraclitus that "it is what opposes that helps" and "from different tones comes the fairest tune" and "all things are produced through strife"; while Empedocles, as well as others, expresses the opposite view that like aims at like. The physical problems we may leave alone (for they do not belong to the present inquiry); let us examine those which are human and involve character and feeling, e. g., whether friendship can arise between any two people or people cannot be friends if they are wicked, and whether there is one species of friendship or more than one. Those who think there is only one because it admits of degrees have relied on an inadequate indication; for even things different in species admit of degree. We have discussed this matter previously.

2. [*Three objects of love.*] The kinds of friendship may perhaps be cleared up if we first come to know the object of love. For not everything seems to be loved but only the lovable, and this is good, pleasant, or useful; but it would seem to be that by which some good or pleasure is produced that is useful, so that it is the good and the useful that are lovable as ends. Do men love, then, *the* good, or what is good for *them?* These sometimes clash. So too with regard to the pleasant. Now it is thought that each loves what is good for himself, and that the good is without qualification lovable,

and what is good for each man is lovable for him; but each man loves not what is good for him but what seems good. This however will make no difference; we shall just have to say that this is "that which seems lovable." Now there are three grounds on which people love; of the love of lifeless objects we do not use the word "friendship"; for it is not mutual love, nor is there a wishing of good to the other (for it would surely be ridiculous to wish wine well; if one wishes anything for it, it is that it may keep, so that one may have it oneself); but to a friend we say we ought to wish what is good for his sake. But to those who thus wish good we ascribe only goodwill, if the wish is not reciprocated; goodwill when it *is* reciprocal being friendship. Or must we add "when it is recognized"? For many people have goodwill to those whom they have not seen but judge to be good or useful; and one of these might return this feeling. These people seem to bear goodwill to each other; but how could one call them friends when they do not know their mutual feelings? To be friends, then, they must be mutually recognized as bearing goodwill and wishing well to each other for one of the aforesaid reasons.

3. [*Three corresponding kinds of friendship*.] Now these reasons differ from each other in kind; so, therefore, do the corresponding forms of love and friendship. There are therefore three kinds of friendship, equal in number to the things that are lovable; for with respect to each there is a mutual and recognized love, and those who love each other wish well to each other in that respect in which they love one another. Now those who love each other for their utility do not love each other for themselves but in virtue of some good which they get from each other. So too with those who love for the sake of pleasure; it is not for their character that men love ready-witted people, but because they find them pleasant. Therefore those who love for the sake of utility love for the sake of what is good for *themselves*, and those who love for the sake of pleasure do so for the sake of what is pleasant to *themselves*, and not in so far as the other is the person loved

but in so far as he is useful or pleasant. And thus these friendships are only incidental; for it is not as being the man he is that the loved person is loved, but as providing some good or pleasure. Such friendships, then, are easily dissolved, if the parties do not remain like themselves; for if the one party is no longer pleasant or useful the other ceases to love him.

Now the useful is not permanent but is always changing. Thus when the motive of the friendship is done away, the friendship is dissolved, inasmuch as it existed only for the ends in question. This kind of friendship seems to exist chiefly between old people (for at that age people pursue not the pleasant but the useful) and, of those who are in their prime or young, between those who pursue utility. And such people do not live much with each other either; for sometimes they do not even find each other pleasant; therefore they do not need such companionship unless they are useful to each other; for they are pleasant to each other only in so far as they rouse in each other hopes of something good to come. Among such friendships people also class the friendship of host and guest. On the other hand the friendship of young people seems to aim at pleasure; for they live under the guidance of emotion, and pursue above all what is pleasant to themselves and what is immediately before them; but with increasing age their pleasures become different. This is why they quickly become friends and quickly cease to be so; their friendship changes with the object that is found pleasant, and such pleasure alters quickly. Young people are amorous too; for the greater part of the friendship of love depends on emotion and aims at pleasure; this is why they fall in love and quickly fall out of love, changing often within a single day. But these people do wish to spend their days and lives together; for it is thus that they attain the purpose of their friendship.

Perfect friendship is the friendship of men who are good, and alike in virtue; for these wish well alike to each other *qua* good, and they are good in themselves. Now those who wish well to their friends for their sake are most truly friends;

for they do this by reason of their own nature and not incidentally; therefore their friendship lasts as long as they are good—and goodness is an enduring thing. And each is good without qualification and to his friend, for the good are both good without qualification and useful to each other. So too they are pleasant; for the good are pleasant both without qualification and to each other, since to each his own activities and others like them are pleasurable, and the actions of the good *are* the same or like. And such a friendship is as might be expected permanent, since there meet in it all the qualities that friends should have. For all friendship is for the sake of good or of pleasure—good or pleasure either in the abstract or such as will be enjoyed by him who has the friendly feeling—and is based on a certain resemblance; and to a friendship of good men all the qualities we have named belong in virtue of the nature of the friends themselves; for in the case of this kind of friendship the other qualities also are alike in both friends, and that which is good without qualification is also without qualification pleasant, and these are the most lovable qualities. Love and friendship therefore are found most and in their best form between such men.

But it is natural that such friendships should be infrequent; for such men are rare. Further, such friendship requires time and familiarity; as the proverb says, men cannot know each other till they have "eaten salt together"; nor can they admit each other to friendship or be friends till each has been found lovable and been trusted by each. Those who quickly show the marks of friendship to each other wish to be friends, but are not friends unless they both are lovable and know the fact; for a wish for friendship may arise quickly, but friendship does not.

4. [*Contrast between the best and the inferior kinds of friendship.*] This kind of friendship, then, is perfect both in respect of duration and in all other respects, and in it each gets from each in all respects the same as, or something like what, he gives; which is what ought to happen between friends. Friendship for the sake of pleasure bears a resemblance to

this kind; for good people too *are* pleasant to each other. So too does friendship for the sake of utility; for the good are also useful to each other. Among men of these inferior sorts too, friendships are most permanent when the friends get the same thing from each other (e. g., pleasure), and not only that but also from the same source, as happens between ready-witted people, not as happens between lover and beloved. For these do not take pleasure in the same things, but the one in seeing the beloved and the other in receiving attentions from his lover; and when the bloom of youth is passing the friendship sometimes passes too (for the one finds no pleasure in the sight of the other, and the other gets no attentions from the first); but many lovers on the other hand are constant, if familiarity has led them to love each other's characters, these being alike. But those who exchange not pleasure but utility in their amour are both less truly friends and less constant. Those who are friends for the sake of utility part when the advantage is at an end; for they were lovers not of each other but of profit.

For the sake of pleasure or utility, then, even bad men may be friends of each other, or good men of bad, or one who is neither good nor bad may be a friend to any sort of person, but for their own sake clearly only good men can be friends; for bad men do not delight in each other unless some advantage come of the relation.

The friendship of the good too and this alone is proof against slander; for it is not easy to trust any one's talk about a man who has long been tested by oneself; and it is among good men that trust and the feeling that "he would never wrong me" and all the other things that are demanded in true friendship are found. In the other kinds of friendship, however, there is nothing to prevent these evils arising.

For men apply the name of friends even to those whose motive is utility, in which sense states are said to be friendly (for the alliances of states seem to aim at advantage), and to those who love each other for the sake of pleasure, in which sense children are called friends. Therefore we too ought perhaps to call such people friends, and say that there are several kinds of friendship—firstly and in the proper sense that of good men *qua* good, and by analogy the other kinds; for it is in virtue of something good and something akin to what is found in true friendship that they are friends, since even the pleasant is good for the lovers of pleasure. But these two kinds of friendship are not often united, nor do the same people become friends for the sake of utility and of pleasure; for things that are only incidentally connected are not often coupled together.

Friendship being divided into these kinds, bad men will be friends for the sake of pleasure or of utility, being in this respect like each other, but good men will be friends for their own sake, i. e., in virtue of their goodness. These, then, are friends without qualification; the others are friends incidentally and through a resemblance to these.

5. [*The state of friendship distinguished from the activity of friendship and the feeling of friendliness.*] As in regard to the virtues some men are called good in respect of a state of character, others in respect of an activity, so too in the case of friendship; for those who live together delight in each other and confer benefits on each other, but those who are asleep or locally separated are not performing, but are disposed to perform, the activities of friendship; distance does not break off the friendship absolutely, but only the activity of it. But if the absence is lasting, it seems actually to make men forget their friendship; hence the saying "out of sight, out of mind." Neither old people nor sour people seem to make friends easily; for there is little that is pleasant in them, and no one can spend his days with one whose company is painful, or not pleasant, since nature seems above all to avoid the painful and to aim at the pleasant. Those, however, who approve of each other but do not live together seem to be well-disposed rather than actual friends. For there is nothing so characteristic of friends as living together (since while it is people who are in need that desire benefits, even those who are supremely happy desire to spend their days together; for solitude suits such people least of all); but people can-

not live together if they are not pleasant and do not enjoy the same things, as friends who are companions seem to do.

The truest friendship, then, is that of the good, as we have frequently said; for that which is without qualification good or pleasant seems to be lovable and desirable, and for each person that which is good or pleasant to him; and the good man is lovable and desirable to the good man for both these reasons. Now it looks as if love were a feeling, friendship a state of character; for love may be felt just as much towards lifeless things, but mutual love involves choice and choice springs from a state of character; and men wish well to those whom they love, for their sake, not as a result of feeling but as a result of a state of character. And in loving a friend men love what is good for themselves; for the good man in becoming a friend becomes a good to his friend. Each, then, both loves what is good for himself, and makes an equal return in goodwill and in pleasantness; for friendship is said to be equality, and both of these are found most in the friendship of the good.

6. [*Various relations between the three kinds of friendship.*] Between sour and elderly people friendship arises less readily, inasmuch as they are less good-tempered and enjoy companionship less; for these are thought to be the greatest marks of friendship and most productive of it. This is why, while young men become friends quickly, old men do not; it is because men do not become friends with those in whom they do not delight; and similarly sour people do not quickly make friends either. But such men may bear goodwill to each other; for they wish one another well and aid one another in need; but they are hardly *friends* because they do not spend their days together nor delight in each other, and these are thought the greatest marks of friendship.

One cannot be a friend to many people in the sense of having friendship of the perfect type with them, just as one cannot be in love with many people at once (for love is a sort of excess of feeling, and it is the nature of such only to be felt towards one person); and it is not easy for many people at the same time to please the same person very greatly, or perhaps even to be good in his eyes. One must, too, acquire some experience of the other person and become familiar with him, and that is very hard. But with a view to utility or pleasure it is possible that many people should please one; for many people are useful or pleasant, and these services take little time.

Of these two kinds that which is for the sake of pleasure is the more like friendship, when both parties get the same things from each other and delight in each other or in the same things, as in the friendships of the young; for generosity is more found in such friendships. Friendship based on utility is for the commercially minded. People who are supremely happy, too, have no need of useful friends, but do need pleasant friends; for they wish to live with *some one* and, though they can endure for a short time what is painful, no one could put up with it continuously, nor even with the Good itself if it were painful to him; this is why they look out for friends who are pleasant. Perhaps they should look out for friends who, being pleasant, are also good, and good for them, too; for so they will have all the characteristics that friends should have.

People in positions of authority seem to have friends who fall into distinct classes; some people are useful to them and others are pleasant, but the same people are rarely both; for they seek neither those whose pleasantness is accompanied by virtue nor those whose utility is with a view to noble objects, but in their desire for pleasure they seek for ready-witted people, and their other friends they choose as being clever at doing what they are told, and these characteristics are rarely combined. Now we have said that the *good* man *is* at the same time pleasant and useful; but such a man does not become the friend of one who surpasses him in station, unless he is surpassed also in virtue; if this is not so, he does not establish equality by being proportionally exceeded in both respects. But people who surpass him in both respects are not so easy to find.

However that may be, the aforesaid friendships involve

equality; for the friends get the same things from one another and wish the same things for one another, or exchange
one thing for another, e. g., pleasure for utility; we have said,
however, that they are both less truly friendships and less
permanent. But it is from their likeness and their unlikeness
to the same thing that they are thought both to be and not to
be friendships. It is by their likeness to the friendship of
virtue that they seem to be friendships (for one of them involves pleasure and the other utility, and these characteristics
belong to the friendship of virtue as well); while it is because
the friendship of virtue is proof against slander and permanent, while these quickly change (besides differing from
the former in many other respects), that they appear *not* to
be friendships; i. e., it is because of their unlikeness to the
friendship of virtue.

7. [*Unequal friendships.*] But there is another kind of friendship, viz., that which involves an inequality between the
parties, e. g., that of father to son and in general of elder to
younger, that of man to wife and in general that of ruler to
subject. And these friendships differ also from each other; for
it is not the same that exists between parents and children
and between rulers and subjects, nor is even that of father
to son the same as that of son to father, nor that of husband
to wife the same as that of wife to husband. For the virtue
and the function of each of these is different, and so are the
reasons for which they love; the love and the friendship are
therefore different also. Each party, then, neither gets the
same from the other, nor ought to seek it; but when children
render to parents what they ought to render to those who
brought them into the world, and parents render what they
should to their children, the friendship of such persons will be
abiding and excellent. In all friendships implying inequality
the love also should be proportional, i. e., the better should
be more loved than he loves, and so should the more useful,
and similarly in each of the other cases; for when the love is
in proportion to the merit of the parties, then in a sense arises

equality, which is certainly held to be characteristic of friendship.

But equality does not seem to take the same form in acts of justice and in friendship; for in acts of justice what is equal in the primary sense is that which is in proportion to merit, while quantitative equality is secondary, but in friendship quantitative equality is primary and proportion to merit secondary. This becomes clear if there is a great interval in respect of virtue or vice or wealth or anything else between the parties; for then they are no longer friends, and do not even expect to be so. And this is most manifest in the case of the gods; for they surpass us most decisively in all good things. But it is clear also in the case of kings; for with them, too, men who are much their inferiors do not expect to be friends; nor do men of no account expect to be friends with the best or wisest men. In such cases it is not possible to define exactly up to what point friends can remain friends; for much can be taken away and friendship remain, but when one party is removed to a great distance, as God is, the possibility of friendship ceases. This is in fact the origin of the question whether friends really wish for their friends the greatest goods, e. g., that of being gods; since in that case their friends will no longer be friends to them, and therefore will not be good things for them (for friends *are* good things). The answer is that if we were right in saying that friend wishes good to friend for his sake, his friend must remain the sort of being he is, whatever that may be; therefore it is for him only so long as he remains a man that he will wish the greatest goods. But perhaps not *all* the greatest goods; for it is for himself most of all that each man wishes what is good.

8. [*Loving is more of the essence of friendship than being loved.*] Most people seem, owing to ambition, to wish to be loved rather than to love; which is why most men love flattery; for the flatterer is a friend in an inferior position, or pretends to be such and to love more than he is loved; and being loved seems to be akin to being honoured, and this is

what most people aim at. But it seems to be not for its own sake that people choose honour, but incidentally. For most people enjoy being honoured by those in positions of authority because of their hopes (for they think that if they want anything they will get it from them; and therefore they delight in honour as a token of favour to come); while those who desire honour from good men, and men who know, are aiming at confirming their own opinion of themselves; they delight in honour, therefore, because they believe in their own goodness on the strength of the judgement of those who speak about them. In being loved, on the other hand, people delight for its own sake; whence it would seem to be better than being honoured, and friendship to be desirable in itself. But it seems to lie in loving rather than in being loved, as is indicated by the delight mothers take in loving; for some mothers hand over their children to be brought up, and so long as they know their fate they love them and do not seek to be loved in return (if they cannot have both), but seem to be satisfied if they see them prospering; and they themselves love their children even if these owing to their ignorance give them nothing of a mother's due. Now since friendship depends more on loving, and it is those who love their friends that are praised, loving seems to be the characteristic virtue of friends, so that it is only those in whom this is found in due measure that are lasting friends, and only their friendship that endures.

It is in this way more than any other that even unequals can be friends; they can be equalized. Now equality and likeness are friendship, and especially the likeness of those who are like in virtue; for being steadfast in themselves they hold fast to each other, and neither ask nor give base services, but (one may say) even prevent them; for it is characteristic of good men neither to go wrong themselves nor to let their friends do so. But wicked men have no steadfastness (for they do not remain even like to themselves), but become friends for a short time because they delight in each other's wickedness. Friends who are useful or pleasant last longer; i. e., as long as they provide each other with enjoyments or advantages. Friendship for utility's sake seems to be that which most easily exists between contraries, e. g., between poor and rich, between ignorant and learned; for what a man actually lacks he aims at, and one gives something else in return. But under this head, too, we might bring lover and beloved, beautiful and ugly. This is why lovers sometimes seem ridiculous, when they demand to be loved as they love; if they are equally lovable their claim can perhaps be justified, but when they have nothing lovable about them it is ridiculous. Perhaps, however, contrary does not even aim at contrary by its own nature, but only incidentally, the desire being for what is intermediate; for that is what is good, e. g., it is good for the dry not to become wet but to come to the intermediate state, and similarly with the hot and in all other cases. These subjects we may dismiss; for they are indeed somewhat foreign to our inquiry.

9. [*Parallelism of friendship and justice.*] Friendship and justice seem, as we have said at the outset of our discussion, to be concerned with the same objects and exhibited between the same persons. For in every community there is thought to be some form of justice, and friendship too; at least men address as friends their fellow voyagers and fellow soldiers, and so too those associated with them in any other kind of community. And the extent of their association is the extent of their friendship, as it is the extent to which justice exists between them. And the proverb "what friends have is common property" expresses the truth; for friendship depends on community. Now brothers and comrades have all things in common, but the others to whom we have referred have definite things in common—some more things, others fewer; for of friendships, too, some are more and others less truly friendships. And the claims of justice differ too; the duties of parents to children and those of brothers to each other are not the same nor those of comrades and those of fellow citizens, and so, too, with the other kinds of friendship. There is a difference, therefore, also between the acts that are unjust towards each of these classes of associates, and the injustice increases

by being exhibited towards those who are friends in a fuller sense; e. g., it is a more terrible thing to defraud a comrade than a fellow citizen, more terrible not to help a brother than a stranger, and more terrible to wound a father than any one else. And the demands of justice also seem to increase with the intensity of the friendship, which implies that friendship and justice exist between the same persons and have an equal extension.

Now all forms of community are like parts of the political community; for men journey together with a view to some particular advantage, and to provide something that they need for the purposes of life; and it is for the sake of advantage that the political community too seems both to have come together originally and to endure, for this is what legislators aim at, and they call just that which is to the common advantage. Now the other communities aim at advantage bit by bit, e. g., sailors at what is advantageous on a voyage with a view to making money or something of the kind, fellow soldiers at what is advantageous in war, whether it is wealth or victory or the taking of a city that they seek, and members of tribes and demes act similarly [Some communities seem to arise for the sake of pleasure, viz., religious guilds and social clubs; for these exist respectively for the sake of offering sacrifice and of companionship. But all these seem to fall under the political community; for it aims not at present advantage but at what is advantageous for life as a whole], offering sacrifices and arranging gatherings for the purpose, and assigning honours to the gods, and providing pleasant relaxations for themselves. For the ancient sacrifices and gatherings seem to take place after the harvest as a sort of firstfruits, because it was at these seasons that people had most leisure. All the communities, then, seem to be parts of the political community; and the particular kinds of friendship will correspond to the particular kinds of community.

10. [*Classification of constitutions.*] There are three kinds of constitution, and an equal number of deviation forms—perversions, as it were, of them. The constitutions are monarchy,

aristocracy, and thirdly that which is based on a property qualification, which it seems appropriate to call timocratic, though most people are wont to call it polity. The best of these is monarchy, the worst timocracy. The deviation from monarchy is tyranny; for both are forms of one-man rule, but there is the greatest difference between them; the tyrant looks to his own advantage, the king to that of his subjects. For a man is not a king unless he is sufficient to himself and excels his subjects in all good things; and such a man needs nothing further; therefore he will not look to his own interests but to those of his subjects; for a king who is not like that would be a mere titular king. Now tyranny is the very contrary of this; the tyrant pursues his own good. And it is clearer in the case of tyranny that it is the worst deviation form; but it is the contrary of the best that is worst. Monarchy passes over into tyranny; for tyranny is the evil form of one-man rule and the bad king becomes a tyrant. Aristocracy passes over into oligarchy by the badness of the rulers, who distribute contrary to equity what belongs to the city—all or most of the good things to themselves, and office always to the same people, paying most regard to wealth; thus the rulers are few and are bad men instead of the most worthy. Timocracy passes over into democracy; for these are coterminous, since it is the ideal even of timocracy to be the rule of the majority, and all who have the property qualification count as equal. Democracy is the least bad of the deviations; for in its case the form of constitution is but a slight deviation. These then are the changes to which constitutions are most subject; for these are the smallest and easiest transitions.

One may find resemblances to the constitutions and, as it were, patterns of them even in households. For the association of a father with his sons bears the form of monarchy, since the father cares for his children; and this is why Homer calls Zeus "father"; it is the ideal of monarchy to be paternal rule. But among the Persians the rule of the father is tyrannical; they use their sons as slaves. Tyrannical too is the rule of a master over slaves; for it is the advantage of the master that is brought about in it. Now this seems to be a correct form of government, but the Persian type is perverted; for the modes of rule appropriate to different relations are diverse. The association of man and wife seems to be aristocratic; for the man rules in accordance with his worth, and in those matters in which a man should rule, but the matters that befit a woman he hands over to her. If the man rules in everything the relation passes over into oligarchy; for in doing so he is not acting in accordance with their respective worth, and not ruling in virtue of his superiority. Sometimes, however, women rule, because they are heiresses; so their rule is not in virtue of excellence but due to wealth and power, as in oligarchies. The association of brothers is like timocracy; for they are equal, except in so far as they differ in age; hence if they differ *much* in age, the friendship is no longer of the fraternal type. Democracy is found chiefly in masterless dwellings (for here every one is on an equality), and in those in which the ruler is weak and every one has license to do as he pleases.

11. [*Corresponding forms of friendship and of justice.*] Each of the constitutions may be seen to involve friendship just in so far as it involves justice. The friendship between a king and his subjects depends on an excess of benefits conferred; for he confers benefits on his subjects if being a good man he cares for them with a view to their well-being, as a shepherd does for his sheep (whence Homer called Agamemnon "shepherd of the peoples"). Such too is the friendship of a father, though this exceeds the other in the greatness of the benefits conferred; for he is responsible for the existence of his children, which is thought the greatest good, and for their nurture and upbringing. These things are ascribed to ancestors as well. Further, by nature a father tends to rule over his sons, ancestors over descendants, a king over his subjects. These friendships imply superiority of one party over the other, which is why ancestors are honoured. The justice therefore that exists between persons so related is not the same on both sides but is in every case proportioned to merit; for that is true of the friendship as well. The friendship of man

and wife, again, is the same that is found in an aristocracy; for it is in accordance with virtue—the better gets more of what is good, and each gets what befits him; and so, too, with the justice in these relations. The friendship of brothers is like that of comrades; for they are equal and of like age, and such persons are for the most part like in their feelings and their character. Like this, too, is the friendship appropriate to timocratic government; for in such a constitution the ideal is for the citizens to be equal and fair; therefore rule is taken in turn, and on equal terms; and the friendship appropriate here will correspond.

But in the deviation forms, as justice hardly exists, so too does friendship. It exists least in the worst form; in tyranny there is little or no friendship. For where there is nothing common to ruler and ruled, there is not friendship either, since there is not justice; e. g., between craftsman and tool, soul and body, master and slave; the latter in each case is benefited by that which uses it, but there is no friendship nor justice towards lifeless things. But neither is there friendship towards a horse or an ox, nor to a slave *qua* slave. For there is nothing common to the two parties; the slave is a living tool and the tool a lifeless slave. *Qua* slave then, one cannot be friends with him. But *qua* man one can; for there seems to be some justice between any man and any other who can share in a system of law or be a party to an agreement; therefore there can also be friendship with him in so far as he is a man. Therefore while in tyrannies friendship and justice hardly exist, in democracies they exist more fully; for where the citizens are equal they have much in common.

* * *

BOOK X

1. [*Two opposed views about pleasure.*] After these matters
we ought perhaps next to discuss pleasure. For it is thought
to be most intimately connected with our human nature,
which is the reason why in educating the young we steer
them by the rudders of pleasure and pain; it is thought, too,
that to enjoy the things we ought and to hate the things we
ought has the greatest bearing on virtue of character. For
these things extend right through life, with a weight and
power of their own in respect both to virtue and to the happy
life, since men choose what is pleasant and avoid what is
painful; and such things, it will be thought, we should least
of all omit to discuss, especially since they admit of much
dispute. For some say pleasure is the good, while others,
on the contrary, say it is thoroughly bad—some no doubt
being persuaded that the facts are so, and others thinking it
has a better effect on our life to exhibit pleasure as a bad
thing even if it is not; for most people (they think) incline
towards it and are the slaves of their pleasures, for which
reason they ought to lead them in the opposite direction, since
thus they will reach the middle state. But surely this is not
correct. For arguments about matters concerned with feelings
and actions are less reliable than facts: and so when they
clash with the facts of perception they are despised, and
discredit the truth as well; if a man who runs down pleasure
is once seen to be aiming at it, his inclining towards it is
thought to imply that it is all worthy of being aimed at; for
most people are not good at drawing distinctions. True arguments seem, then, most useful, not only with a view to knowl-

edge, but with a view to life also; for since they harmonize with the facts they are believed, and so they stimulate those who understand them to live according to them. Enough of such questions; let us proceed to review the opinions that have been expressed about pleasure.

2. [*The view that pleasure is the good.*] Eudoxus thought pleasure was the good because he saw all things, both rational and irrational, aiming at it, and because in all things that which is the object of choice is what is excellent, and that which is most the object of choice the greatest good; thus the fact that all things moved towards the same object indicated that this was for all things the chief good (for each thing, he argued, finds its own good, as it finds its own nourishment); and that which is good for all things and at which all aim was *the* good. His arguments were credited more because of the excellence of his character than for their own sake; he was thought to be remarkably self-controlled, and therefore it was thought that he was not saying what he did say as a friend of pleasure, but that the facts really were so. He believed that the same conclusion followed no less plainly from a study of the contrary of pleasure; pain was in itself an object of aversion to all things, and therefore its contrary must be similarly an object of choice. And again that is most an object of choice which we choose not because or for the sake of something else, and pleasure is admittedly of this nature; for no one asks to what end he is pleased, thus implying that pleasure is in itself an object of choice. Further, he argued that pleasure when added to any good, e. g., to just or temperate action, makes it more worthy of choice, and that it is only by itself that the good can be increased.

This argument seems to show it to be one of the goods, and no more a good than any other; for every good is more worthy of choice along with another good than taken alone. And so it is by an argument of this kind that Plato proves the good *not* to be pleasure; he argues that the pleasant life is more desirable with wisdom than without, and that if the mixture is better, pleasure is not the good; for the good cannot become more desirable by the addition of anything to it. Now it is clear that nothing else, any more than pleasure, can be the good if it is made more desirable by the addition of any of the things that are good in themselves. What, then, is there that satisfies this criterion, which at the same time we can participate in? It is something of this sort that we are looking for.

Those who object that that at which all things aim is not necessarily good are, we may surmise, talking nonsense. For we say that that which every one thinks really is so; and the man who attacks this belief will hardly have anything more credible to maintain instead. If it is senseless creatures that desire the things in question, there might be something in what they say; but if intelligent creatures do so as well, what sense can there be in this view? But perhaps even in inferior creatures there is some natural good stronger than themselves which aims at their proper good.

Nor does the argument about the contrary of pleasure seem to be correct. They say that if pain is an evil it does not follow that pleasure is a good; for evil is opposed to evil and at the same time both are opposed to the neutral state—which is correct enough but does not apply to the things in question. For if both pleasure and pain belonged to the class of evils they ought both to be objects of aversion, while if they belonged to the class of neutrals neither should be an object of aversion or they should both be equally so; but in fact people evidently avoid the one as evil and choose the other as good; that then must be the nature of the opposition between them.

3. [*The view that pleasure is wholly bad.*] Nor again, if pleasure is not a quality, does it follow that it is not a good; for the activities of virtue are not qualities either, nor is happiness.

They say, however, that the good is determinate, while pleasure is indeterminate, because it admits of degrees. Now if it is from the feeling of pleasure that they judge thus, the same will be true of justice and the other virtues, in respect of which we plainly say that people of a certain character are so more or less, and act more or less in accordance with these virtues; for people may be more just or brave, and it is possible also to act justly or temperately more or less. But if their judgement is based on the various pleasures, surely they are not stating the real cause, if in fact some pleasures are unmixed and others mixed. Again, just as health admits of degrees without being indeterminate, why should not pleasure? The same proportion is not found in all things, nor a single proportion always in the same thing, but it may be relaxed and yet persist up to a point, and it may differ in degree. The case of pleasure also may therefore be of this kind.

Again, they assume that the good is perfect while movements and comings into being are imperfect, and try to exhibit pleasure as being a movement and a coming into being. But they do not seem to be right even in saying that it is a movement. For speed and slowness are thought to be proper to every movement, and if a movement, e. g., that of the heavens, has not speed or slowness in itself, it has it in relation to something else; but of pleasure neither of these things is true. For while we may *become* pleased quickly as we may become angry quickly, we cannot *be* pleased quickly, not even in relation to some one else, while we *can* walk, or grow, or the like, quickly. While, then, we can change quickly or slowly into a state of pleasure, we cannot quickly exhibit the activity of pleasure, i. e., be pleased. Again, how can it be a coming into being? It is not thought that any chance thing can come out of any chance thing, but that a thing is dissolved into that out of which it comes into being; and pain would be the destruction of that of which pleasure is the coming into being.

They say, too, that pain is the lack of that which is according to nature, and pleasure is replenishment. But these experiences are bodily. If then pleasure is replenishment with that which is according to nature, that which feels pleasure will be that in which the replenishment takes place, i. e., the body; but that is not thought to be the case; there-

fore the replenishment is not pleasure, though one would
be pleased when replenishment was taking place, just as one
would be pained if one was being operated on. This opinion
seems to be based on the pains and pleasures connected with
nutrition; on the fact that when people have been short of
food and have felt pain beforehand they are pleased by the
replenishment. But this does not happen with all pleasures;
for the pleasures of learning and, among the sensuous pleasures, those of smell, and also many sounds and sights, and
memories and hopes, do not presuppose pain. Of what then
will these be the coming into being? There has not been lack
of anything of which they could be the supplying anew.

In reply to those who bring forward the disgraceful pleasures one may say that these are not pleasant; if things are
pleasant to people of vicious constitution, we must not suppose that they are also pleasant to others than these, just as
we do not reason so about the things that are wholesome or
sweet or bitter to sick people, or ascribe whiteness to the
things that seem white to those suffering from a disease
of the eye. Or one might answer thus—that the pleasures are
desirable, but not from *these* sources, as wealth is desirable,
but not as the reward of betrayal, and health, but not at
the cost of eating anything and everything. Or perhaps pleasures differ in kind; for those derived from noble sources are
different from those derived from base sources, and one cannot get the pleasure of the just man without being just, nor
that of the musical man without being musical, and so on.

The fact, too, that a friend is different from a flatterer
seems to make it plain that pleasure is not a good or that
pleasures are different in kind; for the one is thought to
consort with us with a view to the good, the other with a
view to our pleasure, and the one is reproached for his conduct while the other is praised on the ground that he con-
sorts with us for different ends. And no one would choose
to live with the intellect of a child throughout his life, however much he were to be pleased at the things that children
are pleased at, nor to get enjoyment by doing some most
disgraceful deed, though he were never to feel any pain in

consequence. And there are many things we should be keen about even if they brought no pleasure, e. g., seeing, remembering, knowing, possessing the virtues. If pleasures necessarily do accompany these, that makes no odds; we should choose these even if no pleasure resulted. It seems to be clear, then, that neither is pleasure the good nor is all pleasure desirable, and that some pleasures *are* desirable in themselves being different in kind or in their sources from the others. So much for the things that are said about pleasure and pain.

4. [*Definition of pleasure.*] What pleasure is, or what kind of thing it is, will become plainer if we take up the question again from the beginning. Seeing seems to be at any moment complete, for it does not lack anything which coming into being later will complete its form; and pleasure also seems to be of this nature. For it is a whole, and at no time can one find a pleasure whose form will be completed if the pleasure lasts longer. For this reason, too, it is not a movement. For every movement (e. g., that of building) takes time and is for the sake of an end, and is complete when it has made what it aims at. It is complete, therefore, only in the whole time or at that final moment. In their parts and during the time they occupy, all movements are incomplete, and are different in kind from the whole movement and from each other. For the fitting together of the stones is different from the fluting of the column, and these are both different from the making of the temple; and the making of the temple is complete (for it lacks nothing with a view to the end proposed), but the making of the base or of the triglyph is incomplete; for each is the making of only a part. They differ in kind, then, and it is not possible to find at any and every time a movement complete in form, but if at all, only in the whole time. So, too, in the case of walking and all other movements. For if locomotion is a movement from here to there, it, too, has differences in kind—flying, walking, leaping, and so on. And not only so, but in walking itself there are such differences; for the whence and whither are

not the same in the whole racecourse and in a part of it, nor in one part and in another, nor is it the same thing to traverse this line and that; for one traverses not only a line but one which is in a place, and this one is in a different place from that. We have discussed movement with precision in another work, but it seems that it is not complete at any and every time, but that the many movements are incomplete and different in kind, since the whence and whither give them their form. But of pleasure the form is complete at any and every time. Plainly, then, pleasure and movement must be different from each other, and pleasure must be one of the things that are whole and complete. This would seem to be the case, too, from the fact that it is not possible to move otherwise than in time, but it *is* possible to be pleased; for that which takes place in a moment is a whole.

From these considerations it is clear, too, that these thinkers are not right in saying there is a movement or a coming into being *of* pleasure. For these cannot be ascribed to all things, but only to those that are divisible and not wholes; there is no coming into being of seeing nor of a point nor of a unit, nor is any of these a movement or coming into being; therefore there is no movement or coming into being of pleasure either; for it is a whole.

Since every sense is active in relation to its object, and a sense which is in good condition acts perfectly in relation to the most beautiful of its objects (for perfect activity seems to be ideally of this nature; whether we say that *it* is active, or the organ in which it resides, may be assumed to be immaterial), it follows that in the case of each sense the best activity is that of the best-conditioned organ in relation to the finest of its objects. And this activity will be the most complete and pleasant. For, while there is pleasure in respect of any sense, and in respect of thought and contemplation no less, the most complete is pleasantest, and that of a well-conditioned organ in relation to the worthiest of its objects is the most complete; and the pleasure completes the activity. But the pleasure does not complete it in the same way as the combination of object and sense, both good, just as health and the doctor are not in the same way the cause of a man's being healthy. (That pleasure is produced in respect to each sense is plain; for we speak of sights and sounds as pleasant. It is also plain that it arises most of all when both the sense is at its best and it is active in reference to an object which corresponds; when both object and perceiver are of the best there will always be pleasure, since the requisite agent and patient are both present.) Pleasure completes the activity not as the corresponding permanent state does, by its immanence, but as an end which supervenes as the bloom of youth does on those in the flower of their age. So long, then, as both the intelligible or sensible object and the discriminating or contemplative faculty are as they should be, the pleasure will be involved in the activity; for when both the passive and the active factor are unchanged and are related to each other in the same way, the same result naturally follows.

How, then, is it that no one is continuously pleased? Is it that we grow weary? Certainly all human things are incapable of continuous activity. Therefore pleasure also is not continuous; for it accompanies activity Some things delight us when they are new, but later do so less, for the same reason; for at first the mind is in a state of stimulation and intensely active about them, as people are with respect to their vision when they look hard at a thing, but afterwards our activity is not of this kind, but has grown relaxed; for which reason the pleasure also is dulled.

One might think that all men desire pleasure because they all aim at life; life is an activity, and each man is active about those things and with those faculties that he loves most; e. g., the musician is active with his hearing in reference to tunes, the student with his mind in reference to theoretical questions, and so on in each case; now pleasure completes the activities, and therefore life, which they desire. It is with good reason, then, that they aim at pleasure too, since for every one it completes life, which is desirable. But whether we choose life for the sake of pleasure or pleasure for the sake of life is a question we may dismiss for the present. For they seem to be bound up together and not to admit of separation, since without activity pleasure does not arise, and every activity is completed by the attendant pleasure.

5. [*Criterion of the value of pleasures.*] For this reason pleasures seem, too, to differ in kind. For things different in kind are, we think, completed by different things (we see this to be true both of natural objects and of things produced by art, e. g., animals, trees, a painting, a sculpture, a house, an implement); and, similarly, we think that activities differing in kind are completed by things differing in kind. Now the activities of thought differ from those of the senses, and both differ among themselves, in kind; so, therefore, do the pleasures that complete them.

This may be seen, too, from the fact that each of the pleasures is bound up with the activity it completes. For an activity is intensified by its proper pleasure, since each class of things is better judged of and brought to precision by those who engage in the activity with pleasure; e. g., it is those who enjoy geometrical thinking that become geometers and grasp the various propositions better, and, similarly, those who are fond of music or of building, and so on, make progress in their proper function by enjoying it; so the pleasures intensify the activities, and what intensifies a thing is proper to it, but things different in kind have properties different in kind.

This will be even more apparent from the fact that activities are hindered by pleasures arising from other sources. For people who are fond of playing the flute are incapable of attending to arguments if they overhear some one playing the flute, since they enjoy flute playing more than the activity in hand; so the pleasure connected with flute playing destroys the activity concerned with argument. This happens, similarly, in all other cases, when one is active about two things at once; the more pleasant activity drives out the other, and if it is much more pleasant does so all the more, so that one even ceases from the other. This is why when we enjoy anything very much we do not throw ourselves into anything else, and do one thing only when we are not much pleased by another; e. g., in the theatre the people who eat sweets do so most when the actors are poor. Now since activities are made precise and more enduring and better by their proper pleasure, and injured by alien pleasures, evidently the two kinds of pleasure are far apart. For alien pleasures do pretty much what proper pains do, since activities are destroyed by their proper pains; e. g., if a man finds writing or doing sums unpleasant and painful, he does not write, or does not do sums, because the activity is painful. So an activity suffers contrary effects from its proper pleasures and pains, i. e., from those that supervene on it in virtue of its own nature And alien pleasures have been stated to do much the same as pain; they destroy the activity, only not to the same degree.

Now since activities differ in respect of goodness and badness, and some are worthy to be chosen, others to be avoided, and others neutral, so, too, are the pleasures; for to each activity there is a proper pleasure. The pleasure proper to a worthy activity is good and that proper to an unworthy activity bad; just as the appetites for noble objects are laudable, those for base objects culpable. But the pleasures involved in activities are more proper to them than the desires; for the latter are separated both in time and in nature, while the former are close to the activities, and so hard to distinguish from them that it admits of dispute whether the activity is not the same as the pleasure. (Still, pleasure does not seem to *be* thought or perception—that would be strange; but because they are not found apart they appear to some people the same.) As activities are different, then, so are the corresponding pleasures. Now sight is superior to touch in purity, and hearing and smell to taste; the pleasures, therefore, are similarly superior, and those of thought superior to these, and within each of the two kinds some are superior to others.

Each animal is thought to have a proper pleasure, as it has a proper function; viz., that which corresponds to its activity. If we survey them species by species, too, this will be evident; horse, dog, and man have different pleasures, as Heraclitus says "asses would prefer sweepings to gold"; for food is pleasanter than gold to asses. So the pleasures of creatures different in kind differ in kind, and it is plausible to suppose that those of a single species do not differ. But they vary to no small extent, in the case of men at least; the same things delight some people and pain others, and are painful and odious to some, and pleasant to and liked by others. This happens, too, in the case of sweet things; the same things do not seem sweet to a man in a fever and a healthy man—nor hot to a weak man and one in good condition. The same happens in other cases. But in all such matters that which appears to the good man is thought to be really so. If this is correct, as it seems to be, and virtue and the good man as such are the measure of each thing, those also will be pleasures which appear so to him, and those things pleasant which he enjoys. If the things he finds tiresome seem pleasant to some one, that is nothing surprising; for men may be ruined and spoilt in many ways; but the things are not pleasant, but only pleasant to these people and to people in this condition. Those which are admittedly disgraceful plainly should not be said to be pleasures, except to a perverted taste; but of those that are thought to be good what kind of pleasure or what pleasure should be said to be that proper to man? Is it not plain from the corresponding activities? The pleasures follow these. Whether, then, the perfect and supremely happy man has one or more activities, the pleasures that perfect these will be said in the strict sense to be pleasures proper to man, and the rest will be so in a secondary and fractional way, as are the activities.

6. [*Happiness is good activity, not amusement.*] Now that we have spoken of the virtues, the forms of friendship, and the varieties of pleasure, what remains is to discuss in outline the nature of happiness, since this is what we state the end of human nature to be. Our discussion will be the more concise if we first sum up what we have said already. We said, then, that it is not a disposition; for if it were it might

belong to some one who was asleep throughout his life, living the life of a plant, or, again, to some one who was suffering the greatest misfortunes. If these implications are unacceptable, and we must rather class happiness as an activity, as we have said before, and if some activities are necessary, and desirable for the sake of something else, while others are so in themselves, evidently happiness must be placed among those desirable in themselves, not among those desirable for the sake of something else, for happiness does not lack anything, but is self-sufficient. Now those activities are desirable in themselves from which nothing is sought beyond the activity And of this nature virtuous actions are thought to be; for to do noble and good deeds is a thing desirable for its own sake.

Pleasant amusements also are thought to be of this nature; we choose them not for the sake of other things; for we are injured rather than benefited by them, since we are led to neglect our bodies and our property. But most of the people who are deemed happy take refuge in such pastimes, which is the reason why those who are ready-witted at them are highly esteemed at the courts of tyrants; they make themselves pleasant companions in the tyrants' favourite pursuits, and that is the sort of man they want Now these things are thought to be of the nature of happiness because people in despotic positions spend their leisure in them, but perhaps such people prove nothing; for virtue and reason, from which good activities flow, do not depend on despotic position; nor, if these people, who have never tasted pure and generous pleasure, take refuge in the bodily pleasures, should these for that reason be thought more desirable; for boys, too, think the things that are valued among themselves are the best. It is to be expected, then, that, as different things seem valuable to boys and to men, so they should to bad men and to good. Now, as we have often maintained, those things are both valuable and pleasant which are such to the good man; and to each man the activity in accordance with his own disposition is most desirable, and, therefore, to the good man that which is in accordance with virtue. Happiness, therefore, does not lie in amusement; it would, indeed, be strange if the end were amusement, and one were to take trouble and suffer hardship all one's life in order to amuse oneself. For, in a word, everything that we choose we choose for the sake of something else—except happiness, which is an end. Now to exert oneself and work for the sake of amusement seems silly and utterly childish. But to amuse oneself in order that one may exert oneself, as Anacharsis puts it, seems right; for amusement is a sort of relaxation, and we need relaxation because we cannot work continuously. Relaxation, then, is not an end; for it is taken for the sake of activity.

The happy life is thought to be virtuous; now a virtuous life requires exertion, and does not consist in amusement. And we say that serious things are better than laughable things and those connected with amusement, and that the activity of the better of any two things—whether it be two elements of our being or two men—is the more serious; but the activity of the better is *ipso facto* superior and more of the nature of happiness. And any chance person—even a slave—can enjoy the bodily pleasures no less than the best man; but no one assigns to a slave a share in happiness—unless he assigns to him also a share in human life. For happiness does not lie in such occupations, but, as we have said before, in virtuous activities.

7. [*Happiness in the highest sense is the contemplative life.*] If happiness is activity in accordance with virtue, it is reasonable that it should be in accordance with the highest virtue; and this will be that of the best thing in us. Whether it be reason or something else that is this element which is thought to be our natural ruler and guide and to take thought of things noble and divine, whether it be itself also divine or only the most divine element in us, the activity of this in accordance with its proper virtue will be perfect happiness. That this activity is contemplative we have already said.

Now this would seem to be in agreement both with what we said before and with the truth. For, firstly, this activity is the best (since not only is reason the best thing in us, but the objects of reason are the best of knowable objects); and, secondly, it is the most continuous, since we can contemplate truth more continuously than we can *do* anything. And we think happiness has pleasure mingled with it, but the activity of philosophic wisdom is admittedly the pleasantest of virtuous activities; at all events the pursuit of it is thought to offer pleasures marvellous for their purity and their enduringness, and it is to be expected that those who know will pass their time more pleasantly than those who inquire. And the self-sufficiency that is spoken of must belong most to the contemplative activity. For while a philosopher, as well as a just man or one possessing any other virtue, needs the necessaries of life, when they are sufficiently equipped with things of that sort the just man needs people towards whom and with whom he shall act justly, and the temperate man, the brave man, and each of the others is in the same case, but the philosopher, even when by himself, can contemplate truth, and the better the wiser he is; he can perhaps do so better if he has fellow workers, but still he is the most self-sufficient. And this activity alone would seem to be loved for its own sake; for nothing arises from it apart from the contemplating, while from practical activities we gain more or less apart from the action. And happiness is thought to depend on leisure; for we are busy that we may have leisure, and make war that we may live in peace. Now the activity of the practical virtues is exhibited in political or military affairs, but the actions concerned with these seem to be unleisurely. Warlike actions are completely so (for no one chooses to be at war, or provokes war, for the sake of being at war; any one would seem absolutely murderous if he were to make enemies of his friends in order to bring about battle and slaughter); but the action of the statesman is also unleisurely, and—apart from the political action itself—aims at despotic power and honours, or at all events happiness, for him and his fellow citizens—a happiness different from political action, and evidently sought as being different. So if among virtuous actions political and military actions are distinguished by nobility and greatness, and these are unleisurely and aim at an end and are not desirable for their own sake, but the activity of reason, which is contemplative, seems both to be superior in serious worth and to aim at no end beyond itself, and to have its pleasure proper to itself (and this augments the activity), and the self-sufficiency, leisureliness, unweariedness (so far as this is possible for man), and all the other attributes ascribed to the supremely happy man are evidently those connected with this activity, it follows that this will be the complete happiness of man, if it be allowed a complete term of life (for none of the attributes of happiness is *in*complete).

But such a life would be too high for man; for it is not in so far as he is man that he will live so, but in so far as something divine is present in him; and by so much as this is superior to our composite nature is its activity superior to that which is the exercise of the other kind of virtue. If reason is divine, then, in comparison with man, the life according to it is divine in comparison with human life. But we must not follow those who advise us, being men, to think of human things, and, being mortal, of mortal things, but must, so far as we can, make ourselves immortal, and strain every nerve to live in accordance with the best thing in us; for even if it be small in bulk, much more does it in power and worth surpass everything. This would seem, too, to be each man himself, since it is the authoritative and better part of him. It would be strange, then, if he were to choose not the life of his self but that of something else. And what we said before will apply now; that which is proper to each thing is by nature best and most pleasant for each thing; for man, therefore, the life according to reason is best and pleasantest, since reason more than anything else *is* man. This life therefore is also the happiest.

8. [*Superiority of the contemplative life.*] But in a secondary degree the life in accordance with the other kind of virtue

is happy; for the activities in accordance with this befit our human estate. Just and brave acts, and other virtuous acts, we do in relation to each other, observing our respective duties with regard to contracts and services and all manner of actions and with regard to passions; and all of these seem to be typically human. Some of them seem even to arise from the body, and virtue of character to be in many ways bound up with the passions. Practical wisdom, too, is linked to virtue of character, and this to practical wisdom, since the principles of practical wisdom are in accordance with the moral virtues and rightness in morals is in accordance with practical wisdom. Being connected with the passions also, the moral virtues must belong to our composite nature; and the virtues of our composite nature are human; so, therefore, are the life and the happiness which correspond to these. The excellence of the reason is a thing apart; we must be content to say this much about it, for to describe it precisely is a task greater than our purpose requires. It would seem, however, also to need external equipment but little, or less than moral virtue does. Grant that both need the necessaries, and do so equally, even if the statesman's work is the more concerned with the body and things of that sort; for there will be little difference there; but in what they need for the exercise of their activities there will be much difference. The liberal man will need money for the doing of his liberal deeds, and the just man too will need it for the returning of services (for wishes are hard to discern, and even people who are not just pretend to wish to act justly); and the brave man will need power if he is to accomplish any of the acts that correspond to his virtue, and the temperate man will need opportunity; for how else is either he or any of the others to be recognized? It is debated, too, whether the will or the deed is more essential to virtue, which is assumed to involve both; it is surely clear that its perfection involves both; but for deeds many things are needed, and more, the greater and nobler the deeds are. But the man who is contemplating the truth needs no such thing, at least with a view to the exercise of his activity; indeed they are, one may say, even hindrances, at all events to his contemplation; but in so far as he is a man and lives with a number of people, he chooses to do virtuous acts; he will therefore need such aids to living a human life.

But that perfect happiness is a contemplative activity will appear from the following consideration as well. We assume the gods to be above all other beings blessed and happy; but what sort of actions must we assign to them? Acts of justice? Will not the gods seem absurd if they make contracts and return deposits, and so on? Acts of a brave man, then, confronting dangers and running risks because it is noble to do so? Or liberal acts? To whom will they give? It will be strange if they are really to have money or anything of the kind. And what would their temperate acts be? Is not such praise tasteless, since they have no bad appetites? If we were to run through them all, the circumstances of action would be found trivial and unworthy of gods. Still, every one supposes that they *live* and therefore that they are active; we cannot suppose them to sleep like Endymion. Now if you take away from a living being action, and still more production, what is left but contemplation? Therefore the activity of God, which surpasses all others in blessedness, must be contemplative; and of human activities, therefore, that which is most akin to this must be most of the nature of happiness.

This is indicated, too, by the fact that the other animals have no share in happiness, being completely deprived of such activity. For while the whole life of the gods is blessed, and that of men too in so far as some likeness of such activity belongs to them, none of the other animals is happy, since they in no way share in contemplation. Happiness extends, then, just so far as contemplation does, and those to whom contemplation more fully belongs are more truly happy, not as a mere concomitant but in virtue of the contemplation; for this is in itself precious. Happiness, therefore, must be some form of contemplation.

But, being a man, one will also need external prosperity; for our nature is not self-sufficient for the purpose of contemplation, but our body also must be healthy and must have food and other attention. Still, we must not think that the man who is to be happy will need many things or great things, merely because he cannot be supremely happy without external goods; for self-sufficiency and action do not involve excess, and we can do noble acts without ruling earth and sea; for even with moderate advantages one can act virtuously (this is manifest enough; for private persons are thought to do worthy acts no less than despots—indeed even more); and it is enough that we should have so much as that; for the life of the man who is active in accordance with virtue will be happy. Solon, too, was perhaps sketching well the happy man when he described him as moderately furnished with externals but as having done (as Solon thought) the noblest acts, and lived temperately; for one can with but moderate possessions do what one ought. Anaxagoras also seems to have supposed the happy man not to be rich nor a despot, when he said that he would not be surprised if the happy man were to seem to most people a strange person; for they judge by externals, since these are all they perceive. The opinions of the wise seem, then, to harmonize with our arguments. But while even such things carry some conviction, the truth in practical matters is discerned from the facts of life; for these are the decisive factor. We must therefore survey what we have already said, bringing it to the test of the facts of life, and if it harmonizes with the facts we must accept it, but if it clashes with them we must suppose it to be mere theory. Now he who exercises his reason and cultivates it seems to be both in the best state of mind and most dear to the gods. For if the gods have any care for human affairs, as they are thought to have, it would be reasonable both that they should delight in that which was best and most akin to them (i. e., reason) and that they should reward those who love and honour this most, as caring for the things that are dear to them and acting both rightly and nobly. And that all these attributes belong most of all to the philosopher is manifest. He, therefore, is the dearest to the gods. And he who is that will presumably be

also the happiest; so that in this way too the philosopher will
more than any other be happy.

9. [*Legislation is needed if the end is to be attained:* Politics.] If these matters and the virtues, and also friendship
and pleasure, have been dealt with sufficiently in outline,
are we to suppose that our programme has reached its end?
Surely, as the saying goes, where there are things to be done
the end is not to survey and recognize the various things, but
rather to do them; with regard to virtue, then, it is not
enough to know, but we must try to have and use it, or try
any other way there may be of becoming good. Now if arguments were in themselves enough to make men good, they
would justly, as Theognis says, have won very great rewards,
and such rewards should have been provided; but as things
are, while they seem to have power to encourage and stimulate the generous-minded among our youth, and to make a
character which is gently born, and a true lover of what is
noble, ready to be possessed by virtue, they are not able to
encourage the many to nobility and goodness. For these do
not by nature obey the sense of shame, but only fear, and
do not abstain from bad acts because of their baseness but
through fear of punishment; living by passion they pursue
their own pleasures and the means to them, and avoid the
opposite pains, and have not even a conception of what is
noble and truly pleasant, since they have never tasted it.
What argument would remould such people? It is hard, if not
impossible, to remove by argument the traits that have long
since been incorporated in the character; and perhaps we
must be content if, when all the influences by which we are
thought to become good are present, we get some tincture of
virtue.

Now some think that we are made good by nature, others
by habituation, others by teaching. Nature's part evidently
does not depend on us, but as a result of some divine causes
is present in those who are truly fortunate; while argument
and teaching, we may suspect, are not powerful with all
men, but the soul of the student must first have been culti-

vated by means of habits for noble joy and noble hatred, like earth which is to nourish the seed. For he who lives as passion directs will not hear argument that dissuades him, nor understand it if he does; and how can we persuade one in such a state to change his ways? And in general passion seems to yield not to argument but to force. The character, then, must somehow be there already with a kinship to virtue, loving what is noble and hating what is base.

But it is difficult to get from youth up a right training for virtue if one has not been brought up under right laws; for to live temperately and hardily is not pleasant to most people, especially when they are young. For this reason their nurture and occupations should be fixed by law; for they will not be painful when they have become customary. But it is surely not enough that when they are young they should get the right nurture and attention; since they must, even when they are grown up, practise and be habituated to them, we shall need laws for this as well, and generally speaking to cover the whole of life; for most people obey necessity rather than argument, and punishments rather than the sense of what is noble.

This is why some think that legislators ought to stimulate men to virtue and urge them forward by the motive of the noble, on the assumption that those who have been well advanced by the formation of habits will attend to such influences; and that punishments and penalties should be imposed on those who disobey and are of inferior nature, while the incurably bad should be completely banished. A good man (they think), since he lives with his mind fixed on what is noble, will submit to argument, while a bad man, whose desire is for pleasure, is corrected by pain like a beast of burden. This is, too, why they say the pains inflicted should be those that are most opposed to the pleasures such men love.

However that may be, if (as we have said) the man who is to be good must be well trained and habituated, and go on to spend his time in worthy occupations and neither willingly nor unwillingly do bad actions, and if this can be brought about if men live in accordance with a sort of reason and right order, provided this has force—if this be so, the paternal command indeed has not the required force or compulsive power (nor in general has the command of one man, unless he be a king or something similar), but the law *has* compulsive power, while it is at the same time a rule proceeding from a sort of practical wisdom and reason. And while people hate *men* who oppose their impulses, even if they oppose them rightly, the law in its ordaining of what is good is not burdensome.

In the Spartan state alone, or almost alone, the legislator seems to have paid attention to questions of nurture and occupations; in most states such matters have been neglected, and each man lives as he pleases, Cyclops-fashion, "to his own wife and children dealing law." Now it is best that there should be a public and proper care for such matters; but if they are neglected by the community it would seem right for each man to help his children and friends towards virtue, and that they should have the power, or at least the will, to do this.

It would seem from what has been said that he can do this better if he makes himself capable of legislating. For public control is plainly effected by laws, and good control by good laws; whether written or unwritten would seem to make no difference, nor whether they are laws providing for the education of individuals or of groups—any more than it does in the case of music or gymnastics and other such pursuits. For as in cities laws and prevailing types of character have force, so in households do the injunctions and the habits of the father, and these have even more because of the tie of blood and the benefits he confers; for the children start with a natural affection and disposition to obey. Further, private education has an advantage over public, as private medical treatment has; for while in general rest and abstinence from food are good for a man in a fever, for a particular man they may not be; and a boxer presumably does not prescribe the same style of fighting to all his pupils. It would seem, then, that the detail is worked out with more precision if the control is private; for each person is more likely to get what suits his case.

But the details can be best looked after, one by one, by a doctor or gymnastic instructor or any one else who has the general knowledge of what is good for every one or for people of a certain kind (for the sciences both are said to be, and are, concerned with what is universal); not but what some particular detail may perhaps be well looked after by an unscientific person, if he has studied accurately in the light of experience what happens in each case, just as some people seem to be their own best doctors, though they could give no help to any one else. None the less, it will perhaps be agreed that if a man does wish to become master of an art or science he must go to the universal, and come to know it as well as possible; for, as we have said, it is with this that the sciences are concerned.

And surely he who wants to make men, whether many or few, better by his care must try to become capable of legislating, if it is through laws that we can become good. For to get any one whatever—any one who is put before us—into the right condition is not for the first chance comer; if any one can do it, it is the man who knows, just as in medicine and all other matters which give scope for care and prudence.

Must we not, then, next examine whence or how one can learn how to legislate? Is it, as in all other cases, from statesmen? Certainly it was thought to be a part of statesmanship. Or is a difference apparent between statesmanship and the other sciences and arts? In the others the same people are found offering to teach the arts and practising them, e. g., doctors or painters; but while the sophists profess to teach politics, it is practised not by any of them but by the politicians, who would seem to do so by dint of a certain skill and experience rather than of thought; for they are not found either writing or speaking about such matters (though it were a nobler occupation perhaps than composing speeches for the law courts and the assembly), nor again are they found to have made statesmen of their own sons or any other of their friends. But it was to be expected that they should if they could; for there is nothing better than such a skill that they could have left to their cities, or could prefer to have for themselves, or, therefore, for those dearest to them. Still, experience seems to contribute not a little; else they could not have become politicians by familiarity with politics; and so it seems that those who aim at knowing about the art of politics need experience as well.

But those of the sophists who profess the art seem to be very far from teaching it. For, to put the matter generally, they do not even know what kind of thing it is nor what kinds of things it is about; otherwise they would not have classed it as identical with rhetoric or even inferior to it, nor have thought it easy to legislate by collecting the laws that are thought well of; they say it is possible to select the best laws, as though even the selection did not demand intelligence and as though right judgement were not the greatest thing, as in matters of music. For while people experienced in any department judge rightly the works produced in it, and understand by what means or how they are achieved, and what harmonizes with what, the inexperienced must be content if they do not fail to see whether the work has been well or ill made—as in the case of painting. Now laws are as it were the "works" of the political art; how then can one learn from them to be a legislator, or judge which are best? Even medical men do not seem to be made by a study of textbooks. Yet people try, at any rate, to state not only the treatments, but also how particular classes of people can be cured and should be treated—distinguishing the various habits of body; but while this seems useful to experienced people, to the inexperienced it is valueless. Surely, then, while collections of laws, and of constitutions also, may be serviceable to those who can study them and judge what is good or bad and what enactments suit what circumstances, those who go through such collections without a practised faculty will not have right judgement (unless it be as a spontaneous gift of nature), though they may perhaps become more intelligent in such matters.

Now our predecessors have left the subject of legislation to us unexamined; it is perhaps best, therefore, that we should ourselves study it, and in general study the question of the constitution, in order to complete to the best of our ability our philosophy of human nature. First, then, if anything has been said well in detail by earlier thinkers, let us try to review it; then in the light of the constitutions we have collected let us study what sorts of influence preserve and destroy states, and what sorts preserve or destroy the particular kinds of constitution, and to what causes it is due that some are well and others ill administered. When these have been studied we shall perhaps be more likely to see with a comprehensive view, which constitution is best, and how each must be ordered, and what laws and customs it must use, if it is to be at its best. Let us make a beginning of our discussion.

POLITICS

Translated by Benjamin Jowett

The last paragraph of the NICOMACHEAN ETHICS is not only a transition to the POLITICS but also a brief introduction to it, for Aristotle gives a broad outline of what he intends: to review the contributions of earlier thinkers, to study the various kinds of states and constitutions in order to discover what factors preserve or destroy them, and through this study to decide what the ideal state is and what its laws and customs must be.

Despite the announced program, the POLITICS is not altogether a systematically constructed work, and scholars have proposed various rearrangements designed to give it more coherence. But even in its traditional form, often lacking transitions and basic continuity, Aristotle's treatise on the state is a work of superb insight and analysis. It is founded not only on his direct experience of politics in action but also, we are told, on solid historical research on comparative grounds—his compilation and study of 158 Greek city-state constitutions. In several respects Aristotle may have been the prisoner of his own data. His ideal commonwealth, like the city-states he studied, is founded on the institution of slavery; and, like most of his philosophical contemporaries, he is scornful of trade and labor. Despite these limitations, which are of his own time and country, the

POLITICS remains a classic seminal study of the origins, the forms, and the functions of the state.

Man is a political animal, Aristotle says, and political institutions are neither arbitrary nor merely voluntary associations but are rooted in the basic nature and necessities of man. Having validated this principle, he proceeds, in the selections which follow, to establish the groundwork for the ideal commonwealth. He criticizes in some detail the ideal state proposed by Plato in the REPUBLIC, and he surveys the astounding variety of states and constitutions which fourth-century Greece had to offer. Like Plato, he is vitally concerned with the relationship between education and government, and he makes the clear recommendation that the training and guidance of the young be the cornerstone of the ideal state. As the state is the sum of the goals of its citizens, so, in the Aristotelian scheme of knowledge, politics, which determines goals and conduct, is the supreme practical art.

POLITICS

@@@

BOOK I

1. [*The state is the highest form of community.*] Every state is a community of some kind, and every community is established with a view to some good; for mankind always act in order to obtain that which they think good. But, if all communities aim at some good, the state or political community, which is the highest of all, and which embraces all the rest, aims at good in a greater degree than any other, and at the highest good.

Some people think that the qualifications of a statesman, king, householder, and master are the same, and that they differ, not in kind, but only in the number of their subjects. For example, the ruler over a few is called a master; over more, the manager of a household; over a still larger number, a statesman or king, as if there were no difference between a great household and a small state. The distinction which is made between the king and the statesman is as follows: When the government is personal, the ruler is a king; when, according to the rules of the political science, the citizens rule and are ruled in turn, then he is called a statesman.

But all this is a mistake; for governments differ in kind, as will be evident to any one who considers the matter according to the method which has hitherto guided us. As in other departments of science, so in politics, the compound should always be resolved into the simple elements or least parts of the whole. We must therefore look at the elements of which the state is composed, in order that we may see in what the different kinds of rule differ from one another, and whether any scientific result can be attained about each one of them.

2. [*Components and foundations of the state.*] He who thus considers things in their first growth and origin, whether a state or anything else, will obtain the clearest view of them. In the first place there must be a union of those who cannot exist without each other; namely, of male and female, that the race may continue (and this is a union which is formed, not of deliberate purpose, but because, in common with other animals and with plants, mankind have a natural desire to leave behind them an image of themselves), and of natural ruler and subject, that both may be preserved. For that which can foresee by the exercise of mind is by nature intended to be lord and master, and that which can with its body give effect to such foresight is a subject, and by nature a slave; hence master and slave have the same interest. Now nature has distinguished between the female and the slave. For she is not niggardly, like the smith who fashions the Delphian knife for many uses; she makes each thing for a single use, and every instrument is best made when intended for one and not for many uses. But among barbarians no distinction is made between women and slaves, because there is no natural ruler among them: they are a community of slaves, male and female. Wherefore the poets say:

"It is meet that Hellenes should rule over barbarians";

as if they thought that the barbarian and the slave were by nature one.

Out of these two relationships between man and woman, master and slave, the first thing to arise is the family, and Hesiod is right when he says:

"First house and wife and an ox for the plough,"

for the ox is the poor man's slave. The family is the association established by nature for the supply of men's everyday wants, and the members of it are called by Charondas "companions of the cupboard," and by Epimenides the Cretan, "companions of the manger." But when several families are united, and the association aims at something more than the supply of daily needs, the first society to be formed is the village. And the most natural form of the village appears to be that of a colony from the family, composed of the children and grandchildren, who are said to be "suckled with the same milk." And this is the reason why Hellenic states were originally governed by kings; because the Hellenes were under royal rule before they came together, as the barbarians still are. Every family is ruled by the eldest, and therefore in the colonies of the family the kingly form of government prevailed because they were of the same blood. As Homer says:

"Each one gives law to his children and to his wives."

For they lived dispersedly, as was the manner in ancient times. Wherefore men say that the Gods have a king, because they themselves either are or were in ancient times under the rule of a king. For they imagine, not only the forms of the Gods, but their ways of life to be like their own.

When several villages are united in a single complete community, large enough to be nearly or quite self-sufficing, the state comes into existence, originating in the bare needs of life, and continuing in existence for the sake of a good life. And therefore, if the earlier forms of society are natural, so is the state, for it is the end of them, and the nature of a thing is its end. For what each thing is when fully developed, we call its nature, whether we are speaking of a man, a horse, or a family. Besides, the final cause and end of a thing is the best, and to be self-sufficing is the end and the best.

Hence it is evident that the state is a creation of nature, and that man is by nature a political animal. And he who by nature and not by mere accident is without a state, is either a bad man or above humanity; he is like the

"Tribeless, lawless, heartless one,"

whom Homer denounces—the natural outcast is forthwith a lover of war; he may be compared to an isolated piece at draughts.

Now, that man is more of a political animal than bees or any other gregarious animals is evident. Nature, as we often say, makes nothing in vain, and man is the only animal whom she has endowed with the gift of speech. And whereas mere voice is but an indication of pleasure or pain, and is therefore found in other animals (for their nature attains to the perception of pleasure and pain and the intimation of them to one another, and no further), the power of speech is intended to set forth the expedient and inexpedient, and therefore likewise the just and the unjust. And it is a characteristic of man that he alone has any sense of good and evil, of just and unjust, and the like, and the association of living beings who have this sense makes a family and a state.

Further, the state is by nature clearly prior to the family and to the individual, since the whole is of necessity prior to the part; for example, if the whole body be destroyed, there will be no foot or hand, except in an equivocal sense, as we might speak of a stone hand; for when destroyed the hand will be no better than that. But things are defined by their working and power; and we ought not to say that they are the same when they no longer have their proper quality, but only that they have the same name. The proof that the state is a creation of nature and prior to the individual is that the individual, when isolated, is not self-sufficing; and therefore he is like a part in relation to the whole. But he who is unable to live in society, or who has no need because he is sufficient for himself, must be either a beast or a god; he is no part of a state. A social instinct is implanted in all men by nature, and yet he who first founded the state was the greatest of benefactors. For man, when perfected, is the best of animals, but, when separated from law and justice, he is the worst of all; since armed injustice is the more dangerous, and he is equipped at birth with arms, meant to be used by intelligence and virtue, which he may use for the worst ends. Wherefore, if he have not virtue, he is the most

unholy and the most savage of animals, and the most full
of lust and gluttony. But justice is the bond of men in states,
for the administration of justice, which is the determination
of what is just, is the principle of order in political society.

* * *

BOOK II

1. [*Theories of the ideal state.*] Our purpose is to consider
what form of political community is best of all for those
who are most able to realize their ideal of life. We must
therefore examine not only this but other constitutions, both
such as actually exist in well-governed states, and any theoretical forms which are held in esteem; that what is good
and useful may be brought to light. And let no one suppose
that in seeking for something beyond them we are anxious
to make a sophistical display at any cost; we only undertake
this inquiry because all the constitutions with which we are
acquainted are faulty.

We will begin with the natural beginning of the subject.
Three alternatives are conceivable. The members of a state
must either have (1) all things or (2) nothing in common,
or (3) some things in common and some not. That they
should have nothing in common is clearly impossible, for the
constitution is a community, and must at any rate have a
common place—one city will be in one place, and the citizens
are those who share in that one city. But should a well-
ordered state have all things, as far as may be, in common,
or some only and not others? For the citizens might conceiv-
ably have wives and children and property in common, as

Socrates proposes in the *Republic* of Plato. Which is better, our present condition, or the proposed new order of society?

2. [*Criticism of Plato's theories.*] There are many difficulties in the community of women. And the principle on which Socrates rests the necessity of such an institution evidently is not established by his arguments. Further, as a means to the end which he ascribes to the state, the scheme, taken literally, is impracticable, and how we are to interpret it is nowhere precisely stated. I am speaking of the premiss from which the argument of Socrates proceeds, "that the greater the unity of the state the better." Is it not obvious that a state may at length attain such a degree of unity as to be no longer a state? since the nature of a state is to be a plurality, and in tending to greater unity, from being a state, it becomes a family, and from being a family, an individual; for the family may be said to be more one than the state, and the individual than the family. So that we ought not to attain this greatest unity even if we could, for it would be the destruction of the state. Again, a state is not made up only of so many men, but of different kinds of men; for similars do not constitute a state. It is not like a military alliance. The usefulness of the latter depends upon its quantity even where there is no difference in quality (for mutual protection is the end aimed at), just as a greater weight of anything is more useful than a less (in like manner, a state differs from a nation, when the nation has not its population organized in villages, but lives an Arcadian sort of life); but the elements out of which a unity is to be formed differ in kind. Wherefore the principle of compensation, as I have already remarked in the *Ethics*, is the salvation of states. Even among freemen and equals this is a principle which must be maintained, for they cannot all rule together, but must change at the end of a year or some other period of time or in some order of succession. The result is that upon this plan they all govern; just as if shoemakers and carpenters were to exchange their occupations, and the same persons did not always continue shoemakers and carpenters. And since it is

better that this should be so in politics as well, it is clear that while there should be continuance of the same persons in power where this is possible, yet where this is not possible by reason of the natural equality of the citizens, and at the same time it is just that all should share in the government (whether to govern be a good thing or a bad), an approximation to this is that equals should in turn retire from office and should, apart from official position, be treated alike. Thus the one party rule and the others are ruled in turn, as if they were no longer the same persons. In like manner when they hold office there is a variety in the offices held. Hence it is evident that a city is not by nature one in that sense which some persons affirm; and that what is said to be the greatest good of cities is in reality their destruction; but surely the good of things must be that which preserves them. Again, in another point of view, this extreme unification of the state is clearly not good; for a family is more self-sufficing than an individual, and a city than a family, and a city only comes into being when the community is large enough to be self-sufficing. If then self-sufficiency is to be desired, the lesser degree of unity is more desirable than the greater.

3. [*Criticism of Plato's theories.*] But, even supposing that it were best for the community to have the greatest degree of unity, this unity is by no means proved to follow from the fact "of all men saying 'mine' and 'not mine' at the same instant of time," which, according to Socrates, is the sign of perfect unity in a state. For the word "all" is ambiguous. If the meaning be that every individual says "mine" and "not mine" at the same time, then perhaps the result at which Socrates aims may be in some degree accomplished; each man will call the same person his own son and the same person his own wife, and so of his property and of all that falls to his lot. This, however, is not the way in which people would speak who had their wives and children in common; they would say "all" but not "each." In like manner their property would be described as belonging to them not severally but collectively. There is an obvious fallacy in the term "all": like

some other words, "both," "odd," "even," it is ambiguous, and even in abstract argument becomes a source of logical puzzles. That all persons call the same thing mine in the sense in which each does so may be a fine thing, but it is impracticable; or if the words are taken in the other sense, such a unity in no way conduces to harmony. And there is another objection to the proposal. For that which is common to the greatest number has the least care bestowed upon it. Every one thinks chiefly of his own, hardly at all of the common interest; and only when he is himself concerned as an individual. For besides other considerations, everybody is more inclined to neglect the duty which he expects another to fulfil; as in families many attendants are often less useful than a few. Each citizen will have a thousand sons who will not be his sons individually, but anybody will be equally the son of anybody, and will therefore be neglected by all alike. Further, upon this principle, every one will use the word "mine" of one who is prospering or the reverse, however small a fraction he may himself be of the whole number; the same boy will be "my son," "so and so's son," the son of each of the thousand, or whatever be the number of the citizens; and even about this he will not be positive; for it is impossible to know who chanced to have a child, or whether, if one came into existence, it has survived. But which is better—for each to say "mine" in this way, making a man the same relation to two thousand or ten thousand citizens, or to use the word "mine" in the ordinary and more restricted sense? For usually the same person is called by one man his own son whom another calls his own brother or cousin or kinsman—blood relation or connexion by marriage either of himself or of some relation of his, and yet another his clansman or tribesman; and how much better is it to be the real cousin of somebody than to be a son after Plato's fashion! Nor is there any way of preventing brothers and children and fathers and mothers from sometimes recognizing one another; for children are born like their parents, and they will necessarily be finding indications of their relationship to one another. Geographers declare such to be the fact; they say that in part of Upper Libya, where the women are common, nevertheless the children who are born are assigned to their respective fathers on the ground of their likeness. And some women, like the females of other animals—for example, mares and cows—have a strong tendency to produce offspring resembling their parents, as was the case with the Pharsalian mare called Honest.

4. [*Criticism of Plato's theories.*] Other evils, against which it is not easy for the authors of such a community to guard, will be assaults and homicides, voluntary as well as involuntary, quarrels and slanders, all which are most unholy acts when committed against fathers and mothers and near relations, but not equally unholy when there is no relationship. Moreover, they are much more likely to occur if the relationship is unknown, and, when they have occurred, the customary expiations of them cannot be made. Again, how strange it is that Socrates, after having made the children common, should hinder lovers from carnal intercourse only, but should permit love and familiarities between father and son or between brother and brother, than which nothing can be more unseemly, since even without them love of this sort is improper. How strange, too, to forbid intercourse for no other reason than the violence of the pleasure, as though the relationship of father and son or of brothers with one another made no difference.

This community of wives and children seems better suited to the husbandmen than to the guardians, for if they have wives and children in common, they will be bound to one another by weaker ties, as a subject class should be, and they will remain obedient and not rebel. In a word, the result of such a law would be just the opposite of that which good laws ought to have, and the intention of Socrates in making these regulations about women and children would defeat itself. For friendship we believe to be the greatest good of states and the preservative of them against revolutions; neither is there anything which Socrates so greatly lauds as the unity of the state which he and all the world declare to be created by friendship. But the unity which he commends would be like

that of the lovers in the *Symposium,* who, as Aristophanes
says, desire to grow together in the excess of their affection,
and from being two to become one, in which case one or both
would certainly perish. Whereas in a state having women and
children common, love will be watery; and the father will
certainly not say "my son," or the son "my father." As a little
sweet wine mingled with a great deal of water is imperceptible in the mixture, so, in this sort of community, the idea of
relationship which is based upon these names will be lost;
there is no reason why the so-called father should care about
the son, or the son about the father, or brothers about one
another. Of the two qualities which chiefly inspire regard
and affection—that a thing is your own and that it is your
only one—neither can exist in such a state as this.

Again, the transfer of children as soon as they are born
from the rank of husbandmen or of artisans to that of guardians, and from the rank of guardians into a lower rank, will
be very difficult to arrange; the givers or transferrers cannot
but know whom they are giving and transferring, and to
whom. And the previously mentioned evils, such as assaults,
unlawful loves, homicides, will happen more often amongst
those who are transferred to the lower classes, or who have
a place assigned to them among the guardians; for they will
no longer call the members of the class they have left brothers,
and children, and fathers, and mothers, and will not, therefore, be afraid of committing any crimes by reason of con-
sanguinity. Touching the community of wives and children,
let this be our conclusion.

5. [*Criticism of Plato's theories.*] Next let us consider what
should be our arrangements about property: should the citizens of the perfect state have their possessions in common
or not? This question may be discussed separately from the
enactments about women and children. Even supposing that
the women and children belong to individuals, according to
the custom which is at present universal, may there not be
an advantage in having and using possessions in common?
Three cases are possible: (1) the soil may be appropriated,

but the produce may be thrown for consumption into the common stock; and this is the practice of some nations. Or (2), the soil may be common, and may be cultivated in common, but the produce divided among individuals for their private use; this is a form of common property which is said to exist among certain barbarians. Or (3), the soil and the produce may be alike common.

When the husbandmen are not the owners, the case will be different and easier to deal with; but when they till the ground for themselves the question of ownership will give a world of trouble. If they do not share equally in enjoyments and toils, those who labour much and get little will necessarily complain of those who labour little and receive or consume much. But indeed there is always a difficulty in men living together and having all human relations in common, but especially in their having common property. The partnerships of fellow travellers are an example to the point, for they generally fall out over everyday matters and quarrel about any trifle which turns up. So with servants: we are most liable to take offense at those with whom we most frequently come into contact in daily life.

These are only some of the disadvantages which attend the community of property; the present arrangement, if improved as it might be by good customs and laws, would be far better, and would have the advantages of both systems. Property should be in a certain sense common, but, as a general rule, private; for, when every one has a distinct interest, men will not complain of one another, and they will make more progress, because every one will be attending to his own business. And yet by reason of goodness, and in respect of use, "Friends," as the proverb says, "will have all things common." Even now there are traces of such a principle, showing that it is not impracticable, but, in well-ordered states, exists already to a certain extent and may be carried further. For, although every man has his own property, some things he will place at the disposal of his friends, while of others he shares the use with them. The Lacedaemonians, for example, use one another's slaves, and horses, and dogs, as if they were their own; and when they lack provisions on a journey, they appropriate what they find in the fields throughout the country. It is clearly better that property should be private, but the use of it common; and the special business of the legislator is to create in men this benevolent disposition. Again, how immeasurably greater is the pleasure, when a man feels a thing to be his own; for surely the love of self is a feeling implanted by nature and not given in vain, although selfishness is rightly censured; this, however, is not the mere love of self, but the love of self in excess, like the miser's love of money; for all, or almost all, men love money and other such objects in a measure. And further, there is the greatest pleasure in doing a kindness or service to friends or guests or companions, which can only be rendered when a man has private property. These advantages are lost by excessive unification of the state. The exhibition of two virtues, besides, is visibly annihilated in such a state: first, temperance towards women (for it is an honourable action to abstain from another's wife for temperance' sake); secondly, liberality in the matter of property. No one, when men have all things in common, will any longer set an example of liberality or do any liberal action; for liberality consists in the use which is made of property.

Such legislation may have a specious appearance of benevolence; men readily listen to it, and are easily induced to believe that in some wonderful manner everybody will become everybody's friend, especially when some one is heard denouncing the evils now existing in states, suits about contracts, convictions for perjury, flatteries of rich men and the like, which are said to arise out of the possession of private property. These evils, however, are due to a very different cause—the wickedness of human nature. Indeed, we see that there is much more quarrelling among those who have all things in common, though there are not many of them when compared with the vast numbers who have private property.

Again, we ought to reckon, not only the evils from which the citizens will be saved, but also the advantages which they will lose. The life which they are to lead appears to be quite impracticable. The error of Socrates must be attributed to the false notion of unity from which he starts. Unity there should be, both of the family and of the state, but in some respects only. For there is a point at which a state may attain such a degree of unity as to be no longer a state, or at which, without actually ceasing to exist, it will become an inferior state, like harmony passing into unison, or rhythm which has been reduced to a single foot. The state, as I was saying, is plurality, which should be united and made into a community by education; and it is strange that the author of a system of education which he thinks will make the state virtuous, should expect to improve his citizens by regulations of this sort, and not by philosophy or by customs and laws, like those which prevail at Sparta and Crete respecting common meals, whereby the legislator has made property common. Let us remember that we should not disregard the experience of ages; in the multitude of years these things, if they were good, would certainly not have been unknown; for almost everything has been found out, although sometimes they are not put together; in other cases men do not use the knowledge which they have. Great light would be thrown on this subject if we could see such a form of government in the actual process of construction; for the legislator could not form a state at all without distributing and dividing its constituents into associations for common meals, and into phratries and tribes. But all this legislation ends only in forbidding agriculture to the guardians, a prohibition which the Lacedaemonians try to enforce already.

But, indeed, Socrates has not said, nor is it easy to decide, what in such a community will be the general form of the state. The citizens who are not guardians are the majority, and about them nothing has been determined: are the husbandmen, too, to have their property in common? Or is each individual to have his own? and are the wives and children to be individual or common? If, like the guardians, they are to have all things in common, in what do they differ from them, or what will they gain by submitting to their government? Or, upon what principle would they submit, unless indeed the governing class adopt the ingenious policy of the Cretans, who give their slaves the same institutions as their own, but forbid them gymnastic exercises and the possession of arms. If, on the other hand, the inferior classes are to be like other cities in respect of marriage and property, what will be the form of the community? Must it not contain two states in one, each hostile to the other? He makes the guardians into a mere occupying garrison, while the husbandmen and artisans and the rest are the real citizens. But if so the suits and quarrels, and all the evils which Socrates affirms to exist in other states, will exist equally among them. He says indeed that, having so good an education, the citizens will not need many laws, for example laws about the city or about the markets; but then he confines his education to the guardians. Again, he makes the husbandmen owners of the property upon condition of their paying a tribute. But in that case they are likely to be much more unmanageable and conceited than the Helots, or Penestae, or slaves in general. And whether community of wives and property be necessary for the lower equally with the higher class or not, and the questions akin to this, what will be the education, form of government, laws of the lower class, Socrates has nowhere determined; neither is it easy to discover this, nor is their character of small importance if the common life of the guardians is to be maintained.

Again, if Socrates makes the women common, and retains private property, the men will see to the fields, but who will see to the house? And who will do so if the agricultural class have both their property and their wives in common? Once more: it is absurd to argue, from the analogy of the animals, that men and women should follow the same pursuits, for animals have not to manage a household. The government, too, as constituted by Socrates, contains elements of danger; for he makes the same persons always rule. And if this is often a cause of disturbance among the meaner sort, how much more among high-spirited warriors? But that the persons whom he makes rulers must be the same is evident; for the gold which the God mingles in the souls of men is not at one time given to one, at another time to another, but always to the same; as he says, "God mingles gold in some, and silver in others, from their very birth; but brass and iron in those who are meant to be artisans and husbandmen." Again, he deprives the guardians even of happiness, and says that the legislator ought to make the whole state happy. But the whole cannot be happy unless most, or all, or some of its parts enjoy happiness. In this respect happiness is not like the even principle in numbers, which may exist only in the whole, but in neither of the parts; not so happiness. And if the guardians are not happy, who are? Surely not the artisans, or the common people. The Republic of which Socrates discourses has all these difficulties, and others quite as great.

6. [*Criticism of Plato's later theories.*] The same, or nearly the same, objections apply to Plato's later work, the *Laws*, and therefore we had better examine briefly the constitution which is therein described. In the *Republic*, Socrates has definitely settled in all a few questions only; such as the community of women and children, the community of property, and the constitution of the state. The population is divided into two classes—one of husbandmen, and the other of warriors; from this latter is taken a third class of counsellors and rulers of the state. But Socrates has not determined whether the husbandmen and artisans are to have a share in the government, and whether they, too, are to carry arms and share in military service, or not. He certainly thinks that the women ought to share in the education of the guardians, and to fight by their side. The remainder of the work is filled up with digressions foreign to the main subject, and with discussions about the education of the guardians. In the *Laws* there is hardly anything but laws; not much is said about the constitution. This, which he had intended to make more of the ordinary type, he gradually brings round to the other or ideal form. For with the exception of the community of women and property, he supposes everything to be the same in both states; there is to be the same education; the citizens of both are to live free from servile occupations, and there are to be common meals in both. The only difference

is that in the *Laws*, the common meals are extended to women, and the warriors number 5000, but in the *Republic* only 1000.

The discourses of Socrates are never commonplace; they always exhibit grace and originality and thought; but perfection in everything can hardly be expected. We must not overlook the fact that the number of 5000 citizens, just now mentioned, will require a territory as large as Babylon, or some other huge site, if so many persons are to be supported in idleness, together with their women and attendants, who will be a multitude many times as great. In framing an ideal we may assume what we wish, but should avoid impossibilities.

It is said that the legislator ought to have his eye directed to two points—the people and the country. But neighbouring countries also must not be forgotten by him, firstly because the state for which he legislates is to have a political and not an isolated life. For a state must have such a military force as will be serviceable against her neighbours, and not merely useful at home. Even if the life of action is not admitted to be the best, either for individuals or states, still a city should be formidable to enemies, whether invading or retreating.

There is another point: Should not the amount of property be defined in some way which differs from this by being clearer? For Socrates says that a man should have so much property as will enable him to live temperately, which is only a way of saying "to live well"; this is too general a conception. Further, a man may live temperately and yet miserably. A better definition would be that a man must have so much property as will enable him to live not only temperately but liberally; if the two are parted, liberality will combine with luxury; temperance will be associated with toil. For liberality and temperance are the only eligible qualities which have to do with the use of property. A man cannot use property with mildness or courage, but temperately and liberally he may; and therefore the practice of these virtues is inseparable from property. There is an inconsistency, too, in equalizing the property and not regulating the number of the citizens; the population is to remain unlimited, and he thinks that it will be sufficiently equalized by a certain number of marriages being unfruitful, however many are born to others, because he finds this to be the case in existing states. But greater care will be required than now; for among ourselves, whatever may be the number of citizens, the property is always distributed among them, and therefore no one is in want; but, if the property were incapable of division as in the *Laws*, the supernumeraries, whether few or many, would get nothing. One would have thought that it was even more necessary to limit population than property; and that the limit should be fixed by calculating the chances of mortality in the children, and of sterility in married persons. The neglect of this subject, which in existing states is so common, is a never-failing cause of poverty among the citizens; and poverty is the parent of revolution and crime. Pheidon the Corinthian, who was one of the most ancient legislators, thought that the families and the number of citizens ought to remain the same, although originally all the lots may have been of different sizes; but in the *Laws* the opposite principle is maintained. What in our opinion is the right arrangement will have to be explained hereafter.

There is another omission in the *Laws*: Socrates does not tell us how the rulers differ from their subjects; he only says that they should be related as the warp and the woof, which are made out of different wools. He allows that a man's whole property may be increased fivefold, but why should not his land also increase to a certain extent? Again, will the good management of a household be promoted by his arrangement of homesteads? for he assigns to each individual two homesteads in separate places, and it is difficult to live in two houses.

The whole system of government tends to be neither democracy nor oligarchy, but something in a mean between them, which is usually called a polity, and is composed of the heavy-armed soldiers. Now, if he intended to frame a constitution which would suit the greatest number of states, he was very likely right, but not if he meant to say that this constitutional form came nearest to his first or ideal state; for many would prefer the Lacedaemonian, or, possibly, some other more aristocratic government. Some, indeed, say that the best constitution is a combination of all existing forms, and they praise the Lacedaemonian because it is made up of oligarchy, monarchy, and democracy, the king forming the monarchy, and the council of elders the oligarchy, while the democratic element is represented by the Ephors; for the Ephors are selected from the people. Others, however, declare the Ephoralty to be a tyranny, and find the element of democracy in the common meals and in the habits of daily life. In the *Laws* it is maintained that the best constitution is made up of democracy and tyranny, which are either not constitutions at all, or are the worst of all. But they are nearer the truth who combine many forms; for the constitution is better which is made up of more numerous elements. The constitution proposed in the *Laws* has no element of monarchy at all; it is nothing but oligarchy and democracy, leaning rather to oligarchy. This is seen in the mode of appointing magistrates; for although the appointment of them by lot from among those who have been already selected combines both elements, the way in which the rich are compelled by law to attend the assembly and vote for magistrates or discharge other political duties, while the rest may do as they like, and the endeavour to have the greater number of the magistrates appointed out of the richer classes and the highest officers selected from those who have the greatest incomes, both these are oligarchical features. The oligarchical principle prevails also in the choice of the council, for all are compelled to choose, but the compulsion extends only to the choice out of the first class, and of an equal number out of the second class and out of the third class, but not in this latter case to all the voters but to those of the first three classes; and the selection of candidates out of the fourth class is only compulsory on the first and second. Then, from the persons so chosen, he says that there ought to be an equal number of each class selected. Thus a preponderance will be given to the better sort of people, who have the larger incomes, because many of the lower classes, not being compelled, will not vote. These considerations, and others which will be adduced when the time comes for examining similar polities, tend to show that states like Plato's should not be composed of democracy and monarchy. There is also a danger in electing the magistrates out of a body who are themselves elected; for, if but a small number choose to combine, the elections will always go as they desire. Such is the constitution which is described in the *Laws*.

* * *

BOOK III

1. [*Definition of a citizen.*] He who would inquire into the essence and attributes of various kinds of governments must first of all determine "What is a state?" At present this is a disputed question. Some say that the state has done a certain act; others, no, not the state, but the oligarchy or the tyrant. And the legislator or statesman is concerned entirely with the state; a constitution or government being an arrangement of the inhabitants of a state. But a state is composite, like any other whole made up of many parts; these are the citizens, who compose it. It is evident, therefore, that we must begin by asking, Who is the citizen, and what is the meaning of the term? For here again there may be a difference of opinion. He who is a citizen in a democracy will often not be a citizen in an oligarchy. Leaving out of consideration those who have been made citizens, or who have obtained the name of citizen in any other accidental manner, we may say, first, that a citizen is not a citizen because he lives in a certain place, for

resident aliens and slaves share in the place; nor is he a citizen who has no legal right except that of suing and being sued; for this right may be enjoyed under the provisions of a treaty. Nay, resident aliens in many places do not possess even such rights completely, for they are obliged to have a patron, so that they do but imperfectly participate in citizenship, and we call them citizens only in a qualified sense, as we might apply the term to children who are too young to be on the register, or to old men who have been relieved from state duties. Of these we do not say quite simply that they are citizens, but add in the one case that they are not of age, and in the other, that they are past the age, or something of that sort; the precise expression is immaterial, for our meaning is clear. Similar difficulties to those which I have mentioned may be raised and answered about deprived citizens and about exiles. But the citizen whom we are seeking to define is a citizen in the strictest sense, against whom no such exception can be taken, and his special characteristic is that he shares in the administration of justice, and in offices. Now of offices some are discontinuous, and the same persons are not allowed to hold them twice, or can only hold them after a fixed interval; others have no limit of time—for example, the office of dicast or ecclesiast. It may, indeed, be argued that these are not magistrates at all, and that their functions give them no share in the government. But surely it is ridiculous to say that those who have the supreme power do not govern. Let us not dwell further upon this, which is a purely verbal question; what we want is a common term including both dicast and ecclesiast. Let us, for the sake of distinction, call it "indefinite office," and we will assume that those who share in such office are citizens. This is the most comprehensive definition of a citizen, and best suits all those who are generally so called.

But we must not forget that things of which the underlying principles differ in kind, one of them being first, another second, another third, have, when regarded in this relation, nothing, or hardly anything, worth mentioning in common. Now we see that governments differ in kind, and that some of them are prior and that others are posterior; those which are faulty or perverted are necessarily posterior to those which are perfect. (What we mean by perversion will be hereafter explained.) The citizen then of necessity differs under each form of government; and our definition is best adapted to the citizen of a democracy; but not necessarily to other states. For in some states the people are not acknowledged, nor have they any regular assembly, but only extraordinary ones; and suits are distributed by sections among the magistrates. At Lacedaemon, for instance, the Ephors determine suits about contracts, which they distribute among themselves, while the elders are judges of homicide, and other causes are decided by other magistrates A similar principle prevails at Carthage, there certain magistrates decide all causes. We may, indeed, modify our definition of the citizen so as to include these states. In them it is the holder of a definite, not of an indefinite office, who legislates and judges, and to some or all such holders of definite offices is reserved the right of deliberating or judging about some things or about all things. The conception of the citizen now begins to clear up.

He who has the power to take part in the deliberative or judicial administration of any state is said by us to be a citizen of that state; and, speaking generally, a state is a body of citizens sufficing for the purposes of life.

2. [*Definition of a citizen.*] But in practice a citizen is defined to be one of whom both the parents are citizens; others insist on going further back; say to two or three or more ancestors. This is a short and practical definition; but there are some who raise the further question: How this third or fourth ancestor came to be a citizen? Gorgias of Leontini, partly because he was in a difficulty, partly in irony, said—"Mortars are what is made by the mortar makers, and the citizens of Larissa are those who are made by the magistrates; for it is their trade to make Larissaeans" Yet the question is really simple, for, if according to the definition just given they shared in the government, they were citizens. This is a better

definition than the other. For the words, "born of a father or mother who is a citizen," cannot possibly apply to the first inhabitants or founders of a state.

There is a greater difficulty in the case of those who have been made citizens after a revolution, as by Cleisthenes at Athens after the expulsion of the tyrants, for he enrolled in tribes many metics, both strangers and slaves. The doubt in these cases is, not who is, but whether he who is ought to be a citizen; and there will still be a further doubt, whether he who ought not to be a citizen, is one in fact, for what ought not to be is what is false. Now, there are some who hold office, and yet ought not to hold office, whom we describe as ruling, but ruling unjustly. And the citizen was defined by the fact of his holding some kind of rule or office—he who holds a judicial or legislative office fulfils our definition of a citizen. It is evident, therefore, that the citizens about whom the doubt has arisen must be called citizens.

3. [*Definition of the state.*] Whether they ought to be so or not is a question which is bound up with the previous inquiry. For a parallel question is raised respecting the state, whether a certain act is or is not an act of the state; for example, in the transition from an oligarchy or a tyranny to a democracy. In such cases persons refuse to fulfil their contracts or any other obligations, on the ground that the tyrant, and not the state, contracted them; they argue that some constitutions are established by force, and not for the sake of the common good. But this would apply equally to democracies, for they too may be founded on violence, and then the acts of the democracy will be neither more nor less acts of the state in question than those of an oligarchy or of a tyranny. This question runs up into another: on what principle shall we ever say that the state is the same, or different? It would be a very superficial view which considered only the place and the inhabitants (for the soil and the population may be separated, and some of the inhabitants may live in one place and some in another). This, however, is not a very serious difficulty; we need only remark that the word "state" is ambiguous.

It is further asked: When are men, living in the same place, to be regarded as a single city—what is the limit? Certainly not the wall of the city, for you might surround all Peloponnesus with a wall. Like this, we may say, is Babylon, and every city that has the compass of a nation rather than a city; Babylon, they say, had been taken for three days before some part of the inhabitants became aware of the fact. This difficulty may, however, with advantage be deferred to another occasion; the statesman has to consider the size of the state, and whether it should consist of more than one nation or not.

Again, shall we say that while the race of inhabitants, as well as their place of abode, remain the same, the city is also the same, although the citizens are always dying and being born, as we call rivers and fountains the same, although the water is always flowing away and coming again? Or shall we say that the generations of men, like the rivers, are the same, but that the state changes? For, since the state is a partnership, and is a partnership of citizens in a constitution, when the form of the government changes, and becomes different, then it may be supposed that the state is no longer the same, just as a tragic differs from a comic chorus, although the members of both may be identical And in this manner we speak of every union or composition of elements as different when the form of their composition alters; for example, a scale containing the same sounds is said to be different, accordingly as the Dorian or the Phrygian mode is employed. And if this is true it is evident that the sameness of the state consists chiefly in the sameness of the constitution, and it may be called or not called by the same name, whether the inhabitants are the same or entirely different. It is quite another question, whether a state ought or ought not to fulfil engagements when the form of government changes.

4. [*Civic virtue.*] There is a point nearly allied to the preceding: Whether the virtue of a good man and a good citizen is the same or not. But, before entering on this discussion, we must certainly first obtain some general notion of the virtue of

the citizen. Like the sailor, the citizen is a member of a community. Now, sailors have different functions, for one of them is a rower, another a pilot, and a third a lookout man, a fourth is described by some similar term; and while the precise definition of each individual's virtue applies exclusively to him, there is, at the same time, a common definition applicable to them all. For they have all of them a common object, which is safety in navigation. Similarly, one citizen differs from another, but the salvation of the community is the common business of them all. This community is the constitution; the virtue of the citizen must therefore be relative to the constitution of which he is a member. If, then, there are many forms of government, it is evident that there is not one single virtue of the good citizen which is perfect virtue. But we say that the good man is he who has one single virtue which is perfect virtue. Hence it is evident that the good citizen need not of necessity possess the virtue which makes a good man.

The same question may also be approached by another road, from a consideration of the best constitution. If the state cannot be entirely composed of good men, and yet each citizen is expected to do his own business well, and must therefore have virtue, still, inasmuch as all the citizens cannot be alike, the virtue of the citizen and of the good man cannot coincide. All must have the virtue of the good citizen—thus, and thus only, can the state be perfect; but they will not have the virtue of a good man, unless we assume that in the good state all the citizens must be good.

Again, the state, as composed of unlikes, may be compared to the living being; as the first elements into which a living being is resolved are soul and body, as soul is made up of rational principle and appetite, the family of husband and wife, property of master and slave, so of all these, as well as other dissimilar elements, the state is composed; and, therefore, the virtue of all the citizens cannot possibly be the same, any more than the excellence of the leader of a chorus is the same as that of the performer who stands by his side. I have said enough to show why the two kinds of virtue cannot be absolutely and always the same.

But will there then be no case in which the virtue of the good citizen and the virtue of the good man coincide? To this we answer that the good *ruler* is a good and wise man, and that he who would be a statesman must be a wise man. And some persons say that even the education of the ruler should be of a special kind; for are not the children of kings instructed in riding and military exercises? As Euripides says:

"No subtle arts for me, but what the state requires."

As though there were a special education needed by a ruler. If then the virtue of a good ruler is the same as that of a good man, and we assume further that the subject is a citizen as well as the ruler, the virtue of the good citizen and the virtue of the good man cannot be absolutely the same, although in some cases they may; for the virtue of a ruler differs from that of a citizen. It was the sense of this difference which made Jason say that "he felt hungry when he was not a tyrant," meaning that he could not endure to live in a private station. But, on the other hand, it may be argued that men are praised for knowing both how to rule and how to obey, and he is said to be a citizen of approved virtue who is able to do both. Now if we suppose the virtue of a good man to be that which rules, and the virtue of the citizen to include ruling and obeying, it cannot be said that they are equally worthy of praise. Since, then, it is sometimes thought that the ruler and the ruled must learn different things and not the same, but that the citizen must know and share in them both, the inference is obvious. There is, indeed, the rule of a master, which is concerned with menial offices: the master need not know how to perform these, but may employ others in the execution of them—the other would be degrading; and by the other I mean the power actually to do menial duties, which vary much in character and are executed by various classes of slaves, such, for example, as handicraftsmen, who, as their name signifies, live by the labour of their hands; under these the mechanic is included. Hence in ancient times, and among some nations, the working classes had no share in the government—a privilege which they only acquired under the extreme democracy. Certainly the good man and the statesman and the good citizen ought not to learn the crafts of inferiors except for their own occasional use; if they habitually practise them, there will cease to be a distinction between master and slave.

This is not the rule of which we are speaking; but there is a rule of another kind, which is exercised over freemen and equals by birth—a constitutional rule, which the ruler must learn by obeying, as he would learn the duties of a general of cavalry by being under the orders of a general of cavalry, or the duties of a general of infantry by being under the orders of a general of infantry, and by having had the command of a regiment and of a company. It has been well said that "he who has never learned to obey cannot be a good commander." The two are not the same, but the good citizen ought to be capable of both; he should know how to govern like a freeman, and how to obey like a freeman—these are the virtues of a citizen. And, although the temperance and justice of a ruler are distinct from those of a subject, the virtue of a good man will include both; for the virtue of the good man who is free and also a subject, e. g., his justice, will not be one but will comprise distinct kinds, the one qualifying him to rule, the other to obey, and differing as the temperance and courage of men and women differ. For a man would be thought a coward if he had no more courage than a courageous woman, and a woman would be thought loquacious if she imposed no more restraint on her conversation than the good man; and indeed their part in the management of the household is different, for the duty of the one is to acquire, and of the other to preserve. Practical wisdom only is characteristic of the ruler: it would seem that all other virtues must equally belong to ruler and subject. The virtue of the subject is certainly not wisdom, but only true opinion; he may be compared to the maker of the flute, while his master is like the flute player or user of the flute.

From these considerations may be gathered the answer to the question, whether the virtue of the good man is the same as that of the good citizen, or different, and how far the same, and how far different.

5. [*Limitations on citizenship.*] There still remains one more question about the citizen: Is he only a true citizen who has a share of office, or is the mechanic to be included? If they who hold no office are to be deemed citizens, not every citizen can have this virtue of ruling and obeying; for this man is a citizen. And if none of the lower class are citizens, in which part of the state are they to be placed? For they are not resident aliens, and they are not foreigners. May we not reply, that as far as this objection goes there is no more absurdity in excluding them than in excluding slaves and freedmen from any of the above-mentioned classes? It must be admitted that we cannot consider all those to be citizens who are necessary to the existence of the state; for example, children are not citizens equally with grown-up men, who are citizens absolutely, but children, not being grown up, are only citizens on a certain assumption. Nay, in ancient times, and among some nations, the artisan class *were* slaves or foreigners, and therefore the majority of them are so now. The best form of state will not admit them to citizenship; but if they are admitted, then our definition of the virtue of a citizen will not apply to every citizen, nor to every free man as such, but only to those who are freed from necessary services. The necessary people are either slaves who minister to the wants of individuals, or mechanics and labourers who are the servants of the community. These reflections carried a little further will explain their position; and indeed what has been said already is of itself, when understood, explanation enough.

Since there are many forms of government there must be many varieties of citizens, and especially of citizens who are subjects; so that under some governments the mechanic and the labourer will be citizens, but not in others, as, for example, in aristocracy or the so-called government of the best (if there be such an one), in which honours are given according to virtue and merit; for no man can practise virtue who is living the life of a mechanic or labourer. In oligarchies the qualification for office is high, and therefore no labourer can ever be a citizen; but a mechanic may, for an actual majority of them are rich. At Thebes there was a law that no man could hold office who had not retired from business for ten years. But in many states the law goes to the length of admitting aliens; for in some democracies a man is a citizen though his mother only be a citizen; and a similar principle is applied to illegitimate children; the law is relaxed when there is a dearth of population. But when the number of citizens increases, first the children of a male or a female slave are excluded; then those whose mothers only are citizens; and at last the right of citizenship is confined to those whose fathers and mothers are both citizens.

Hence, as is evident, there are different kinds of citizens; and he is a citizen in the highest sense who shares in the honours of the state. Compare Homer's words "like some dishonoured stranger"; he who is excluded from the honours of the state is no better than an alien. But when this exclusion is concealed, then the object is that the privileged class may deceive their fellow inhabitants.

As to the question whether the virtue of the good man is the same as that of the good citizen, the considerations already adduced prove that in some states the good man and the good citizen are the same, and in others different. When they are the same it is not every citizen who is a good man, but only the statesman and those who have or may have, alone or in conjunction with others, the conduct of public affairs.

6. [*The aims of the state are two.*] Having determined these questions, we have next to consider whether there is only one form of government or many, and if many, what they are, and how many, and what are the differences between them.

A constitution is the arrangement of magistracies in a state, especially of the highest of all. The government is everywhere sovereign in the state, and the constitution is in fact the government. For example, in democracies the people are supreme, but in oligarchies, the few; and, therefore, we say that these two forms of government also are different; and so in other cases.

First, let us consider what is the purpose of a state, and how many forms of government there are by which human society is regulated. We have already said, in the first part of this treatise, when discussing household management and the rule of a master, that man is by nature a political animal. And therefore, men, even when they do not require one another's help, desire to live together; not but that they are also brought together by their common interests in proportion as they severally attain to any measure of well-being. This is certainly the chief end, both of individuals and of states. And also for the sake of mere life (in which there is possibly some noble element so long as the evils of existence do not greatly overbalance the good) mankind meet together and maintain the political community. And we all see that men cling to life even at the cost of enduring great misfortune, seeming to find in life a natural sweetness and happiness.

There is no difficulty in distinguishing the various kinds of authority; they have been often defined already in discussions outside the school. The rule of a master, although the slave by nature and the master by nature have in reality the same interests, is nevertheless exercised primarily with a view to the interest of the master, but accidentally considers the slave, since, if the slave perish, the rule of the master perishes with him. On the other hand, the government of a wife and children and of a household, which we have called household management, is exercised in the first instance for the good of the governed or for the common good of both parties, but essentially for the good of the governed, as we see to be the case in medicine, gymnastic, and the arts in general, which are only accidentally concerned with the good of the artists themselves. For there is no reason why the trainer may not sometimes practise gymnastics, and the helmsman is always one of the crew. The trainer or the helmsman considers the good of those committed to his care. But, when he is one of the persons taken care of, he accidentally participates in the advantage, for the helmsman is also a sailor, and the trainer becomes one of those in training. And so in politics. When the state is framed upon the principle of equality and likeness, the citizens think that they ought to hold office by turns. Formerly, as is natural, every one would take his turn of service; and then again, somebody else would look after his interest, just as he, while in office, had looked after theirs. But nowadays, for the sake of the advantage which is to be gained from the public revenues and from office, men want to be always in office. One might imagine that the rulers, being sickly, were only kept in health while they continued in office; in that case we may be sure that they would be hunting after places. The conclusion is evident: that governments which have a regard to the common interest are constituted in accordance with strict principles of justice, and are therefore true forms; but those which regard only the interest of the rulers are all defective and perverted forms, for they are despotic, whereas a state is a community of freemen.

7. [*Good and bad constitutions.*] Having determined these points, we have next to consider how many forms of government there are, and what they are; and in the first place what are the true forms, for when they are determined the perversions of them will at once be apparent. The words constitution and government have the same meaning, and the government, which is the supreme authority in states, must be in the hands of one, or of a few, or of the many. The true forms of government, therefore, are those in which the one, or the few, or the many, govern with a view to the common interest; but governments which rule with a view to the private interest, whether of the one, or of the few, or of the many, are perversions. For the members of a state, if they are truly citizens, ought to participate in its advantages. Of forms of government in which one rules, we call that which regards the common interests, kingship or royalty; that in which more than one, but not many, rule, aristocracy; and it is so called, either because the rulers are the best men, or because they have at heart the best interests of the state and of the

citizens. But when the citizens at large administer the state for the common interest, the government is called by the generic name—a constitution. And there is a reason for this use of language. One man or a few may excel in virtue; but as the number increases it becomes more difficult for them to attain perfection in every kind of virtue, though they may in military virtue, for this is found in the masses. Hence in a constitutional government the fighting men have the supreme power, and those who possess arms are the citizens.

Of the above-mentioned forms, the perversions are as follows: of royalty, tyranny; of aristocracy, oligarchy; of constitutional government, democracy. For tyranny is a kind of monarchy which has in view the interest of the monarch only; oligarchy has in view the interest of the wealthy; democracy, of the needy: none of them the common good of all.

8. [*Democracy and oligarchy.*] But there are difficulties about these forms of government, and it will therefore be necessary to state a little more at length the nature of each of them. For he who would make a philosophical study of the various sciences, and does not regard practice only, ought not to overlook or omit anything, but to set forth the truth in every particular. Tyranny, as I was saying, is monarchy exercising the rule of a master over the political society; oligarchy is when men of property have the government in their hands; democracy, the opposite, when the indigent, and not the men of property, are the rulers. And here arises the first of our difficulties, and it relates to the distinction just drawn. For democracy is said to be the government of the many. But what if the many are men of property and have the power in their hands? In like manner oligarchy is said to be the government of the few; but what if the poor are fewer than the rich, and have the power in their hands because they are stronger? In these cases the distinction which we have drawn between these different forms of government would no longer hold good.

Suppose, once more, that we add wealth to the few and poverty to the many, and name the governments accordingly

—an oligarchy is said to be that in which the few and the wealthy, and a democracy that in which the many and the poor are the rulers—there will still be a difficulty. For, if the only forms of government are the ones already mentioned, how shall we describe those other governments also just mentioned by us, in which the rich are the more numerous and the poor are the fewer, and both govern in their respective states?

The argument seems to show that, whether in oligarchies or in democracies, the number of the governing body, whether the greater number, as in a democracy, or the smaller number, as in an oligarchy, is an accident due to the fact that the rich everywhere are few, and the poor numerous. But if so, there is a misapprehension of the causes of the difference between them. For the real difference between democracy and oligarchy is poverty and wealth. Wherever men rule by reason of their wealth, whether they be few or many, that is an oligarchy, and where the poor rule, that is a democracy. But as a fact the rich are few and the poor many; for few are well-to-do, whereas freedom is enjoyed by all, and wealth and freedom are the grounds on which the oligarchical and democratical parties respectively claim power in the state.

9. [*Democracy and oligarchy.*] Let us begin by considering the common definitions of oligarchy and democracy, and what is justice oligarchical and democratical. For all men cling to justice of some kind, but their conceptions are imperfect and they do not express the whole idea. For example, justice is thought by them to be, and is, equality, not, however, for all, but only for equals. And inequality is thought to be, and is, justice; neither is this for all, but only for unequals. When the persons are omitted, then men judge erroneously. The reason is that they are passing judgement on themselves, and most people are bad judges in their own case. And whereas justice implies a relation to persons as well as to things, and a just distribution, as I have already said in the *Ethics*, implies the same ratio between the persons and between the things, they agree about the equality of the things, but dis-

pute about the equality of the persons, chiefly for the reason which I have just given—because they are bad judges in their own affairs; and secondly, because both the parties to the argument are speaking of a limited and partial justice, but imagine themselves to be speaking of absolute justice. For the one party, if they are unequal in one respect, for example wealth, consider themselves to be unequal in all; and the other party, if they are equal in one respect, for example free birth, consider themselves to be equal in all. But they leave out the capital point. For if men met and associated out of regard to wealth only, their share in the state would be proportioned to their property, and the oligarchical doctrine would then seem to carry the day. It would not be just that he who paid one mina should have the same share of a hundred minae, whether of the principal or of the profits, as he who paid the remaining ninety-nine. But a state exists for the sake of a good life, and not for the sake of life only; if life only were the object, slaves and brute animals might form a state, but they cannot, for they have no share in happiness or in a life of free choice. Nor does a state exist for the sake of alliance and security from injustice, nor yet for the sake of exchange and mutual intercourse; for then the Tyrrhenians and the Carthaginians, and all who have commercial treaties with one another, would be the citizens of one state. True, they have agreements about imports, and engagements that they will do no wrong to one another, and written articles of alliance. But there are no magistracies common to the contracting parties who will enforce their engagements; different states have each their own magistracies. Nor does one state take care that the citizens of the other are such as they ought to be, nor see that those who come under the terms of the treaty do no wrong or wickedness at all, but only that they do no injustice to one another. Whereas, those who care for good government take into consideration virtue and vice in states. Whence it may be further inferred that virtue must be the care of a state which is truly so called, and not merely enjoys the name; for without this end the community becomes a mere alliance which differs only in place from alliances of which the members live apart; and law is only a convention, "a surety to one another of justice," as the sophist Lycophron says, and has no real power to make the citizens good and just.

This is obvious; for suppose distinct places, such as Corinth and Megara, to be brought together so that their walls touched, still they would not be one city, not even if the citizens had the right to intermarry, which is one of the rights peculiarly characteristic of states. Again, if men dwelt at a distance from one another, but not so far off as to have no intercourse, and there were laws among them that they should not wrong each other in their exchanges, neither would this be a state. Let us suppose that one man is a carpenter, another a husbandman, another a shoemaker, and so on, and that their number is ten thousand; nevertheless, if they have nothing in common but exchange, alliance, and the like, that would not constitute a state. Why is this? Surely not because they are at a distance from one another: for even supposing that such a community were to meet in one place, but that each man had a house of his own, which was in a manner his state, and that they made alliance with one another, but only against evildoers; still an accurate thinker would not deem this to be a state, if their intercourse with one another was of the same character after as before their union. It is clear then that a state is not a mere society, having a common place, established for the prevention of mutual crime and for the sake of exchange. These are conditions without which a state cannot exist; but all of them together do not constitute a state, which is a community of families and aggregations of families in well-being, for the sake of a perfect and self-sufficing life. Such a community can only be established among those who live in the same place and intermarry. Hence arise in cities family connexions, brotherhoods, common sacrifices, amusements which draw men together. But these are created by friendship, for the will to live together is friendship. The end of the state is the good life, and these are the means towards it. And the state is the union of families and villages in a perfect and self-sufficing life, by which we mean a happy and honourable life.

Our conclusion, then, is that political society exists for the sake of noble actions, and not of mere companionship. Hence they who contribute most to such a society have a greater share in it than those who have the same or a greater freedom or nobility of birth but are inferior to them in political virtue; or than those who exceed them in wealth but are surpassed by them in virtue.

From what has been said it will be clearly seen that all the partisans of different forms of government speak of a part of justice only.

* * *

BOOK IV

1. [*Aims of political science.*] In all arts and sciences which embrace the whole of any subject, and do not come into being in a fragmentary way, it is the province of a single art or science to consider all that appertains to a single subject. For example, the art of gymnastic considers not only the suitableness of different modes of training to different bodies (2), but what sort is absolutely the best (1); (for the absolutely best must suit that which is by nature best and best furnished with the means of life), and also what common form of training is adapted to the great majority of men (4). And if a man does not desire the best habit of body, or the greatest skill in gymnastics, which might be attained by him, still the trainer or the teacher of gymnastic should be able to impart any lower degree of either (3). The same principle

equally holds in medicine and shipbuilding, and the making of clothes, and in the arts generally.

Hence it is obvious that government too is the subject of a single science, which has to consider what government is best and of what sort it must be, to be most in accordance with our aspirations, if there were no external impediment, and also what kind of government is adapted to particular states. For the best is often unattainable, and therefore the true legislator and statesman ought to be acquainted, not only with (1) that which is best in the abstract, but also with (2) that which is best relatively to circumstances. We should be able further to say how a state may be constituted under any given conditions (3); both how it is originally formed and, when formed, how it may be longest preserved; the supposed state being so far from having the best constitution that it is unprovided even with the conditions necessary for the best; neither is it the best under the circumstances, but of an inferior type.

He ought, moreover, to know (4) the form of government which is best suited to states in general; for political writers, although they have excellent ideas, are often unpractical. We should consider, not only what form of government is best, but also what is possible and what is easily attainable by all. There are some who would have none but the most perfect; for this many natural advantages are required. Others, again, speak of a more attainable form, and, although they reject the constitution under which they are living, they extol some one in particular, for example the Lacedaemonian. Any change of government which has to be introduced should be one which men, starting from their existing constitutions, will be both willing and able to adopt, since there is quite as much trouble in the reformation of an old constitution as in the establishment of a new one, just as to unlearn is as hard as to learn. And therefore, in addition to the qualifications of the statesman already mentioned, he should be able to find remedies for the defects of existing constitutions, as has been said before. This he cannot do unless he knows how many forms of government there are. It is often supposed that there is only one kind of democracy and one of oligarchy. But this is a mistake; and, in order to avoid such mistakes, we must ascertain what differences there are in the constitutions of states, and in how many ways they are combined. The same political insight will enable a man to know which laws are the best, and which are suited to different constitutions; for the laws are, and ought to be, relative to the constitution, and not the constitution to the laws. A constitution is the organization of offices in a state, and determines what is to be the governing body, and what is the end of each community. But laws are not to be confounded with the principles of the constitution; they are the rules according to which the magistrates should administer the state, and proceed against offenders. So that we must know the varieties, and the number of varieties, of each form of government, if only with a view to making laws. For the same laws cannot be equally suited to all oligarchies or to all democracies, since there is certainly more than one form both of democracy and of oligarchy.

2. [*Other types of state.*] In our original discussion about governments we divided them into three true forms: kingly rule, aristocracy, and constitutional government, and three corresponding perversions—tyranny, oligarchy, and democracy. Of kingly rule and of aristocracy we have already spoken, for the inquiry into the perfect state is the same thing with the discussion of the two forms thus named, since both imply a principle of virtue provided with external means. We have already determined in what aristocracy and kingly rule differ from one another, and when the latter should be established. In what follows we have to describe the so-called constitutional government, which bears the common name of all constitutions, and the other forms, tyranny, oligarchy, and democracy.

It is obvious which of the three perversions is the worst, and which is the next in badness. That which is the perversion of the first and most divine is necessarily the worst. And just as a royal rule, if not a mere name, must exist by virtue of some great personal superiority in the king, so tyranny, which

is the worst of governments, is necessarily the farthest removed from a well-constituted form; oligarchy is little better,
for it is a long way from aristocracy, and democracy is the
most tolerable of the three.

A writer who preceded me has already made these distinctions, but his point of view is not the same as mine. For he
lays down the principle that when all the constitutions are
good (the oligarchy and the rest being virtuous), democracy
is the worst, but the best when all are bad. Whereas we maintain that they are in any case defective, and that one oligarchy is not to be accounted better than another, but only
less bad.

Not to pursue this question further at present, let us begin
by determining (1) how many varieties of constitution there
are (since of democracy and oligarchy there are several); (2)
what constitution is the most generally acceptable, and what
is eligible in the next degree after the perfect state; and besides this what other there is which is aristocratical and well-
constituted, and at the same time adapted to states in general; (3) of the other forms of government to whom each is
suited. For democracy may meet the needs of some better
than oligarchy, and conversely. In the next place (4) we have
to consider in what manner a man ought to proceed who desires to establish some one among these various forms, whether
of democracy or of oligarchy; and lastly, (5) having briefly
discussed these subjects to the best of our power, we will
endeavour to ascertain the modes of ruin and preservation
both of constitutions generally and of each separately, and to
what causes they are to be attributed.

3. [*Democracy and oligarchy.*] The reason why there are
many forms of government is that every state contains many
elements. In the first place we see that all states are made up of
families, and in the multitude of citizens there must be some
rich and some poor, and some in a middle condition; the rich
are heavy-armed, and the poor not. Of the common people,
some are husbandmen, and some traders, and some artisans.
There are also among the notables differences of wealth and

property—for example, in the number of horses which they keep, for they cannot afford to keep them unless they are rich. And therefore in old times the cities whose strength lay in their cavalry were oligarchies, and they used cavalry in wars against their neighbours; as was the practice of the Eretrians and Chalcidians, and also of the Magnesians on the river Maeander, and of other peoples in Asia. Besides differences of wealth there are differences of rank and merit, and there are some other elements which were mentioned by us when in treating of aristocracy we enumerated the essentials of a state. Of these elements, sometimes all, sometimes the lesser and sometimes the greater number, have a share in the government. It is evident then that there must be many forms of government, differing in kind, since the parts of which they are composed differ from each other in kind. For a constitution is an organization of offices, which all the citizens distribute among themselves, according to the power which different classes possess, for example the rich or the poor, or according to some principle of equality which includes both. There must therefore be as many forms of government as there are modes of arranging the offices, according to the superiorities and the differences of the parts of the state.

There are generally thought to be two principal forms; as men say of the winds that there are but two—north and south, and that the rest of them are only variations of these, so of governments there are said to be only two forms—democracy and oligarchy. For aristocracy is considered to be a kind of oligarchy, as being the rule of a few, and the so-called constitutional government to be really a democracy, just as among the winds we make the west a variation of the north, and the east of the south wind. Similarly of musical modes there are said to be two kinds, the Dorian and the Phrygian; the other arrangements of the scale are comprehended under one or other of these two. About forms of government this is a very favourite notion. But in either case the better and more exact way is to distinguish, as I have done, the one or two which are true forms, and to regard the others as perver-

sions, whether of the most perfectly attempered mode or of
the best form of government: we may compare the severer
and more overpowering modes to the oligarchical forms, and
the more relaxed and gentler ones to the democratic.

4. [*Four kinds of democracies.*] It must not be assumed, as
some are fond of saying, that democracy is simply that form
of government in which the greater number are sovereign,
for in oligarchies, and indeed in every government, the majority rules; nor again is oligarchy that form of government in
which a few are sovereign. Suppose the whole population of
a city to be 1300, and that of these 1000 are rich, and do not
allow the remaining 300 who are poor, but free, and in all
other respects their equals, a share of the government—no one
will say that this is a democracy. In like manner, if the poor
were few and the masters of the rich who outnumber them,
no one would ever call such a government, in which the
rich majority have no share of office, an oligarchy. Therefore
we should rather say that democracy is the form of government in which the free are rulers, and oligarchy in which
the rich; it is only an accident that the free are the many and
the rich are the few. Otherwise a government in which the
offices were given according to stature, as is said to be the
case in Ethiopia, or according to beauty, would be an oligarchy; for the number of tall or good-looking men is small.
And yet oligarchy and democracy are not sufficiently distinguished merely by these two characteristics of wealth and
freedom. Both of them contain many other elements, and
therefore we must carry our analysis further, and say that
the government is not a democracy in which the freemen,
being few in number, rule over the many who are not free,
as at Apollonia, on the Ionian Gulf, and at Thera (for in each
of these states the nobles, who were also the earliest settlers,
were held in chief honour, although they were but a few out
of many). Neither is it a democracy when the rich have the
government because they exceed in number; as was the case
formerly at Colophon, where the bulk of the inhabitants
were possessed of large property before the Lydian War. But

the form of government is a democracy when the free, who are also poor and the majority, govern, and an oligarchy when the rich and the noble govern, they being at the same time few in number.

I have said that there are many forms of government, and have explained to what causes the variety is due. Why there are more than those already mentioned, and what they are, and whence they arise, I will now proceed to consider, starting from the principle already admitted, which is that every state consists, not of one, but of many parts. If we were going to speak of the different species of animals, we should first of all determine the organs which are indispensable to every animal, as for example some organs of sense and the instruments of receiving and digesting food, such as the mouth and the stomach, besides organs of locomotion. Assuming now that there are only so many kinds of organs, but that there may be differences in them—I mean different kinds of mouths, and stomachs, and perceptive and locomotive organs—the possible combinations of these differences will necessarily furnish many varieties of animals. (For animals cannot be the same which have different kinds of mouths or of ears.) And when all the combinations are exhausted, there will be as many sorts of animals as there are combinations of the necessary organs. The same, then, is true of the forms of government which have been described; states, as I have repeatedly said, are composed, not of one, but of many elements. One element is the food-producing class, who are called husbandmen; a second, the class of mechanics who practise the arts without which a city cannot exist; of these arts some are absolutely necessary, others contribute to luxury or to the grace of life. The third class is that of traders, and by traders I mean those who are engaged in buying and selling, whether in commerce or in retail trade. A fourth class is that of the serfs or labourers. The warriors make up the fifth class, and they are as necessary as any of the others, if the country is not to be the slave of every invader. For how can a state which has any title to the name be of a slavish nature? The state is independent and self-sufficing, but a slave

is the reverse of independent. Hence we see that this subject, though ingeniously, has not been satisfactorily treated in
the *Republic*. Socrates says that a state is made up of four
sorts of people who are absolutely necessary; these are a
weaver, a husbandman, a shoemaker, and a builder; afterwards, finding that they are not enough, he adds a smith, and
again a herdsman, to look after the necessary animals; then
a merchant, and then a retail trader. All these together form
the complement of the first state, as if a state were established
merely to supply the necessaries of life, rather than for the
sake of the good, or stood equally in need of shoemakers and
of husbandmen. But he does not admit into the state a military class until the country has increased in size, and is beginning to encroach on its neighbour's land, whereupon they
go to war. Yet even amongst his four original citizens, or
whatever be the number of those whom he associates in the
state, there must be some one who will dispense justice and
determine what is just. And as the soul may be said to be
more truly part of an animal than the body, so the higher
parts of states, that is to say, the warrior class, the class engaged in the administration of justice, and that engaged in
deliberation, which is the special business of political common sense—these are more essential to the state than the parts
which minister to the necessaries of life. Whether their several functions are the functions of different citizens, or of
the same—for it may often happen that the same persons are
both warriors and husbandmen—is immaterial to the argument. The higher as well as the lower elements are to be
equally considered parts of the state, and if so, the military
element at any rate must be included. There are also the
wealthy who minister to the state with their property; these
form the seventh class. The eighth class is that of magistrates
and of officers; for the state cannot exist without rulers. And
therefore some must be able to take office and to serve the
state, either always or in turn. There only remains the class
of those who deliberate and who judge between disputants;
we were just now distinguishing them. If presence of all
these elements, and their fair and equitable organization, is

necessary to states, then there must also be persons who have the ability of statesmen. Different functions appear to be often combined in the same individual; for example, the warrior may also be a husbandman, or an artisan; or, again, the counsellor a judge. And all claim to possess political ability, and think that they are quite competent to fill most offices. But the same persons cannot be rich and poor at the same time. For this reason the rich and the poor are regarded in an especial sense as parts of a state. Again, because the rich are generally few in number, while the poor are many, they appear to be antagonistic, and as the one or the other prevails they form the government. Hence arises the common opinion that there are two kinds of government—democracy and oligarchy.

I have already explained that there are many forms of constitution, and to what causes the variety is due. Let me now show that there are different forms both of democracy and oligarchy, as will indeed be evident from what has preceded. For both in the common people and in the notables various classes are included; of the common people, one class are husbandmen, another artisans; another traders, who are employed in buying and selling; another are the seafaring class, whether engaged in war or in trade, as ferrymen or as fishermen. (In many places any one of these classes forms quite a large population; for example, fishermen at Tarentum and Byzantium, crews of triremes at Athens, merchant seamen at Aegina and Chios, ferrymen at Tenedos.) To the classes already mentioned may be added day labourers, and those who, owing to their needy circumstances, have no leisure, or those who are not of free birth on both sides; and there may be other classes as well. The notables again may be divided according to their wealth, birth, virtue, education, and similar differences.

Of forms of democracy first comes that which is said to be based strictly on equality. In such a democracy the law says that it is just for the poor to have no more advantage than the rich; and that neither should be masters, but both equal. For if liberty and equality, as is thought by some, are chiefly to be found in democracy, they will be best attained when all persons alike share in the government to the utmost. And since the people are the majority, and the opinion of the majority is decisive, such a government must necessarily be a democracy. Here then is one sort of democracy. There is another, in which the magistrates are elected according to a certain property qualification, but a low one; he who has the required amount of property has a share in the government, but he who loses his property loses his rights. Another kind is that in which all the citizens who are under no disqualification share in the government, but still the law is supreme. In another, everybody, if he be only a citizen, is admitted to the government, but the law is supreme as before. A fifth form of democracy, in other respects the same, is that in which, not the law, but the multitude, have the supreme power, and supersede the law by their decrees. This is a state of affairs brought about by the demagogues. For in democracies which are subject to the law the best citizens hold the first place, and there are no demagogues; but where the laws are not supreme, there demagogues spring up. For the people becomes a monarch, and is many in one; and the many have the power in their hands, not as individuals, but collectively. Homer says that "it is not good to have a rule of many," but whether he means this corporate rule, or the rule of many individuals, is uncertain. At all events this sort of democracy, which is now a monarch, and no longer under the control of law, seeks to exercise monarchical sway, and grows into a despot; the flatterer is held in honour; this sort of democracy being relatively to other democracies what tyranny is to other forms of monarchy. The spirit of both is the same, and they alike exercise a despotic rule over the better citizens. The decrees of the demos correspond to the edicts of the tyrant; and the demagogue is to the one what the flatterer is to the other. Both have great power; the flatterer with the tyrant, the demagogue with democracies of the kind which we are describing. The demagogues make the decrees of the people override the laws, by referring all things to the popular assembly. And therefore they grow great, because the people have all things in their hands, and they hold in their hands the votes of the people, who are too ready to listen to them. Further, those who have any complaint to bring against the magistrates say, "let the people be judges"; the people are too happy to accept the invitation; and so the authority of every office is undermined. Such a democracy is fairly open to the objection that it is not a constitution at all; for where the laws have no authority, there is no constitution. The law ought to be supreme over all, and the magistracies should judge of particulars, and only this should be considered a constitution. So that if democracy be a real form of government, the sort of system in which all things are regulated by decrees is clearly not even a democracy in the true sense of the word, for decrees relate only to particulars.

5. [*Four kinds of oligarchies.*] Of oligarchies, too, there are different kinds: one where the property qualification for office is such that the poor, although they form the majority, have no share in the government, yet he who acquires a qualification may obtain a share. Another sort is when there is a qualification for office, but a high one, and the vacancies in the governing body are filled by co-optation. If the election is made out of all the qualified persons, a constitution of this kind inclines to an aristocracy, if out of a privileged class, to an oligarchy. Another sort of oligarchy is when the son succeeds the father. There is a fourth form, likewise hereditary, in which the magistrates are supreme and not the law. Among oligarchies this is what tyranny is among monarchies, and the last-mentioned form of democracy among democracies; and in fact this sort of oligarchy receives the name of a dynasty (or rule of powerful families).

These are the different sorts of oligarchies and democracies. It should however be remembered that in many states the constitution which is established by law, although not democratic, owing to the education and habits of the people may be administered democratically, and conversely in other states the established constitution may incline to democracy, but may be administered in an oligarchical spirit. This most often happens after a revolution; for governments do not change at once; at first the dominant party are content with encroaching a little upon their opponents. The laws which existed previously continue in force, but the authors of the revolution have the power in their hands.

6. [*Circumstances under which these variations arise.*] From what has been already said we may safely infer that there are so many different kinds of democracies and of oligarchies. For it is evident that either all the classes whom we mentioned must share in the government, or some only and not others. When the class of husbandmen and of those who possess moderate fortunes have the supreme power, the government is administered according to law. For the citizens being compelled to live by their labour have no leisure; and so they set up the authority of the law, and attend assemblies only when necessary. They all obtain a share in the government when they have acquired the qualification which is fixed by the law—the absolute exclusion of any class would be a step towards oligarchy; hence all who have acquired the property qualification are admitted to a share in the constitution. But leisure cannot be provided for them unless there are revenues to support them. This is one sort of democracy, and these are the causes which give birth to it. Another kind is based on the distinction which naturally comes next in order; in this, every one to whose birth there is no objection is eligible, but actually shares in the government only if he can find leisure. Hence in such a democracy the supreme power is vested in the laws, because the state has no means of paying the citizens. A third kind is when all freemen have a right to share in the government, but do not actually share, for the reason which has been already given; so that in this form again the law must rule. A fourth kind of democracy is that which comes latest in the history of states. In our own day, when cities have far outgrown their original size, and their revenues have increased, all the citizens have a place in the government, through the great

preponderance of the multitude; and they all, including the poor who receive pay, and therefore have leisure to exercise their rights, share in the administration. Indeed, when they are paid, the common people have the most leisure, for they are not hindered by the care of their property, which often fetters the rich, who are thereby prevented from taking part in the assembly or in the courts, and so the state is governed by the poor, who are a majority, and not by the laws. So many kinds of democracies there are, and they grow out of these necessary causes.

Of oligarchies, one form is that in which the majority of the citizens have some property, but not very much; and this is the first form, which allows to any one who obtains the required amount the right of sharing in the government. The sharers in the government being a numerous body, it follows that the law must govern, and not individuals. For in proportion as they are further removed from a monarchical form of government, and in respect of property have neither so much as to be able to live without attending to business, nor so little as to need state support, they must admit the rule of law and not claim to rule themselves. But if the men of property in the state are fewer than in the former case, and own more property, there arises a second form of oligarchy. For the stronger they are, the more power they claim, and having this object in view, they themselves select those of the other classes who are to be admitted to the government; but, not being as yet strong enough to rule without the law, they make the law represent their wishes. When this power is intensified by a further diminution of their numbers and increase of their property, there arises a third and further stage of oligarchy, in which the governing class keep the offices in their own hands, and the law ordains that the son shall succeed the father. When, again, the rulers have great wealth and numerous friends, this sort of family despotism approaches a monarchy; individuals rule and not the law. This is the fourth sort of oligarchy, and is analogous to the last sort of democracy.

7. [*Aristocracy.*] There are still two forms besides democracy and oligarchy; one of them is universally recognized and included among the four principal forms of government, which are said to be (1) monarchy, (2) oligarchy, (3) democracy, and (4) the so-called aristocracy or government of the best. But there is also a fifth, which retains the generic name of polity or constitutional government; this is not common, and therefore has not been noticed by writers who attempt to enumerate the different kinds of government; like Plato, in their books about the state, they recognize four only. The term "aristocracy" is rightly applied to the form of government which is described in the first part of our treatise; for that only can be rightly called aristocracy which is a government formed of the best men absolutely, and not merely of men who are good when tried by any given standard. In the perfect state the good man is absolutely the same as the good citizen; whereas in other states the good citizen is only good relatively to his own form of government. But there are some states differing from oligarchies and also differing from the so-called polity or constitutional government; these are termed aristocracies, and in them magistrates are certainly chosen, both according to their wealth and according to their merit. Such a form of government differs from each of the two just now mentioned, and is termed an aristocracy. For indeed in states which do not make virtue the aim of the community, men of merit and reputation for virtue may be found. And so where a government has regard to wealth, virtue, and numbers, as at Carthage, that is aristocracy; and also where it has regard only to two out of the three, as at Lacedaemon, to virtue and numbers, and the two principles of democracy and virtue temper each other. There are these two forms of aristocracy in addition to the first and perfect state, and there is a third form, viz., the constitutions which incline more than the so-called polity towards oligarchy.

8. [*Polity.*] I have yet to speak of the so-called polity and of tyranny. I put them in this order, not because a polity

or constitutional government is to be regarded as a perversion any more than the above-mentioned aristocracies. The truth is, that they all fall short of the most perfect form of government, and so they are reckoned among perversions, and the really perverted forms are perversions of these, as I said in the original discussion. Last of all I will speak of tyranny, which I place last in the series because I am inquiring into the constitutions of states, and this is the very reverse of a constitution.

Having explained why I have adopted this order, I will proceed to consider constitutional government; of which the nature will be clearer now that oligarchy and democracy have been defined. For polity or constitutional government may be described generally as a fusion of oligarchy and democracy; but the term is usually applied to those forms of government which incline towards democracy, and the term aristocracy to those which incline towards oligarchy, because birth and education are commonly the accompaniments of wealth. Moreover, the rich already possess the external advantages the want of which is a temptation to crime, and hence they are called noblemen and gentlemen. And inasmuch as aristocracy seeks to give predominance to the best of the citizens, people say also of oligarchies that they are composed of noblemen and gentlemen. Now it appears to be an impossible thing that the state which is governed not by the best citizens but by the worst should be well-governed, and equally impossible that the state which is ill-governed should be governed by the best. But we must remember that good laws, if they are not obeyed, do not constitute good government. Hence there are two parts of good government; one is the actual obedience of citizens to the laws, the other part is the goodness of the laws which they obey; they may obey bad laws as well as good. And there may be a further subdivision; they may obey either the best laws which are attainable to them, or the best absolutely.

The distribution of offices according to merit is a special characteristic of aristocracy, for the principle of an aristocracy is virtue, as wealth is of an oligarchy, and freedom of a democracy. In all of them there of course exists the right of the majority, and whatever seems good to the majority of those who share in the government has authority. Now in most states the form called polity exists, for the fusion goes no further than the attempt to unite the freedom of the poor and the wealth of the rich, who commonly take the place of the noble. But as there are three grounds on which men claim an equal share in the government, freedom, wealth, and virtue (for the fourth or good birth is the result of the two last, being only ancient wealth and virtue), it is clear that the admixture of the two elements, that is to say, of the rich and poor, is to be called a polity or constitutional government; and the union of the three is to be called aristocracy or the government of the best, and more than any other form of government, except the true and ideal, has a right to this name.

Thus far I have shown the existence of forms of states other than monarchy, democracy, and oligarchy, and what they are, and in what aristocracies differ from one another, and polities from aristocracies—that the two latter are not very unlike is obvious.

9. [*Polity.*] Next we have to consider how by the side of oligarchy and democracy the so-called polity or constitutional government springs up, and how it should be organized. The nature of it will be at once understood from a comparison of oligarchy and democracy; we must ascertain their different characteristics, and taking a portion from each, put the two together, like the parts of an indenture. Now there are three modes in which fusions of government may be effected. In the first mode we must combine the laws made by both governments, say concerning the administration of justice. In oligarchies they impose a fine on the rich if they do not serve as judges, and to the poor they give no pay; but in democracies they give pay to the poor and do not fine the rich. Now (1) the union of these two modes is a common or middle term between them, and is therefore characteristic of a constitutional government, for it is a combination of both.

This is one mode of uniting the two elements. Or (2) a mean may be taken between the enactments of the two; thus democracies require no property qualification, or only a small one, from members of the assembly, oligarchies a high one; here neither of these is the common term, but a mean between them. (3) There is a third mode, in which something is borrowed from the oligarchical and something from the democratical principle. For example, the appointment of magistrates by lot is thought to be democratical, and the election of them oligarchical; democratical again when there is no property qualification, oligarchical when there is. In the aristocratical or constitutional state, one element will be taken from each—from oligarchy the principle of electing to offices, from democracy the disregard of qualification. Such are the various modes of combination.

There is a true union of oligarchy and democracy when the same state may be termed either a democracy or an oligarchy; those who use both names evidently feel that the fusion is complete. Such a fusion there is also in the mean; for both extremes appear in it. The Lacedaemonian constitution, for example, is often described as a democracy, because it has many democratical features. In the first place the youth receive a democratical education. For the sons of the poor are brought up with the sons of the rich, who are educated in such a manner as to make it possible for the sons of the poor to be educated like them. A similar equality prevails in the following period of life, and when the citizens are grown up to manhood the same rule is observed; there is no distinction between the rich and poor. In like manner they all have the same food at their public tables, and the rich wear only such clothing as any poor man can afford. Again, the people elect to one of the two greatest offices of state, and in the other they share; for they elect the Senators and share in the Ephoralty. By others the Spartan constitution is said to be an oligarchy, because it has many oligarchical elements. That all offices are filled by election and none by lot, is one of these oligarchical characteristics; that the power of inflicting death or banishment rests with a few persons is another; and there are others. In a well-attempered polity there should appear to be both elements and yet neither; also the government should rely on itself, and not on foreign aid, and on itself not through the good will of a majority—they might be equally well-disposed when there is a vicious form of government—but through the general willingness of all classes in the state to maintain the constitution.

Enough of the manner in which a constitutional government, and in which the so-called aristocracies ought to be framed.

10. [*Three kinds of tyranny.*] Of the nature of tyranny I have still to speak, in order that it may have its place in our inquiry (since even tyranny is reckoned by us to be a form of government), although there is not much to be said about it. I have already in the former part of this treatise discussed royalty or kingship according to the most usual meaning of the term, and considered whether it is or is not advantageous to states, and what kind of royalty should be established, and from what source, and how.

When speaking of royalty we also spoke of two forms of tyranny, which are both according to law, and therefore easily pass into royalty. Among Barbarians there are elected monarchs who exercise a despotic power; despotic rulers were also elected in ancient Hellas, called Aesymnetes or dictators. These monarchies, when compared with one another, exhibit certain differences. And they are, as I said before, royal, in so far as the monarch rules according to law over willing subjects; but they are tyrannical in so far as he is despotic and rules according to his own fancy. There is also a third kind of tyranny, which is the most typical form, and is the counterpart of the perfect monarchy. This tyranny is just that arbitrary power of an individual which is responsible to no one, and governs all alike, whether equals or better, with a view to its own advantage, not to that of its subjects, and therefore against their will. No freeman, if he can escape from it, will endure such a government.

The kinds of tyranny are such and so many, and for the reasons which I have given.

11. [*The best state.*] We have now to inquire what is the best constitution for most states, and the best life for most men, neither assuming a standard of virtue which is above ordinary persons, nor an education which is exceptionally favoured by nature and circumstances, nor yet an ideal state which is an aspiration only, but having regard to the life in which the majority are able to share, and to the form of government which states in general can attain. As to those aristocracies, as they are called, of which we were just now speaking, they either lie beyond the possibilities of the greater number of states, or they approximate to the so-called constitutional government, and therefore need no separate discussion. And in fact the conclusion at which we arrive respecting all these forms rests upon the same grounds. For if what was said in the *Ethics* is true, that the happy life is the life according to virtue lived without impediment, and that virtue is a mean, then the life which is in a mean, and in a mean attainable by every one, must be the best. And the same principles of virtue and vice are characteristic of cities and of constitutions; for the constitution is in a figure the life of the city.

Now in all states there are three elements: one class is very rich, another very poor, and a third in a mean. It is admitted that moderation and the mean are best, and therefore it will clearly be best to possess the gifts of fortune in moderation; for in that condition of life men are most ready to follow rational principle. But he who greatly excels in beauty, strength, birth, or wealth, or on the other hand who is very poor, or very weak, or very much disgraced, finds it difficult to follow rational principle. Of these two the one sort grow into violent and great criminals, the others into rogues and petty rascals. And two sorts of offences correspond to them, the one committed from violence, the other from roguery. Again, the middle class is least likely to shrink from rule, or to be overambitious for it; both of which are injuries to the state. Again, those who have too much of the goods of fortune, strength, wealth, friends, and the like, are neither willing nor able to submit to authority. The evil begins at home; for when they are boys, by reason of the luxury in which they are brought up, they never learn, even at school, the habit of obedience. On the other hand, the very poor, who are in the opposite extreme, are too degraded. So that the one class cannot obey, and can only rule despotically; the other knows not how to command and must be ruled like slaves. Thus arises a city, not of freemen, but of masters and slaves, the one despising, the other envying; and nothing can be more fatal to friendship and good fellowship in states than this; for good fellowship springs from friendship; when men are at enmity with one another, they would rather not even share the same path. But a city ought to be composed, as far as possible, of equals and similars; and these are generally the middle classes. Wherefore the city which is composed of middle-class citizens is necessarily best constituted in respect of the elements of which we say the fabric of the state naturally consists. And this is the class of citizens which is most secure in a state, for they do not, like the poor, covet their neighbours' goods; nor do others covet theirs, as the poor covet the goods of the rich; and as they neither plot against others, nor are themselves plotted against, they pass through life safely. Wisely then did Phocylides pray: "Many things are best in the mean; I desire to be of a middle condition in my city."

Thus it is manifest that the best political community is formed by citizens of the middle class, and that those states are likely to be well-administered, in which the middle class is large, and stronger if possible than both the other classes, or at any rate than either singly; for the addition of the middle class turns the scale, and prevents either of the extremes from being dominant. Great then is the good fortune of a state in which the citizens have a moderate and sufficient property; for where some possess much, and the others nothing, there may arise an extreme democracy, or a pure oligarchy; or a tyranny may grow out of either extreme—

either out of the most rampant democracy, or out of an oligarchy; but it is not so likely to arise out of the middle constitutions and those akin to them. I will explain the reason of this hereafter, when I speak of the revolutions of states. The mean condition of states is clearly best, for no other is free from faction; and where the middle class is large, there are least likely to be factions and dissensions. For a similar reason large states are less liable to faction than small ones, because in them the middle class is large; whereas in small states it is easy to divide all the citizens into two classes who are either rich or poor, and to leave nothing in the middle. And democracies are safer and more permanent than oligarchies, because they have a middle class which is more numerous and has a greater share in the government; for when there is no middle class, and the poor greatly exceed in number, troubles arise, and the state soon comes to an end. A proof of the superiority of the middle class is that the best legislators have been of a middle condition; for example, Solon, as his own verses testify; and Lycurgus, for he was not a king; and Charondas, and almost all legislators.

These considerations will help us to understand why most governments are either democratical or oligarchical. The reason is that the middle class is seldom numerous in them, and whichever party, whether the rich or the common people, transgresses the mean and predominates, draws the constitution its own way, and thus arises either oligarchy or democracy. There is another reason—the poor and the rich quarrel with one another, and whichever side gets the better, instead of establishing a just or popular government, regards political supremacy as the prize of victory, and the one party sets up a democracy and the other an oligarchy. Further, both the parties which had the supremacy in Hellas looked only to the interest of their own form of government, and established in states, the one, democracies, and the other, oligarchies; they thought of their own advantage, of the public not at all. For these reasons the middle form of government has rarely, if ever, existed, and among a very few only. One man alone of all who ever ruled in Hellas was induced to give this middle constitution to states. But it has now become a habit among the citizens of states, not even to care about equality; all men are seeking for dominion, or, if conquered, are willing to submit.

What then is the best form of government, and what makes it the best, is evident; and of other constitutions, since we say that there are many kinds of democracy and many of oligarchy, it is not difficult to see which has the first and which the second or any other place in the order of excellence, now that we have determined which is the best. For that which is nearest to the best must of necessity be better, and that which is furthest from it worse, if we are judging absolutely and not relatively to given conditions. I say "relatively to given conditions," since a particular government may be preferable, but another form may be better for some people.

12. [*The best state.*] We have now to consider what and what kind of government is suitable to what and what kind of men. I may begin by assuming, as a general principle common to all governments, that the portion of the state which desires the permanence of the constitution ought to be stronger than that which desires the reverse. Now every city is composed of quality and quantity. By quality I mean freedom, wealth, education, good birth, and by quantity, superiority of numbers. Quality may exist in one of the classes which make up the state, and quantity in the other. For example, the meanly born may be more in number than the well-born, or the poor than the rich, yet they may not so much exceed in quantity as they fall short in quality; and therefore there must be a comparison of quantity and quality. Where the number of the poor is more than proportioned to the wealth of the rich, there will naturally be a democracy, varying in form with the sort of people who compose it in each case. If, for example, the husbandmen exceed in number, the first form of democracy will then arise; if the artisans and labouring class, the last; and so with the intermediate forms. But where the rich and the notables exceed

in quality more than they fall short in quantity, there oligarchy arises, similarly assuming various forms according to the kind of superiority possessed by the oligarchs.

The legislator should always include the middle class in his government; if he makes his laws oligarchical, to the middle class let him look; if he makes them democratical, he should equally by his laws try to attach this class to the state. There only can the government ever be stable where the middle class exceeds one or both of the others, and in that case there will be no fear that the rich will unite with the poor against the rulers. For neither of them will ever be willing to serve the other, and if they look for some form of government more suitable to both, they will find none better than this, for the rich and the poor will never consent to rule in turn, because they mistrust one another. The arbiter is always the one trusted, and he who is in the middle is an arbiter. The more perfect the admixture of the political elements, the more lasting will be the constitution. Many even of those who desire to form aristocratical governments make a mistake, not only in giving too much power to the rich, but in attempting to overreach the people. There comes a time when out of a false good there arises a true evil, since the encroachments of the rich are more destructive to the constitution than those of the people.

* * *

◎◎◎◎◎◎◎◎◎◎◎◎◎◎◎◎◎◎◎◎◎◎◎◎◎◎◎◎◎◎◎◎◎◎◎◎◎◎

BOOK VIII

1. [*Education.*] No one will doubt that the legislator should direct his attention above all to the education of youth; for the neglect of education does harm to the constitution. The

citizen should be moulded to suit the form of government under which he lives. For each government has a peculiar character which originally formed and which continues to preserve it. The character of democracy creates democracy, and the character of oligarchy creates oligarchy; and always the better the character, the better the government.

Again, for the exercise of any faculty or art a previous training and habituation are required; clearly therefore for the practice of virtue. And since the whole city has one end, it is manifest that education should be one and the same for all, and that it should be public, and not private—not as at present, when every one looks after his own children separately, and gives them separate instruction of the sort which he thinks best; the training in things which are of common interest should be the same for all. Neither must we suppose that any one of the citizens belongs to himself, for they all belong to the state, and are each of them a part of the state, and the care of each part is inseparable from the care of the whole. In this particular as in some others the Lacedaemonians are to be praised, for they take the greatest pains about their children, and make education the business of the state.

2. [*Education.*] That education should be regulated by law and should be an affair of state is not to be denied, but what should be the character of this public education, and how young persons should be educated, are questions which remain to be considered. As things are, there is disagreement about the subjects. For mankind are by no means agreed about the things to be taught, whether we look to virtue or the best life. Neither is it clear whether education is more concerned with intellectual or with moral virtue. The existing practice is perplexing; no one knows on what principle we should proceed—should the useful in life, or should virtue, or should the higher knowledge, be the aim of our training; all three opinions have been entertained. Again, about the means there is no agreement; for different persons, starting with different ideas about the nature of virtue, naturally

disagree about the practice of it. There can be no doubt that children should be taught those useful things which are really necessary, but not all useful things; for occupations are divided into liberal and illiberal; and to young children should be imparted only such kinds of knowledge as will be useful to them without vulgarizing them. And any occupation, art, or science, which makes the body or soul or mind of the freeman less fit for the practice or exercise of virtue, is vulgar; wherefore we call those arts vulgar which tend to deform the body, and likewise all paid employments, for they absorb and degrade the mind. There are also some liberal arts quite proper for a freeman to acquire, but only in a certain degree, and if he attend to them too closely, in order to attain perfection in them, the same evil effects will follow. The object also which a man sets before him makes a great difference; if he does or learns anything for his own sake or for the sake of his friends, or with a view to excellence, the action will not appear illiberal; but if done for the sake of others, the very same action will be thought menial and servile. The received subjects of instruction, as I have already remarked, are partly of a liberal and partly of an illiberal character.

3. [*Education.*] The customary branches of education are in number four; they are: (1) reading and writing, (2) gymnastic exercises, (3) music, to which is sometimes added (4) drawing. Of these, reading and writing and drawing are regarded as useful for the purposes of life in a variety of ways, and gymnastic exercises are thought to infuse courage. Concerning music a doubt may be raised—in our own day most men cultivate it for the sake of pleasure, but originally it was included in education, because nature herself, as has been often said, requires that we should be able, not only to work well, but to use leisure well; for, as I must repeat once again, the first principle of all action is leisure. Both are required, but leisure is better than occupation and is its end; and therefore the question must be asked, what ought we to do when at leisure? Clearly we ought not to be amus-

ing ourselves, for then amusement would be the end of life. But if this is inconceivable, and amusement is needed more amid serious occupations than at other times (for he who is hard at work has need of relaxation, and amusement gives relaxation, whereas occupation is always accompanied with exertion and effort), we should introduce amusements only at suitable times, and they should be our medicines, for the emotion which they create in the soul is a relaxation, and from the pleasure we obtain rest. But leisure of itself gives pleasure and happiness and enjoyment of life, which are experienced, not by the busy man, but by those who have leisure. For he who is occupied has in view some end which he has not attained; but happiness is an end, since all men deem it to be accompanied with pleasure and not with pain. This pleasure, however, is regarded differently by different persons, and varies according to the habit of individuals; the pleasure of the best man is the best, and springs from the noblest sources. It is clear then that there are branches of learning and education which we must study merely with a view to leisure spent in intellectual activity, and these are to be valued for their own sake; whereas those kinds of knowledge which are useful in business are to be deemed necessary, and exist for the sake of other things. And therefore our fathers admitted music into education, not on the ground either of its necessity or utility, for it is not necessary, nor indeed useful in the same manner as reading and writing, which are useful in money-making, in the management of a household, in the acquisition of knowledge and in political life, nor like drawing, useful for a more correct judgement of the works of artists, nor again like gymnastic, which gives health and strength; for neither of these is to be gained from music. There remains, then, the use of music for intellectual enjoyment in leisure; which is in fact evidently the reason of its introduction, this being one of the ways in which it is thought that a freeman should pass his leisure; as Homer says:

"But he who alone should be called to the pleasant feast,"

and afterwards he speaks of others whom he describes as inviting

"The bard who would delight them all."

And in another place Odysseus says there is no better way of passing life than when men's hearts are merry and

"The banqueters in the hall, sitting in order, hear the voice of the minstrel."

It is evident, then, that there is a sort of education in which parents should train their sons, not as being useful or necessary, but because it is liberal or noble. Whether this is of one kind only, or of more than one, and if so, what they are, and how they are to be imparted, must hereafter be determined. Thus much we are now in a position to say, that the ancients witness to us; for their opinion may be gathered from the fact that music is one of the received and traditional branches of education. Further, it is clear that children should be instructed in some useful things—for example, in reading and writing—not only for their usefulness, but also because many other sorts of knowledge are acquired through them. With a like view they may be taught drawing, not to prevent their making mistakes in their own purchases, or in order that they may not be imposed upon in the buying or selling of articles, but perhaps rather because it makes them judges of the beauty of the human form. To be always seeking after the useful does not become free and exalted souls. Now it is clear that in education practice must be used before theory, and the body be trained before the mind; and therefore boys should be handed over to the trainer, who creates in them the proper habit of body, and to the wrestling master, who teaches them their exercises.

* * *

POETICS

Translated by Ingram Bywater

Aristotle's treatise on poetry is a brief, incomplete work. The second book has been lost, and the one surviving book deals quite fully with tragedy but only slightly with the epic and hardly at all with comedy and other forms. Yet this little treatise has had an extraordinary influence on dramatic theory and practice and on theories of the fine arts in general. It is packed with ideas which have been argued for centuries and have become basic tools of criticism. Among these are the theory of poetry as imitation, and of tragedy, specifically, as an imitation of incidents arousing pity and fear; the theory of the purgative function of tragedy (*catharsis*), which stresses the beneficent value of the drama in arousing pity and fear in order to purge them; the unified plot, one which has a beginning, middle, and end; the concept of the tragic hero as a man of prosperity and reputation whose misfortune is brought upon him "not by vice and depravity but by some error of judgement." Some of these theories have been notoriously misused; Aristotle's tentative commentary on plot and duration became, in the hands of neoclassical critics and dramatists, the unbreakable unities of time, place, and action.

It is vital to remember that Aristotle's POETICS is

based on his observation of the dramatic practice of his day and that he intended it partly as a handbook for aspiring practitioners of a particular mode of writing. But dramatic and literary practice changes from century to century, and now the value of Aristotle's treatise lies not so much in the answers it gives as in the questions it raises, the ideas it provokes.

The text that follows has been somewhat abridged through the omission of references to lost or obscure plays of Aristotle's time and of the purely technical material on Greek grammar, etymology, spelling, and phonetics.

POETICS

∞∞

1. [*The poetic arts distinguished by their means.*] Our subject being Poetry, I propose to speak not only of the art in general but also of its species and their respective capacities; of the structure of plot required for a good poem; of the number and nature of the constituent parts of a poem; and likewise of any other matters in the same line of inquiry. Let us follow the natural order and begin with the primary facts.

Epic poetry and Tragedy, as also Comedy, Dithyrambic poetry, and most flute playing and lyre playing, are all, viewed as a whole, modes of imitation. But at the same time they differ from one another in three ways, either by a difference of kind in their means, or by differences in the objects, or in the manner of their imitations.

I. Just as colour and form are used as means by some, who (whether by art or constant practice) imitate and portray many things by their aid, and the voice is used by others; so also in the above-mentioned group of arts, the means with them as a whole are rhythm, language, and harmony—used, however, either singly or in certain combinations. A combination of harmony and rhythm alone is the means in flute playing and lyre playing, and any other arts there may be of the same description, e. g., imitative piping. Rhythm alone, without harmony, is the means in the dancer's imitations; for even he, by the rhythms of his attitudes, may represent men's characters, as well as what they do and suffer. There is further an art which imitates by language alone, without harmony, in prose or in verse, and if in verse, either in some one or in a plurality of metres. This form of imitation is to this day without a name. We have no common name for a mime of Sophron or Xenarchus and a Socratic Conversation; and we should still be without one even if the imitation in the two instances were in trimeters or elegiacs or some other kind of verse—though it is the way with people to tack on "poet" to the name of a metre, and talk of elegiac poets and epic poets, thinking that they call them poets not by reason of the imitative nature of their work, but indiscriminately by reason of the metre they write in. Even if a theory of medicine or physical philosophy be put forth in a metrical form, it is usual to describe the writer in this way; Homer and Empedocles, however, have really nothing in common apart from their metre; so that, if the one is to be called a poet, the other should be termed a physicist rather than a poet. We should be in the same position also, if the imitation in these instances were in all the metres, like the *Centaur* (a rhapsody in a medley of all metres) of Chaeremon; and Chaeremon one has to recognize as a poet. So much, then, as to these arts. There are, lastly, certain other arts, which combine all the means enumerated, rhythm, melody, and verse, e. g., Dithyrambic and Nomic poetry, Tragedy and Comedy; with this difference, however, that the three kinds of means are in some of them all employed together, and in others brought in separately, one after the other. These elements of difference in the above arts I term the means of their imitation.

2. [*The poetic arts distinguished by their objects.*] II. The objects the imitator represents are actions, with agents who are necessarily either good men or bad—the diversities of human character being nearly always derivative from this primary distinction, since the line between virtue and vice is one dividing the whole of mankind. It follows, therefore, that the agents represented must be either above our own level of goodness, or beneath it, or just such as we are; in

the same way as, with the painters, the personages of Polygnotus are better than we are, those of Pauson worse, and
those of Dionysius just like ourselves. It is clear that each
of the above-mentioned arts will admit of these differences,
and that it will become a separate art by representing objects with this point of difference. Even in dancing, flute
playing, and lyre playing such diversities are possible; and
they are also possible in the nameless art that uses language,
prose or verse without harmony, as its means; Homer's personages, for instance, are better than we are; Cleophon's
are on our own level; and those of Hegemon of Thasos, the
first writer of parodies, and Nicochares, the author of the
Diliad, are beneath it. The same is true of the Dithyramb
and the Nome: the personages may be presented in them
with the difference exemplified in the . . . of . . . and Argas,
and in the Cyclopses of Timotheus and Philoxenus. This
difference it is that distinguishes Tragedy and Comedy also;
the one would make its personages worse, and the other
better, than the men of the present day.

3. [*The poetic arts distinguished by the manner of their imitations.*] III. A third difference in these arts is in the manner in which each kind of object is represented. Given both
the same means and the same kind of object for imitation,
one may either (1) speak at one moment in narrative and at
another in an assumed character, as Homer does; or (2) one
may remain the same throughout, without any such change;
or (3) the imitators may represent the whole story dramati-
cally, as though they were actually doing the things described.

As we said at the beginning, therefore, the differences in
the imitation of these arts come under three heads, their
means, their objects, and their manner.

So that as an imitator Sophocles will be on one side akin
to Homer, both portraying good men; and on another to
Aristophanes, since both present their personages as acting
and doing. This in fact, according to some, is the reason for
plays being termed dramas, because in a play the personages
act the story. Hence too both Tragedy and Comedy are

claimed by the Dorians as their discoveries; Comedy by the
Megarians—by those in Greece as having arisen when Megara
became a democracy, and by the Sicilian Megarians on the
ground that the poet Epicharmus was of their country, and
a good deal earlier than Chionides and Magnes; even Tragedy also is claimed by certain of the Peloponnesian Dorians.
In support of this claim they point to the words "comedy"
and "drama." Their word for the outlying hamlets, they say,
is *comae*, whereas Athenians call them *demes*—thus assuming
that comedians got the name not from their *comoe* or revels,
but from their strolling from hamlet to hamlet, lack of ap-
preciation keeping them out of the city. Their word also for
"to act," they say, is *dran*, whereas Athenians use *prattein*.

So much, then, as to the number and nature of the points
of difference in the imitation of these arts.

4. [*Origin and development of poetry and its kinds.*] It is
clear that the general origin of poetry was due to two causes,
each of them part of human nature. Imitation is natural to
man from childhood, one of his advantages over the lower
animals being this, that he is the most imitative creature in
the world, and learns at first by imitation. And it is also
natural for all to delight in works of imitation. The truth
of this second point is shown by experience: though the
objects themselves may be painful to see, we delight to view
the most realistic representations of them in art, the forms
for example of the lowest animals and of dead bodies. The
explanation is to be found in a further fact: to be learning
something is the greatest of pleasures not only to the philosopher but also to the rest of mankind, however small their
capacity for it; the reason of the delight in seeing the picture
is that one is at the same time learning—gathering the meaning of things, e. g., that the man there is so-and-so; for if
one has not seen the thing before, one's pleasure will not be
in the picture as an imitation of it, but will be due to the
execution or colouring or some similar cause. Imitation, then,
being natural to us—as also the sense of harmony and
rhythm, the metres being obviously species of rhythms—it

was through their original aptitude, and by a series of improvements for the most part gradual on their first efforts, that they created poetry out of their improvisations.

Poetry, however, soon broke up into two kinds according to the differences of character in the individual poets; for the graver among them would represent noble actions, and those of noble personages; and the meaner sort the actions of the ignoble. The latter class produced invectives at first, just as others did hymns and panegyrics. We know of no such poem by any of the pre-Homeric poets, though there were probably many such writers among them; instances, however, may be found from Homer downwards, e. g., his *Margites*, and the similar poems of others. In this poetry of invective its natural fitness brought an iambic metre into use; hence our present term "iambic," because it was the metre of their "iambs" or invectives against one another. The result was that the old poets became some of them writers of heroic and others of iambic verse. Homer's position, however, is peculiar: just as he was in the serious style the poet of poets, standing alone not only through the literary excellence, but also through the dramatic character of his imitations, so too he was the first to outline for us the general forms of Comedy by producing not a dramatic invective, but a dramatic picture of the Ridiculous; his *Margites* in fact stands in the same relation to our comedies as the *Iliad* and *Odyssey* to our tragedies. As soon, however, as Tragedy and Comedy appeared in the field, those naturally drawn to the one line of poetry became writers of comedies instead of iambs, and those naturally drawn to the other, writers of tragedies instead of epics, because these new modes of art were grander and of more esteem than the old.

If it be asked whether Tragedy is now all that it need be in its formative elements, to consider that, and decide it theoretically and in relation to the theatres, is a matter for another inquiry.

It certainly began in improvisations—as did also Comedy; the one originating with the authors of the Dithyramb, the other with those of the phallic songs, which still survive as institutions in many of our cities. And its advance after that was little by little, through their improving on whatever they had before them at each stage. It was in fact only after a long series of changes that the movement of Tragedy stopped on its attaining to its natural form. (1) The number of actors was first increased to two by Aeschylus, who curtailed the business of the Chorus, and made the dialogue, or spoken portion, take the leading part in the play. (2) A third actor and scenery were due to Sophocles. (3) Tragedy acquired also its magnitude. Discarding short stories and a ludicrous diction, through its passing out of its satyric stage, it assumed, though only at a late point in its progress, a tone of dignity; and its metre changed then from trochaic to iambic. The reason for their original use of the trochaic tetrameter was that their poetry was satyric and more connected with dancing than it now is. As soon, however, as a spoken part came in, nature herself found the appropriate metre. The iambic, we know, is the most speakable of metres, as is shown by the fact that we very often fall into it in conversation, whereas we rarely talk hexameters, and only when we depart from the speaking tone of voice. (4) Another change was a plurality of episodes or acts. As for the remaining matters, the superadded embellishments and the account of their introduction, these must be taken as said, as it would probably be a long piece of work to go through the details.

5. [*Comic and Epic poetry.*] As for Comedy, it is (as has been observed) an imitation of men worse than the average; worse, however, not as regards any and every sort of fault, but only as regards one particular kind, the Ridiculous, which is a species of the Ugly. The Ridiculous may be defined as a mistake or deformity not productive of pain or harm to others; the mask, for instance, that excites laughter, is something ugly and distorted without causing pain.

Though the successive changes in Tragedy and their authors are not unknown, we cannot say the same of Comedy; its early stages passed unnoticed, because it was not as yet taken up in a serious way. It was only at a late point in its progress that a chorus of comedians was officially granted by the archon; they used to be mere volunteers. It had also already certain definite forms at the time when the record of those termed comic poets begins. Who it was who supplied it with masks, or prologues, or a plurality of actors and the like, has remained unknown. The invented Fable, or Plot, however, originated in Sicily with Epicharmus and Phormis; of Athenian poets Crates was the first to drop the Comedy of invective and frame stories of a general and non-personal nature, in other words, Fables or Plots.

Epic poetry, then, has been seen to agree with Tragedy to this extent, that of being an imitation of serious subjects in a grand kind of verse. It differs from it, however, (1) in that it is in one kind of verse and in narrative form; and (2) in its length—which is due to its action having no fixed limit of time, whereas Tragedy endeavours to keep as far as possible within a single circuit of the sun, or something near that. This, I say, is another point of difference between them, though at first the practice in this respect was just the same in tragedies as in epic poems. They differ also (3) in their constituents, some being common to both and others peculiar to Tragedy—hence a judge of good and bad in Tragedy is a judge of that in epic poetry also. All the parts of an epic are included in Tragedy; but those of Tragedy are not all of them to be found in the Epic.

6. [*Definition and analysis of Tragedy.*] Reserving hexameter poetry and Comedy for consideration hereafter, let us proceed now to the discussion of Tragedy; before doing so, however, we must gather up the definition resulting from what has been said. A tragedy, then, is the imitation of an action that is serious and also, as having magnitude, complete in itself; in language with pleasurable accessories, each kind brought in separately in the parts of the work; in a dramatic, not in a narrative form; with incidents arousing pity and fear, wherewith to accomplish its catharsis of such emotions. Here by "language with pleasurable accessories" I

mean that with rhythm and harmony or song superadded; and by "the kinds separately" I mean that some portions are worked out with verse only, and others in turn with song.

I. As they act the stories, it follows that in the first place the Spectacle (or stage appearance of the actors) must be some part of the whole; and in the second Melody and Diction, these two being the means of their imitation. Here by "Diction" I mean merely this, the composition of the verses; and by "Melody," what is too completely understood to require explanation. But further: the subject represented also is an action; and the action involves agents, who must necessarily have their distinctive qualities both of character and thought, since it is from these that we ascribe certain qualities to their actions. There are in the natural order of things, therefore, two causes, Thought and Character, of their actions, and consequently of their success or failure in their lives. Now the action (that which was done) is represented in the play by the Fable or Plot. The Fable, in our present sense of the term, is simply this, the combination of the incidents, or things done in the story; whereas Character is what makes us ascribe certain moral qualities to the agents; and Thought is shown in all they say when proving a particular point or, it may be, enunciating a general truth. There are six parts consequently of every tragedy, as a whole (that is) of such or such quality, viz., a Fable or Plot, Characters, Diction, Thought, Spectacle, and Melody; two of them arising from the means, one from the manner, and three from the objects of the dramatic imitation; and there is nothing else besides these six. Of these, its formative elements, then, not a few of the dramatists have made due use, as every play, one may say, admits of Spectacle, Character, Fable, Diction, Melody, and Thought.

II. The most important of the six is the combination of the incidents of the story. Tragedy is essentially an imitation not of persons but of action and life, of happiness and misery. All human happiness or misery takes the form of action; the end for which we live is a certain kind of activity, not a quality. Character gives us qualities, but it is in our actions—

what we do—that we are happy or the reverse. In a play accordingly they do not act in order to portray the Characters; they include the Characters for the sake of the action. So that it is the action in it, i. e., its Fable or Plot, that is the end and purpose of the tragedy; and the end is everywhere the chief thing. Besides this, a tragedy is impossible without action, but there may be one without Character. The tragedies of most of the moderns are characterless—a defect common among poets of all kinds, and with its counterpart in painting in Zeuxis as compared with Polygnotus; for whereas the latter is strong in character, the work of Zeuxis is devoid of it. And again: one may string together a series of characteristic speeches of the utmost finish as regards Diction and Thought, and yet fail to produce the true tragic effect; but one will have much better success with a tragedy which, however inferior in these respects, has a Plot, a combination of incidents, in it. And again: the most powerful elements of attraction in Tragedy, the Peripeties and Discoveries, are parts of the Plot. A further proof is in the fact that beginners succeed earlier with the Diction and Characters than with the construction of a story; and the same may be said of nearly all the early dramatists. We maintain, therefore, that the first essential, the life and soul, so to speak, of Tragedy is the Plot; and that the Characters come second—compare the parallel in painting, where the most beautiful colours laid on without order will not give one the same pleasure as a simple black-and-white sketch of a portrait. We maintain that Tragedy is primarily an imitation of action, and that it is mainly for the sake of the action that it imitates the personal agents. Third comes the element of Thought, i. e., the power of saying whatever can be said, or what is appropriate to the occasion. This is what, in the speeches in Tragedy, falls under the arts of Politics and Rhetoric; for the older poets make their personages discourse like statesmen, and the modern like rhetoricians. One must not confuse it with Character. Character in a play is that which reveals the moral purpose of the agents, i. e., the sort of thing they seek or avoid, where that is not obvious—hence there is no room for Character in a speech on a purely indifferent subject. Thought, on the other hand, is shown in all they say when proving or disproving some particular point, or enunciating some universal proposition. Fourth among the literary elements is the Diction of the personages, i.e., as before explained, the expression of their thoughts in words, which is practically the same thing with verse as with prose. As for the two remaining parts, the Melody is the greatest of the pleasurable accessories of Tragedy. The Spectacle, though an attraction, is the least artistic of all the parts, and has least to do with the art of poetry. The tragic effect is quite possible without a public performance and actors; and besides, the getting-up of the Spectacle is more a matter for the costumier than the poet.

7. [*Tragedy: arrangement and length of the play.*] Having thus distinguished the parts, let us now consider the proper construction of the Fable or Plot, as that is at once the first and the most important thing in Tragedy. We have laid it down that a tragedy is an imitation of an action that is complete in itself, as a whole of some magnitude; for a whole may be of no magnitude to speak of. Now a whole is that which has beginning, middle, and end. A beginning is that which is not itself necessarily after anything else, and which has naturally something else after it; an end is that which is naturally after something itself, either as its necessary or usual consequent, and with nothing else after it; and a middle, that which is by nature after one thing and has also another after it. A well-constructed Plot, therefore, cannot either begin or end at any point one likes; beginning and end in it must be of the forms just described. Again: to be beautiful, a living creature, and every whole made up of parts, must not only present a certain order in its arrangement of parts, but also be of a certain definite magnitude. Beauty is a matter of size and order, and therefore impossible either (1) in a very minute creature, since our perception becomes indistinct as it approaches instantaneity; or (2) in a creature of vast size—one, say, 1000 miles long—as in that case, instead of the object being seen all at once, the unity and wholeness

of it is lost to the beholder. Just in the same way, then, as a beautiful whole made up of parts, or a beautiful living creature, must be of some size, but a size to be taken in by the eye, so a story or Plot must be of some length, but of a length to be taken in by the memory. As for the limit of its length, so far as that is relative to public performances and spectators, it does not fall within the theory of poetry. If they had to perform a hundred tragedies, they would be timed by water clocks, as they are said to have been at one period. The limit, however, set by the actual nature of the thing is this: the longer the story, consistently with its being comprehensible as a whole, the finer it is by reason of its magnitude. As a rough general formula, "a length which allows of the hero passing by a series of probable or necessary stages from misfortune to happiness, or from happiness to misfortune," may suffice as a limit for the magnitude of the story.

8. [*Tragedy: Unity of action.*] The Unity of a Plot does not consist, as some suppose, in its having one man as its subject. An infinity of things befall that one man, some of which it is impossible to reduce to unity; and in like manner there are many actions of one man which cannot be made to form one action. One sees, therefore, the mistake of all the poets who have written a *Heracleid*, a *Theseid*, or similar poems; they suppose that, because Heracles was one man, the story also of Heracles must be one story. Homer, however, evidently understood this point quite well, whether by art or instinct, just in the same way as he excels the rest in every other respect. In writing an *Odyssey*, he did not make the poem cover all that ever befell his hero—it befell him, for instance, to get wounded on Parnassus and also to feign madness at the time of the call to arms, but the two incidents had no necessary or probable connexion with one another—instead of doing that, he took as the subject of the *Odyssey*, as also of the *Iliad*, an action with a Unity of the kind we are describing. The truth is that, just as in the other imitative arts one imitation is always of one thing, so in poetry the story, as an imitation of action, must represent one action, a complete

whole, with its several incidents so closely connected that the transposal or withdrawal of any one of them will disjoin and dislocate the whole. For that which makes no perceptible difference by its presence or absence is no real part of the whole.

9. [*Tragedy: the probable and universal.*] From what we have said it will be seen that the poet's function is to describe, not the thing that has happened, but a kind of thing that might happen, i. e., what is possible as being probable or necessary. The distinction between historian and poet is not in the one writing prose and the other verse—you might put the work of Herodotus into verse, and it would still be a species of history; it consists really in this, that the one describes the thing that has been, and the other a kind of thing that might be. Hence poetry is something more philosophic and of graver import than history, since its statements are of the nature rather of universals, whereas those of history are singulars. By a universal statement I mean one as to what such or such a kind of man will probably or necessarily say or do—which is the aim of poetry, though it affixes proper names to the characters; by a singular statement, one as to what, say, Alcibiades did or had done to him. In Comedy this has become clear by this time; it is only when their plot is already made up of probable incidents that they give it a basis of proper names, choosing for the purpose any names that may occur to them, instead of writing like the old iambic poets about particular persons. In Tragedy, however, they still adhere to the historic names; and for this reason: what convinces is the possible; now whereas we are not yet sure as to the possibility of that which has not happened, that which has happened is manifestly possible, else it would not have come to pass. Nevertheless even in Tragedy there are some plays with but one or two known names in them, the rest being inventions; and there are some without a single known name, e. g., Agathon's *Antheus,* in which both incidents and names are of the poet's invention; and it is no less delightful on that account. So that one must not aim at a rigid adher-

ence to the traditional stories on which tragedies are based. It would be absurd, in fact, to do so, as even the known stories are only known to a few, though they are a delight none the less to all.

It is evident from the above that the poet must be more the poet of his stories or Plots than of his verses, inasmuch as he is a poet by virtue of the imitative element in his work, and it is actions that he imitates. And if he should come to take a subject from actual history, he is none the less a poet for that; since some historic occurrences may very well be in the probable and possible order of things; and it is in that aspect of them that he is their poet.

Of simple Plots and actions the episodic are the worst. I call a Plot episodic when there is neither probability nor necessity in the sequence of its episodes. Actions of this sort bad poets construct through their own fault, and good ones on account of the players. His work being for public performance, a good poet often stretches out a Plot beyond its capabilities, and is thus obliged to twist the sequence of incident.

Tragedy, however, is an imitation not only of a complete action, but also of incidents arousing pity and fear. Such incidents have the very greatest effect on the mind when they occur unexpectedly and at the same time in consequence of one another; there is more of the marvellous in them then than if they happened of themselves or by mere chance. Even matters of chance seem most marvellous if there is an appearance of design as it were in them; as for instance the statue of Mitys at Argos killed the author of Mitys' death by falling down on him when a looker-on at a public spectacle; for incidents like that we think to be not without a meaning. A Plot, therefore, of this sort is necessarily finer than others.

10. [*Tragedy: simple and complex Plots.*] Plots are either simple or complex, since the actions they represent are naturally of this twofold description. The action, proceeding in the way defined, as one continuous whole, I call simple, when the change in the hero's fortunes takes place without Peripety

or Discovery; and complex, when it involves one or the other, or both. These should each of them arise out of the structure of the Plot itself, so as to be the consequence, necessary or probable, of the antecedents. There is a great difference between a thing happening *propter hoc* and *post hoc*.

11. [*Tragedy: Peripety, Discovery, and Suffering.*] A Peripety is the change of the kind described from one state of things within the play to its opposite, and that too in the way we are saying, in the probable or necessary sequence of events; as it is for instance in *Oedipus*: here the opposite state of things is produced by the Messenger, who, coming to gladden Oedipus and to remove his fears as to his mother, reveals the secret of his birth. And in *Lynceus*: just as he is being led off for execution, with Danaus at his side to put him to death, the incidents preceding this bring it about that he is saved and Danaus put to death. A Discovery is, as the very word implies, a change from ignorance to knowledge, and thus to either love or hate, in the personages marked for good or evil fortune. The finest form of Discovery is one attended by Peripeties, like that which goes with the Discovery in *Oedipus*. There are no doubt other forms of it; what we have said may happen in a way in reference to inanimate things, even things of a very casual kind; and it is also possible to discover whether some one has done or not done something. But the form most directly connected with the Plot and the action of the piece is the first-mentioned. This, with a Peripety, will arouse either pity or fear—actions of that nature being what Tragedy is assumed to represent; and it will also serve to bring about the happy or unhappy ending. The Discovery, then, being of persons, it may be that of one party only to the other, the latter being already known; or both the parties may have to discover themselves. Iphigenia, for instance, was discovered to Orestes by sending the letter; and another Discovery was required to reveal him to Iphigenia.

Two parts of the Plot, then, Peripety and Discovery, are on matters of this sort. A third part is Suffering; which we may define as an action of a destructive or painful nature, such as

murders on the stage, tortures, woundings, and the like. The
other two have been already explained.

12. [*The quantitative parts of a tragedy.*] The parts of Tragedy to be treated as formative elements in the whole were
mentioned in a previous Chapter [6]. From the point of
view, however, of its quantity, i. e., the separate sections into
which it is divided, a tragedy has the following parts: Prologue, Episode, Exode, and a choral portion, distinguished
into Parode and Stasimon; these two are common to all tragedies, whereas songs from the stage and *Commoe* are only
found in some. The Prologue is all that precedes the Parode
of the chorus; an Episode all that comes in between two
whole choral songs; the Exode all that follows after the last
choral song. In the choral portion the Parode is the whole
first statement of the chorus; a Stasimon, a song of the chorus
without anapaests or trochees; a *Commos*, a lamentation
sung by chorus and actor in concert. The parts of Tragedy to
be used as formative elements in the whole we have already
mentioned; the above are its parts from the point of view
of its quantity, or the separate sections into which it is
divided.

13. [*The tragic hero.*] The next points after what we have
said above will be these: (1) What is the poet to aim at, and
what is he to avoid, in constructing his Plots? and (2) What
are the conditions on which the tragic effect depends?

We assume that, for the finest form of Tragedy, the Plot
must be not simple but complex; and further, that it must
imitate actions arousing fear and pity, since that is the distinctive function of this kind of imitation. It follows, therefore,
that there are three forms of Plot to be avoided. (1) A good
man must not be seen passing from happiness to misery, or
(2) a bad man from misery to happiness. The first situation
is not fear inspiring or piteous, but simply odious to us. The
second is the most untragic that can be; it has no one of the
requisites of Tragedy; it does not appeal either to the human
feeling in us, or to our pity, or to our fears. Nor, on the other

hand, should (3) an extremely bad man be seen falling from happiness into misery. Such a story may arouse the human feeling in us, but it will not move us to either pity or fear; pity is occasioned by undeserved misfortune, and fear by that of one like ourselves; so that there will be nothing either piteous or fear inspiring in the situation. There remains, then, the intermediate kind of personage, a man not pre-eminently virtuous and just, whose misfortune, however, is brought upon him not by vice and depravity but by some error of judgement, of the number of those in the enjoyment of great reputation and prosperity; e. g., Oedipus, Thyestes, and the men of note of similar families. The perfect Plot, accordingly, must have a single, and not (as some tell us) a double issue; the change in the hero's fortunes must be not from misery to happiness, but on the contrary from happiness to misery; and the cause of it must lie not in any depravity, but in some great error on his part; the man himself being either such as we have described, or better, not worse, than that. Fact also confirms our theory. Though the poets began by accepting any tragic story that came to hand, in these days the finest tragedies are always on the story of some few houses, on that of Alcmeon, Oedipus, Orestes, Meleager, Thyestes, Telephus, or any others that may have been involved, as either agents or sufferers, in some deed of horror. The theoretically best tragedy, then, has a Plot of this description. The critics, therefore, are wrong who blame Euripides for taking this line in his tragedies, and giving many of them an unhappy ending. It is, as we have said, the right line to take. The best proof is this: on the stage, and in the public performances, such plays, properly worked out, are seen to be the most truly tragic; and Euripides, even if his execution be faulty in every other point, is seen to be nevertheless the most tragic certainly of the dramatists. After this comes the construction of Plot which some rank first, one with a double story (like the *Odyssey*) and an opposite issue for the good and the bad personages. It is ranked as first only through the weakness of the audiences; the poets merely follow their public, writing as its wishes dictate. But the pleasure here is not that of

Tragedy. It belongs rather to Comedy, where the bitterest enemies in the piece (e. g., Orestes and Aegisthus) walk off good friends at the end, with no slaying of any one by any one.

14. [*The tragic deed.*] The tragic fear and pity may be aroused by the Spectacle; but they may also be aroused by the very structure and incidents of the play—which is the better way and shows the better poet. The Plot in fact should be so framed that, even without seeing the things take place, he who simply hears the account of them shall be filled with horror and pity at the incidents; which is just the effect that the mere recital of the story in *Oedipus* would have on one. To produce this same effect by means of the Spectacle is less artistic, and requires extraneous aid. Those, however, who make use of the Spectacle to put before us that which is merely monstrous and not productive of fear, are wholly out of touch with Tragedy; not every kind of pleasure should be required of a tragedy, but only its own proper pleasure.

The tragic pleasure is that of pity and fear, and the poet has to produce it by a work of imitation; it is clear, therefore, that the causes should be included in the incidents of his story. Let us see, then, what kinds of incident strike one as horrible, or rather as piteous. In a deed of this description the parties must necessarily be either friends, or enemies, or indifferent to one another. Now when enemy does it on enemy, there is nothing to move us to pity either in his doing or in his meditating the deed, except so far as the actual pain of the sufferer is concerned; and the same is true when the parties are indifferent to one another. Whenever the tragic deed, however, is done within the family—when murder or the like is done or meditated by brother on brother, by son on father, by mother on son, or son on mother—these are the situations the poet should seek after. The traditional stories, accordingly, must be kept as they are, e. g., the murder of Clytaemnestra by Orestes and of Eriphyle by Alcmeon. At the same time even with these there is something left to the poet himself; it is for him to devise the right way of treating them. Let us explain more clearly what we mean by "the right way." The deed of horror may be done by the doer knowingly and consciously, as in the old poets, and in Medea's murder of her children in Euripides. Or he may do it, but in ignorance of his relationship, and discover that afterwards, as does the Oedipus in Sophocles. Here the deed is outside the play; but it may be within it, like the act of the Alcmeon in Astydamas, or that of the Telegonus in *Ulysses Wounded.* A third possibility is for one meditating some deadly injury to another, in ignorance of his relationship, to make the discovery in time to draw back. These exhaust the possibilities, since the deed must necessarily be either done or not done, and either knowingly or unknowingly.

The worst situation is when the personage is with full knowledge on the point of doing the deed, and leaves it undone. It is odious and also (through the absence of suffering) untragic; hence it is that no one is made to act thus except in some few instances, e. g., Haemon and Creon in *Antigone.* Next after this comes the actual perpetration of the deed meditated. A better situation than that, however, is for the deed to be done in ignorance, and the relationship discovered afterwards, since there is nothing odious in it, and the Discovery will serve to astound us. But the best of all is the last; what we have in *Cresphontes,* for example, where Merope, on the point of slaying her son, recognizes him in time; in *Iphigenia,* where sister and brother are in a like position; and in *Helle,* where the son recognizes his mother, when on the point of giving her up to her enemy.

This will explain why our tragedies are restricted (as we said just now) to such a small number of families. It was accident rather than art that led the poets in quest of subjects to embody this kind of incident in their Plots. They are still obliged, accordingly, to have recourse to the families in which such horrors have occurred.

On the construction of the Plot, and the kind of Plot required for Tragedy, enough has now been said.

15. [*The character of the tragic personages.*] In the Characters there are four points to aim at. First and foremost, that they shall be good. There will be an element of character in the play, if (as has been observed) what a personage says or does reveals a certain moral purpose; and a good element of character, if the purpose so revealed is good. Such goodness is possible in every type of personage, even in a woman or a slave, though the one is perhaps an inferior, and the other a wholly worthless being. The second point is to make them appropriate. The Character before us may be, say, manly; but it is not appropriate in a female Character to be manly, or clever. The third is to make them like the reality, which is not the same as their being good and appropriate, in our sense of the term. The fourth is to make them consistent and the same throughout; even if inconsistency be part of the man before one for imitation as presenting that form of character, he should still be consistently inconsistent. We have an instance of baseness of character, not required for the story, in the Menelaus in *Orestes*; of the incongruous and unbefitting in the lamentation of Ulysses in *Scylla,* and in the (clever) speech of Melanippe; and of inconsistency in *Iphigenia at Aulis,* where Iphigenia the suppliant is utterly unlike the later Iphigenia. The right thing, however, is in the Characters just as in the incidents of the play to endeavour always after the necessary or the probable; so that whenever such-and-such a personage says or does such-and-such a thing, it shall be the necessary or probable outcome of his character; and whenever this incident follows on that, it shall be either the necessary or the probable consequence of it. From this one sees (to digress for a moment) that the Dénouement also should arise out of the plot itself, and not depend on a stage artifice, as in *Medea,* or in the story of the (arrested) departure of the Greeks in the *Iliad.* The artifice must be reserved for matters outside the play—for past events beyond human knowledge, or events yet to come, which require to be foretold or announced; since it is the privilege of the Gods to know everything. There should be nothing improbable among the actual incidents. If it be unavoidable,

however, it should be outside the tragedy, like the improbability in the *Oedipus* of Sophocles. But to return to the Characters. As Tragedy is an imitation of personages better than the ordinary man, we in our way should follow the example of good portrait painters, who reproduce the distinctive features of a man, and at the same time, without losing the likeness, make him handsomer than he is. The poet in like manner, in portraying men quick or slow to anger, or with similar infirmities of character, must know how to represent them as such, and at the same time as good men, as Agathon and Homer have represented Achilles.

All these rules one must keep in mind throughout, and, further, those also for such points of stage effect as directly depend on the art of the poet, since in these too one may often make mistakes. Enough, however, has been said on the subject in one of our published writings.

16. [*The various forms of Discovery.*] Discovery in general has been explained already. As for the species of Discovery, the first to be noted is (1) the least artistic form of it, of which the poets make most use through mere lack of invention, Discovery by signs or marks. Of these signs some are congenital, like the "lance-head which the Earth-born have on them," or "stars," such as Carcinus brings in his *Thyestes;* others acquired after birth—these latter being either marks on the body, e.g., scars, or external tokens, like necklaces, or (to take another sort of instance) the ark in the Discovery in *Tyro.* Even these, however, admit of two uses, a better and a worse; the scar of Ulysses is an instance; the Discovery of him through it is made in one way by the nurse and in another by the swineherds. A Discovery using signs as a means of assurance is less artistic, as indeed are all such as imply reflection; whereas one bringing them in all of a sudden, as in the *Bath-story,* is of a better order. Next after these are (2) Discoveries made directly by the poet; which are inartistic for that very reason; e. g., Orestes' Discovery of himself in *Iphigenia*: whereas his sister reveals who she is by the letter, Orestes is made to say himself what the poet

rather than the story demands. This, therefore, is not far
removed from the first-mentioned fault, since he might have
presented certain tokens as well. Another instance is the
"shuttle's voice" in the *Tereus* of Sophocles. (3) A third
species is Discovery through memory, from a man's consciousness being awakened by something seen. Thus in *The Cy-
prioe* of Dicaeogenes, the sight of the picture makes the man
burst into tears; and in the *Tale of Alcinous*, hearing the
harper Ulysses is reminded of the past and weeps; the Discovery of them being the result. (4) A fourth kind is Discovery through reasoning; e. g., in *The Choephoroe*: "One
like me is here; there is no one like me but Orestes; he, therefore, must be here." Or that which Polyidus the Sophist suggested for *Iphigenia*; since it was natural for Orestes to
reflect: "My sister was sacrificed, and I am to be sacrificed
like her." Or that in the *Tydeus* of Theodectes: "I came to
find a son, and am to die myself." Or that in *The Phinidae*:
on seeing the place the women inferred their fate, that they
were to die there, since they had also been exposed there.
(5) There is, too, a composite Discovery arising from bad
reasoning on the side of the other party. An instance of it is
in *Ulysses the False Messenger*: he said he should know the
bow—which he had not seen; but to suppose from that that
he would know it again (as though he had once seen it) was
bad reasoning. (6) The best of all Discoveries, however, is
that arising from the incidents themselves, when the great
surprise comes about through a probable incident like that
in the *Oedipus* of Sophocles; and also in *Iphigenia*; for it was
not improbable that she should wish to have a letter taken
home. These last are the only Discoveries independent of the
artifice of signs and necklaces. Next after them come Discoveries through reasoning.

17. [*Additional rules for the construction of a play.*] At the
time when he is constructing his Plots, and engaged on the
Diction in which they are worked out, the poet should remember (1) to put the actual scenes as far as possible before his eyes. In this way, seeing everything with the vivid-

ness of an eyewitness as it were, he will devise what is appropriate, and be least likely to overlook incongruities. This is shown by what was censured in Carcinus, the return of Amphiaraus from the sanctuary; it would have passed unnoticed, if it had not been actually seen by the audience; but on the stage his play failed, the incongruity of the incident offending the spectators. (2) As far as may be, too, the poet should even act his story with the very gestures of his personages. Given the same natural qualifications, he who feels the emotions to be described will be the most convincing; distress and anger, for instance, are portrayed most truthfully by one who is feeling them at the moment. Hence it is that poetry demands a man with a special gift for it, or else one with a touch of madness in him; the former can easily assume the required mood, and the latter may be actually beside himself with emotion. (3) His story, again, whether already made or of his own making, he should first simplify and reduce to a universal form, before proceeding to lengthen it out by the insertion of episodes. The following will show how the universal element in *Iphigenia*, for instance, may be viewed: A certain maiden having been offered in sacrifice, and spirited away from her sacrificers into another land, where the custom was to sacrifice all strangers to the Goddess, she was made there the priestess of this rite. Long after that the brother of the priestess happened to come; the fact, however, of the oracle having for a certain reason bidden him go thither, and his object in going, are outside the Plot of the play. On his coming he was arrested, and about to be sacrificed, when he revealed who he was—either as Euripides puts it, or (as suggested by Polyidus) by the not improbable exclamation, "So I too am doomed to be sacrificed, as my sister was"; and the disclosure led to his salvation. This done, the next thing, after the proper names have been fixed as a basis for the story, is to work in episodes or accessory incidents. One must mind, however, that the episodes are appropriate, like the fit of madness in Orestes, which led to his arrest, and the purifying, which brought about his salvation. In plays, then, the episodes are short; in epic poetry

they serve to lengthen out the poem. The argument of the
Odyssey is not a long one. A certain man has been abroad
many years; Poseidon is ever on the watch for him, and he
is all alone. Matters at home too have come to this, that his
substance is being wasted and his son's death plotted by
suitors to his wife. Then he arrives there himself after his
grievous sufferings; reveals himself, and falls on his enemies;
and the end is his salvation and their death. This being all
that is proper to the *Odyssey*, everything else in it is episode.

18. [*Additional rules for the construction of a play.*] (4)
There is a further point to be borne in mind. Every tragedy
is in part Complication and in part Dénouement; the incidents before the opening scene, and often certain also of
those within the play, forming the Complication; and the rest
the Dénouement. By Complication I mean all from the beginning of the story to the point just before the change in
the hero's fortunes; by Dénouement, all from the beginning of
the change to the end. In the *Lynceus* of Theodectes, for instance, the Complication includes, together with the presupposed incidents, the seizure of the child and that in turn
of the parents; and the Dénouement all from the indictment
for the murder to the end. Now it is right, when one speaks
of a tragedy as the same or not the same as another, to do so
on the ground before all else of their Plot, i. e., as having
the same or not the same Complication and Dénouement. Yet
there are many dramatists who, after a good Complication,
fail in the Dénouement. But it is necessary for both points of
construction to be always duly mastered. (5) There are four
distinct species of Tragedy—that being the number of the
constituents also that have been mentioned: first, the complex Tragedy, which is all Peripety and Discovery; second,
the Tragedy of suffering, e. g., the *Ajaxes* and *Ixions;* third,
the Tragedy of character, e. g., *The Phthiotides* and *Peleus.*
The fourth constituent is that of "Spectacle," exemplified in
The Phorcides, in *Prometheus,* and in all plays with the
scene laid in the nether world. The poet's aim, then, should
be to combine every element of interest, if possible, or else

the more important and the major part of them. This is now especially necessary owing to the unfair criticism to which the poet is subjected in these days. Just because there have been poets before him strong in the several species of tragedy, the critics now expect the one man to surpass that which was the strong point of each one of his predecessors. (6) One should also remember what has been said more than once, and not write a tragedy on an epic body of incident (i. e., one with a plurality of stories in it), by attempting to dramatize, for instance, the entire story of the *Iliad*. In the epic owing to its scale every part is treated at proper length; with a drama, however, on the same story the result is very disappointing. This is shown by the fact that all who have dramatized the fall of Ilium in its entirety, and not part by part, like Euripides, or the whole of the Niobe story, instead of a portion, like Aeschylus, either fail utterly or have but ill success on the stage; for that and that alone was enough to ruin even a play by Agathon. Yet in their Peripeties, as also in their simple plots, the poets I mean show wonderful skill in aiming at the kind of effect they desire—a tragic situation that arouses the human feeling in one, like the clever villain (e. g., Sisyphus) deceived, or the brave wrongdoer worsted. This is probable, however, only in Agathon's sense, when he speaks of the probability of even improbabilities coming to pass. (7) The Chorus too should be regarded as one of the actors; it should be an integral part of the whole, and take a share in the action—that which it has in Sophocles, rather than in Euripides. With the later poets, however, the songs in a play of theirs have no more to do with the Plot of that than of any other tragedy. Hence it is that they are now singing intercalary pieces, a practice first introduced by Agathon. And yet what real difference is there between singing such intercalary pieces, and attempting to fit in a speech, or even a whole act, from one play into another?

19. [*The Thought of the tragic personages.*] The Plot and Characters having been discussed, it remains to consider the Diction and Thought. As for the Thought, we may assume

what is said of it in our Art of Rhetoric, as it belongs more
properly to that department of inquiry. The Thought of the
personages is shown in everything to be effected by their
language—in every effort to prove or disprove, to arouse
emotion (pity, fear, anger, and the like), or to maximize or
minimize things. It is clear, also, that their mental procedure
must be on the same lines in their actions likewise, whenever
they wish them to arouse pity or horror, or to have a look of
importance or probability. The only difference is that with the
act the impression has to be made without explanation;
whereas with the spoken word it has to be produced by the
speaker, and result from his language. What, indeed, would
be the good of the speaker, if things appeared in the required
light even apart from anything he says?

As regards the Diction, one subject for inquiry under this
head is the turns given to the language when spoken; e. g.,
the difference between command and prayer, simple statement and threat, question and answer, and so forth. The
theory of such matters, however, belongs to Elocution and
the professors of that art. Whether the poet knows these
things or not, his art as a poet is never seriously criticized
on that account. What fault can one see in Homer's "Sing of
the wrath, Goddess"?—which Protagoras has criticized as being
a command where a prayer was meant, since to bid one do or
not do, he tells us, is a command. Let us pass over this, then,
as appertaining to another art, and not to that of poetry.

20. [*The ultimate constituents of language.*] The Diction
viewed as a whole is made up of the following parts: the
Letter (or ultimate element), the Syllable, the Conjunction,
the Article, the Noun, the Verb, the Case, and the Speech.
(1) The Letter is an indivisible sound of a particular kind,
one that may become a factor in an intelligible sound. Indivisible sounds are uttered by the brutes also, but no one of
these is a Letter in our sense of the term. These elementary
sounds are either vowels, semi-vowels, or mutes. A vowel is
a Letter having an audible sound without the addition of another Letter. A semi-vowel, one having an audible sound by

the addition of another Letter; e. g., S and R. A mute, one having no sound at all by itself, but becoming audible by an addition, that of one of the Letters which have a sound of some sort of their own; e. g., G and D. The Letters differ in various ways: as produced by different conformations or in different regions of the mouth; as aspirated, not aspirated, or sometimes one and sometimes the other; as long, short, or of variable quantity; and further as having an acute, grave, or intermediate accent. The details of these matters we must leave to the metricians. (2) A Syllable is a nonsignificant composite sound, made up of a mute and a Letter having a sound (a vowel or semi-vowel); for GR, without an A, is just as much a Syllable as GRA, with an A. The various forms of the Syllable also belong to the theory of metre. (3) A Conjunction is (a) a nonsignificant sound which, when one significant sound is formable out of several, neither hinders nor aids the union, and which, if the Speech thus formed stands by itself (apart from other Speeches), must not be inserted at the beginning of it. . . . Or (b) a nonsignificant sound capable of combining two or more significant sounds into one. . . . (4) An Article is a nonsignificant sound marking the beginning, end, or dividing point of a Speech, its natural place being either at the extremities or in the middle. (5) A Noun or name is a composite significant sound not involving the idea of time, with parts which have no significance by themselves in it. It is to be remembered that in a compound we do not think of the parts as having a significance also by themselves. . . . (6) A Verb is a composite significant sound involving the idea of time, with parts which (just as in the Noun) have no significance by themselves in it. Whereas the word "man" or "white" does not imply *when*, "walks" and "has walked" involve in addition to the idea of walking that of time present or time past. (7) A Case of a Noun or Verb is when the word means "of" or "to" a thing, and so forth, or for one or many (e. g., "man" and "men"); or it may consist merely in the mode of utterance, e. g., in question, command, etc. "Walked?" and "Walk!" are Cases of the verb "to walk" of this last kind. (8) A Speech is a composite

significant sound, some of the parts of which have a certain
significance by themselves. It may be observed that a Speech
is not always made up of Noun and Verb; it may be without
a Verb, like the definition of man; but it will always have some
part with a certain significance by itself. In the Speech "Cleon
walks," "Cleon" is an instance of such a part. A Speech is
said to be one in two ways, either as signifying one thing, or
as a union of several Speeches made into one by conjunction.
Thus the *Iliad* is one Speech by conjunction of several; and
the definition of man is one through its signifying one thing.

21. [*The different kinds of terms.*] Nouns are of two kinds,
either (1) simple, i. e., made up of nonsignificant parts, like
the word γῆ, or (2) double; in the latter case the word may
be made up either of a significant and a nonsignificant part
(a distinction which disappears in the compound), or of two
significant parts. It is possible also to have triple, quadruple,
or higher compounds, like most of our amplified names; e. g.,
"Hermocaïcoxanthus" and the like.

Whatever its structure, a Noun must always be either (1)
the ordinary word for the thing, or (2) a strange word, or (3)
a metaphor, or (4) an ornamental word, or (5) a coined
word, or (6) a word lengthened out, or (7) curtailed, or (8)
altered in form. By the ordinary word I mean that in general
use in a country; and by a strange word, one in use elsewhere. So that the same word may obviously be at once
strange and ordinary, though not in reference to the same
people; σίγυνον, for instance, is an ordinary word in Cyprus,
and a strange word with us. Metaphor consists in giving the
thing a name that belongs to something else; the transference
being either from genus to species, or from species to genus,
or from species to species, or on grounds of analogy. That
from genus to species is exemplified in "Here stands my
ship"; for lying at anchor is the "standing" of a particular kind
of thing. That from species to genus in "Truly ten thousand
good deeds has Ulysses wrought," where "ten thousand,"
which is a particular large number, is put in place of the

generic "a large number." That from species to species in "Drawing the life with the bronze," in "Severing with the enduring bronze," where the poet uses "draw" in the sense of "sever" and "sever" in that of "draw," both words meaning to "take away" something. That from analogy is possible whenever there are four terms so related that the second (B) is to the first (A), as the fourth (D) to the third (C); for one may then metaphorically put D in lieu of B, and B in lieu of D. Now and then, too, they qualify the metaphor by adding on to it that to which the word it supplants is relative. Thus a cup (B) is in relation to Dionysus (A) what a shield (D) is to Ares (C). The cup accordingly will be metaphorically described as the "shield *of Dionysus*" (D + A), and the shield as the "cup *of Ares*" (B + C). Or to take another instance: As old age (D) is to life (C), so is evening (B) to day (A). One will accordingly describe evening (B) as the "old age *of the day*" (D + A)—or by the Empedoclean equivalent; and old age (D) as the "evening" or "sunset *of life*" (B + C). It may be that some of the terms thus related have no special name of their own, but for all that they will be metaphorically described in just the same way. Thus to cast forth seed corn is called "sowing"; but to cast forth its flame, as said of the sun, has no special name. This nameless act (B), however, stands in just the same relation to its object, sunlight (A), as sowing (D) to the seed corn (C). Hence the expression in the poet, "sowing around a god-created *flame*" (D + A). There is also another form of qualified metaphor. Having given the thing the alien name, one may by a negative addition deny of it one of the attributes naturally associated with its new name. An instance of this would be to call the shield not the "cup *of Ares*," as in the former case, but a "cup *that holds no wine*. . . ." A coined word is a name which, being quite unknown among a people, is given by the poet himself. . . .

22. [*The characteristics of the language of poetry.*] The perfection of Diction is for it to be at once clear and not mean. The clearest indeed is that made up of the ordinary

words for things, but it is mean, as is shown by the poetry of
Cleophon and Sthenelus. On the other hand the Diction becomes distinguished and non-prosaic by the use of unfamiliar
terms, i. e., strange words, metaphors, lengthened forms, and
everything that deviates from the ordinary modes of speech.
But a whole statement in such terms will be either a riddle or
a barbarism, a riddle, if made up of metaphors, a barbarism,
if made up of strange words. The very nature indeed of a
riddle is this, to describe a fact in an impossible combination
of words (which cannot be done with the real names for
things, but can be with their metaphorical substitutes); e. g.,
"I saw a man glue brass on another with fire," and the like.
The corresponding use of strange words results in a barbarism. A certain admixture, accordingly, of unfamiliar terms is
necessary. These, the strange word, the metaphor, the ornamental equivalent, etc., will save the language from seeming
mean and prosaic, while the ordinary words in it will secure
the requisite clearness. What helps most, however, to render
the Diction at once clear and non-prosaic is the use of the
lengthened, curtailed, and altered forms of words. Their deviation from the ordinary words will, by making the language
unlike that in general use, give it a non-prosaic appearance;
and their having much in common with the words in general
use will give it the quality of clearness. It is not right, then,
to condemn these modes of speech, and ridicule the poet for
using them, as some have done; e. g., the elder Euclid, who
said it was easy to make poetry if one were to be allowed to
lengthen the words in the statement itself as much as one
likes. . . . A too apparent use of these licenses has certainly a
ludicrous effect, but they are not alone in that; the rule of
moderation applies to all the constituents of the poetic vo-
cabulary; even with metaphors, strange words, and the rest,
the effect will be the same, if one uses them improperly and
with a view to provoking laughter. The proper use of them
is a very different thing. To realize the difference one should
take an epic verse and see how it reads when the normal
words are introduced. The same should be done too with the
strange word, the metaphor, and the rest; for one has only

to put the ordinary words in their place to see the truth of what we are saying. The same iambic, for instance, is found in Aeschylus and Euripides, and as it stands in the former it is a poor line; whereas Euripides, by the change of a single word, the substitution of a strange for what is by usage the ordinary word, has made it seem a fine one. . . .

The mere fact of their not being in ordinary speech gives the Diction a non-prosaic character; but Ariphrades was unaware of that. It is a great thing, indeed, to make a proper use of these poetical forms, as also of compounds and strange words. But the greatest thing by far is to be a master of metaphor. It is the one thing that cannot be learnt from others; and it is also a sign of genius, since a good metaphor implies an intuitive perception of the similarity in dissimilars.

Of the kinds of words we have enumerated it may be observed that compounds are most in place in the dithyramb, strange words in heroic, and metaphors in iambic poetry. Heroic poetry, indeed, may avail itself of them all. But in iambic verse, which models itself as far as possible on the spoken language, only those kinds of words are in place which are allowable also in an oration, i. e., the ordinary word, the metaphor, and the ornamental equivalent.

Let this, then, suffice as an account of Tragedy, the art imitating by means of action on the stage.

23. [*The Epic must preserve Unity of action.*] As for the poetry which merely narrates, or imitates by means of versified language (without action), it is evident that it has several points in common with Tragedy.

I. The construction of its stories should clearly be like that in a drama; they should be based on a single action, one that is a complete whole in itself, with a beginning, middle, and end, so as to enable the work to produce its own proper pleasure with all the organic unity of a living creature. Nor should one suppose that there is anything like them in our usual histories. A history has to deal not with one action, but with one period and all that happened in that to one or more persons, however disconnected the several events may have been. Just as two events may take place at the same time, e. g., the sea fight off Salamis and the battle with the Carthaginians in Sicily, without converging to the same end, so too of two consecutive events one may sometimes come after the other with no one end as their common issue. Nevertheless most of our epic poets, one may say, ignore the distinction.

Herein, then, to repeat what we have said before, we have a further proof of Homer's marvellous superiority to the rest. He did not attempt to deal even with the Trojan war in its entirety, though it was a whole with a definite beginning and end—through a feeling apparently that it was too long a story to be taken in in one view, or if not that, too complicated from the variety of incident in it. As it is, he has singled out one section of the whole; many of the other incidents, however, he brings in as episodes, using the Catalogue of the Ships, for instance, and other episodes to relieve the uniformity of his narrative. As for the other epic poets, they treat of one man, or one period; or else of an action which, although one, has a multiplicity of parts in it. This last is what the authors of the *Cypria* and *Little Iliad* have done. And the result is that, whereas the *Iliad* or *Odyssey* supplies materials for only one, or at most two tragedies, the *Cypria* does that for several and the *Little Iliad* for more than eight: for an *Adjudgement of Arms,* a *Philoctetes,* a *Neoptolemus,* a *Eurypylus,* a *Ulysses as Beggar,* a *Laconian Women,* a *Fall of Ilium,* and a *Departure of the Fleet;* as also a *Sinon,* and a *Women of Troy.*

24. [*Comparison of Epic and Tragedy.*] II. Besides this, Epic poetry must divide into the same species as Tragedy; it must be either simple or complex, a story of character or one of suffering. Its parts, too, with the exception of Song and Spectacle, must be the same, as it requires Peripeties, Discoveries, and scenes of suffering just like Tragedy. Lastly, the Thought and Diction in it must be good in their way. All these elements appear in Homer first; and he has made due use of them. His two poems are each examples of con-

struction, the *Iliad* simple and a story of suffering, the *Odyssey* complex (there is Discovery throughout it) and a story of character. And they are more than this, since in Diction and Thought too they surpass all other poems.

There is, however, a difference in the Epic as compared with Tragedy, (1) in its length, and (2) in its metre. (1) As to its length, the limit already suggested will suffice: it must be possible for the beginning and end of the work to be taken in in one view—a condition which will be fulfilled if the poem be shorter than the old epics, and about as long as the series of tragedies offered for one hearing. For the extension of its length epic poetry has a special advantage, of which it makes large use. In a play one cannot represent an action with a number of parts going on simultaneously; one is limited to the part on the stage and connected with the actors. Whereas in epic poetry the narrative form makes it possible for one to describe a number of simultaneous incidents; and these, if germane to the subject, increase the body of the poem. This then is a gain to the Epic, tending to give it grandeur, and also variety of interest and room for episodes of diverse kinds. Uniformity of incident by the satiety it soon creates is apt to ruin tragedies on the stage. (2) As for its metre, the heroic has been assigned it from experience; were any one to attempt a narrative poem in some one, or in several, of the other metres, the incongruity of the thing would be apparent. The heroic in fact is the gravest and weightiest of metres—which is what makes it more tolerant than the rest of strange words and metaphors, that also being a point in which the narrative form of poetry goes beyond all others. The iambic and trochaic, on the other hand, are metres of movement, the one representing that of life and action, the other that of the dance. Still more unnatural would it appear, if one were to write an epic in a medley of metres, as Chaeremon did. Hence it is that no one has ever written a long story in any but heroic verse; nature herself, as we have said, teaches us to select the metre appropriate to such a story.

Homer, admirable as he is in every other respect, is especially so in this, that he alone among epic poets is not un-aware of the part to be played by the poet himself in the poem. The poet should say very little *in propria persona,* as he is no imitator when doing that. Whereas the other poets are perpetually coming forward in person, and say but little, and that only here and there, as imitators, Homer after a brief preface brings in forthwith a man, a woman, or some other Character—no one of them characterless, but each with distinctive characteristics.

The marvellous is certainly required in Tragedy. The Epic, however, affords more opening for the improbable, the chief factor in the marvellous, because in it the agents are not visibly before one. The scene of the pursuit of Hector would be ridiculous on the stage—the Greeks halting instead of pursuing him, and Achilles shaking his head to stop them; but in the poem the absurdity is overlooked. The marvellous, however, is a cause of pleasure, as is shown by the fact that we all tell a story with additions, in the belief that we are doing our hearers a pleasure.

Homer more than any other has taught the rest of us the art of framing lies in the right way. I mean the use of paralogism. Whenever, if A is or happens, a consequent, B, is or happens, men's notion is that, if the B is, the A also is—but that is a false conclusion. Accordingly, if A is untrue, but there is something else, B, that on the assumption of its truth follows as its consequent, the right thing then is to add on the B. Just because we know the truth of the consequent, we are in our own minds led on to the erroneous inference of the truth of the antecedent. Here is an instance, from the *Bath-story* in the *Odyssey*.

A likely impossibility is always preferable to an uncon-vincing possibility. The story should never be made up of improbable incidents; there should be nothing of the sort in it. If, however, such incidents are unavoidable, they should be outside the piece, like the hero's ignorance in *Oedipus* of the circumstances of Laius' death; not within it, like the report of the Pythian games in *Electra*, or the man's having come to Mysia from Tegea without uttering a word on the way, in *The Mysians*. So that it is ridiculous to say that one's Plot would have been spoilt without them, since it is fundamentally wrong to make up such Plots. If the poet has taken such a Plot, however, and one sees that he might have put it in a more probable form, he is guilty of absurdity as well as a fault of art. Even in the *Odyssey* the improbabilities in the setting ashore of Ulysses would be clearly intolerable in the hands of an inferior poet. As it is, the poet conceals them, his other excellences veiling their absurdity. Elaborate Diction, however, is required only in places where there is no action, and no Character or Thought to be revealed. Where there is Character or Thought, on the other hand, an overornate Diction tends to obscure them.

25. [*Possible criticisms of an Epic or Tragedy.*] As regards Problems and their Solutions, one may see the number and nature of the assumptions on which they proceed by viewing the matter in the following way. (1) The poet being an imitator just like the painter or other maker of likenesses, he must necessarily in all instances represent things in one or other of three aspects, either as they were or are, or as they are said or thought to be or to have been, or as they ought to be. (2) All this he does in language, with an admixture, it may be, of strange words and metaphors, as also of the various modified forms of words, since the use of these is conceded in poetry. (3) It is to be remembered, too, that there is not the same kind of correctness in poetry as in politics, or indeed any other art. There is, however, within the limits of poetry itself a possibility of two kinds of error, the one directly, the other only accidentally connected with the art. If the poet meant to describe the thing correctly, and failed through lack of power of expression, his art itself is at fault. But if it was through his having meant to describe it in some incorrect way (e. g., to make the horse in movement have both right legs thrown forward) that the technical error (one in a matter of, say, medicine or some other special science), or impossibilities of whatever kind they may be, have got into his description, his error in that case

is not in the essentials of the poetic art. These, therefore, must be the premises of the Solutions in answer to the criticisms involved in the Problems.

I. As to the criticisms relating to the poet's art itself. Any impossibilities there may be in his descriptions of things are faults. But from another point of view they are justifiable, if they serve the end of poetry itself—if (to assume what we have said of that end) they make the effect of either that very portion of the work or some other portion more astounding. The Pursuit of Hector is an instance in point. If, however, the poetic end might have been as well or better attained without sacrifice of technical correctness in such matters, the impossibility is not to be justified, since the description should be, if it can, entirely free from error. One may ask, too, whether the error is in a matter directly or only accidentally connected with the poetic art; since it is a lesser error in an artist not to know, for instance, that the hind has no horns, than to produce an unrecognizable picture of one.

II. If the poet's description be criticized as not true to fact, one may urge perhaps that the object ought to be as described—an answer like that of Sophocles, who said that he drew men as they ought to be, and Euripides as they were. If the description, however, be neither true nor of the thing as it ought to be, the answer must be then, that it is in accordance with opinion. The tales about Gods, for instance, may be as wrong as Xenophanes thinks, neither true nor the better thing to say; but they are certainly in accordance with opinion. Of other statements in poetry one may perhaps say, not that they are better than the truth, but that the fact was so at the time—e. g., the description of the arms: "their spears stood upright, butt end upon the ground"; for that was the usual way of fixing them then, as it is still with the Illyrians. As for the question whether something said or done in a poem is morally right or not, in dealing with that one should consider not only the intrinsic quality of the actual word or deed, but also the person who says or does it, the person to whom he says or does it, the time, the means, and the motive of the agent—whether he does it to attain a greater good, or to avoid a greater evil.

* * *

Speaking generally, one has to justify (1) the Impossible by reference to the requirements of poetry, or to the better, or to opinion. For the purposes of poetry a convincing impossibility is preferable to an unconvincing possibility; and if men such as Zeuxis depicted be impossible, the answer is that it is better they should be like that, as the artist ought to improve on his model. (2) The Improbable one has to justify either by showing it to be in accordance with opinion, or by urging that at times it is not improbable; for there is a probability of things happening also against probability. (3) The contradictions found in the poet's language one should first test as one does an opponent's confutation in a dialetical argument, so as to see whether he means the same thing, in the same relation, and in the same sense, before admitting that he has contradicted either something he has said himself or what a man of sound sense assumes as true. But there is no possible apology for improbability of Plot or depravity of character, when they are not necessary and no use is made of them, like the improbability in the appearance of Aegeus in *Medea* and the baseness of Menelaus in *Orestes*.

The objections, then, of critics start with faults of five kinds. The allegation is always that something is either (1) impossible, (2) improbable, (3) corrupting, (4) contradictory, or (5) against technical correctness. The answers to these objections must be sought under one or other of the above-mentioned heads, which are twelve in number.

26. [*Tragedy artistically superior to Epic poetry.*] The question may be raised whether the epic or the tragic is the higher form of imitation. It may be argued that, if the less vulgar is the higher, and the less vulgar is always that which addresses the better public, an art addressing any and every one is of a very vulgar order. It is a belief that their public cannot see the meaning, unless they add something them-

selves, that causes the perpetual movements of the perform-
ers—bad flute players, for instance, rolling about, if quoit
throwing is to be represented, and pulling at the conductor,
if Scylla is the subject of the piece. Tragedy, then, is said to
be an art of this order—to be in fact just what the later actors
were in the eyes of their predecessors; for Mynniscus used
to call Callippides "the ape," because he thought he so over-
acted his parts; and a similar view was taken of Pindarus
also. All Tragedy, however, is said to stand to the Epic as
the newer to the older school of actors. The one, accordingly,
is said to address a cultivated audience, which does not need
the accompaniment of gesture; the other, an uncultivated
one. If, therefore, Tragedy is a vulgar art, it must clearly be
lower than the Epic.

The answer to this is twofold. In the first place, one may
urge (1) that the censure does not touch the art of the dramatic poet, but only that of his interpreter; for it is quite
possible to overdo the gesturing even in an epic recital, as
did Sosistratus, and in a singing contest, as did Mnasitheus
of Opus. (2) That one should not condemn all movement,
unless one means to condemn even the dance, but only that
of ignoble people—which is the point of the criticism passed
on Callippides and in the present day on others, that their
women are not like gentlewomen. (3) That Tragedy may
produce its effect even without movement or action in just
the same way as Epic poetry; for from the mere reading of a
play its quality may be seen. So that, if it be superior in all
other respects, this element of inferiority is no necessary part
of it.

In the second place, one must remember (1) that Tragedy
has everything that the Epic has (even the epic metre being
admissible), together with a not inconsiderable addition in
the shape of the Music (a very real factor in the pleasure of
the drama) and the Spectacle. (2) That its reality of pres-
entation is felt in the play as read, as well as in the play
as acted. (3) That the tragic imitation requires less space
for the attainment of its end; which is a great advantage,
since the more concentrated effect is more pleasurable than

one with a large admixture of time to dilute it—consider the
Oedipus of Sophocles, for instance, and the effect of expand-
ing it into the number of lines of the *Iliad*. (4) That there
is less unity in the imitation of the epic poets, as is proved by
the fact that any one work of theirs supplies matter for
several tragedies; the result being that, if they take what is
really a single story, it seems curt when briefly told, and
thin and waterish when on the scale of length usual with
their verse. In saying that there is less unity in an epic, I
mean an epic made up of a plurality of actions, in the same
way as the *Iliad* and *Odyssey* have many such parts, each
one of them in itself of some magnitude; yet the structure
of the two Homeric poems is as perfect as can be, and the
action in them is as nearly as possible one action. If, then,
Tragedy is superior in these respects, and also, besides these,
in its poetic effect (since the two forms of poetry should give
us, not any or every pleasure, but the very special kind we
have mentioned), it is clear that, as attaining the poetic effect
better than the Epic, it will be the higher form of art.

So much for Tragedy and Epic poetry—for these two arts
in general and their species; the number and nature of their
constituent parts; the causes of success and failure in them;
the Objections of the critics, and the Solutions in answer to
them.

SUGGESTIONS FOR FURTHER READING

~~~~~~~~~~~~~~~~~~~~~~~~~~~~~~~~~~~~~~~

Editions of Aristotle:

THE WORKS OF ARISTOTLE, translated into English under the editorship of W. D. Ross. Twelve volumes. Oxford University Press. The standard English translation.

THE BASIC WORKS OF ARISTOTLE, edited by Richard McKeon. Random House. A convenient, comprehensive selection, based on the Oxford translation.

Commentary:

Werner Jaeger, ARISTOTLE: FUNDAMENTALS OF THE HISTORY OF HIS DEVELOPMENT. Translated by Richard Robinson. Oxford University Press. The evolution of Aristotle's scientific and philosophic doctrines, studied chronologically.

W. D. Ross, ARISTOTLE. Charles Scribner's Sons. A classic account of the main features of Aristotle's philosophy.

Bertrand Russell, A HISTORY OF WESTERN PHILOSOPHY. Simon and Schuster. Contains an unfriendly but highly provocative critique.

A. E. Taylor, ARISTOTLE. Dover Publications. Aristotle as seen by a dedicated Platonist.

Immerse yourself in the writings of the
world's greatest philosophers. In paperback
from Washington Square Press.

___54729 **PSYCHOTHERAPY AND EXISTENTIALISM**
Viktor E. Frankl $3.95
___64670 **MAN'S SEARCH FOR MEANING** (revised)
Viktor E. Frankl $4.50
___54163 **THE UNHEARD CRY FOR MEANING**
Viktor E. Frankl $3.95
___49606 **BEING AND NOTHINGNESS** Jean–Paul Satre $6.95
___52524 **DIALOGUES OF PLATO** ed. Justin E. Kaplan $5.95
___49952 **COMMUNIST MANIFESTO**
Karl Marx and Friedrich Engels $2.95
___60171 **POCKET AQUINAS** ed. V. Bourke $4.95
___46377 **POCKET ARISTOTLE** ed. Justin E. Kaplan $5.95
___62858 **SOCIAL CONTRACT AND DISCOURSE ON THE**
ORIGIN OF INEQUALITY
Jean Jacques Rousseau $4.95
___44048 **THE SOCIAL PHILOSOPHERS**
Robert Nisbet $5.95
___49415 **STORY OF PHILOSOPHY** Will Durant $5.95

WSP

Simon & Schuster, Mail Order Dept. PHI
200 Old Tappan Rd., Old Tappan, N.J. 07675

Please send me the books I have checked above. I am enclosing $_____ (please add 75¢ to cover
postage and handling for each order. N.Y.S. and N.Y.C. residents please add appropriate sales tax). Send
check or money order—no cash or C.O.D.'s please. Allow up to six weeks for delivery. For purchases
over $10.00 you may use VISA: card number, expiration date and customer signature must be included.

Name_____

Address _____

City _____ State/Zip _____

VISA Card No. _____ Exp. Date_____

Signature _____ 578

In this volume of selections from Aristotle, the editor, Justin D. Kaplan, has included the most widely read, studied and quoted works of the great philosopher. The monumental Oxford translation, by authorities including W. D. Ross, Benjamin Jowett and Ingram Bywater, has been used. The editor's prefatory notes give the reader a convenient and concise review of each work and present the main ideas of a man who has often been called the world's most important thinker.

In his introduction, Mr. Kaplan says of Aristotle: ". . . he offers his own unique and lasting rewards: directness of thought and expression; astounding nimbleness of analysis and reasoning; a dedication to tracing things from their beginnings; a system which embraced, and attempted to unify, both science and philosophy. He impresses us not only by his pioneering ambition and scope, by his quest for unity, but by the role he played in shaping Western thought."